Architectural Guide
Chicago

A Critic's Guide to 100 Post-Modern Buildings
in Chicago from 1978 to 2025

Architectural Guide
Chicago

A Critic's Guide to 100 Post-Modern Buildings
in Chicago from 1978 to 2025

Vladimir Belogolovsky

DOM
publishers

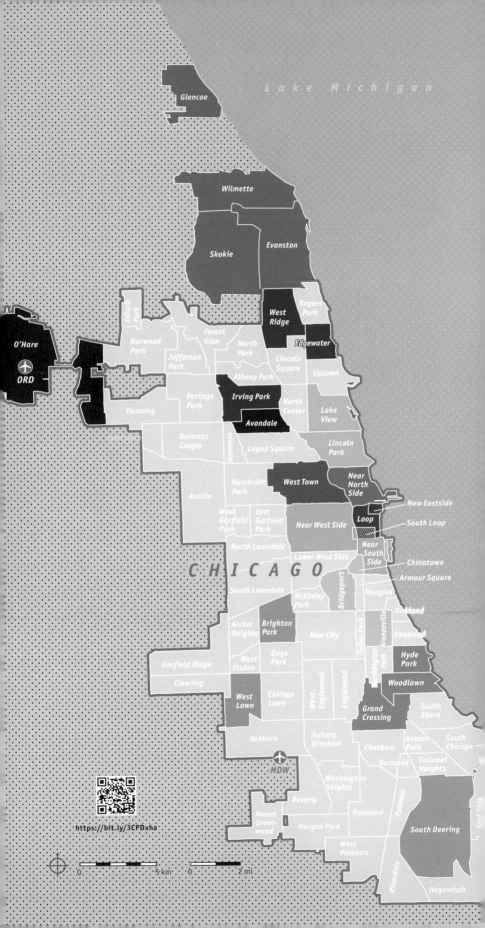

Lake Michigan

Glencoe

Wilmette

Skokie

Evanston

West Ridge

Rogers Park

Edgewater

O'Hare
✈ ORD

Edison Park

Norwood Park

Forest Glen

North Park

Lincoln Square

Uptown

Jefferson Park

Albany Park

Irving Park

North Center

Lake View

Portage Park

Dunning

Avondale

Belmont Cragin

Hermosa

Logan Square

Lincoln Park

Humboldt Park

West Town

Near North Side

New Eastside

Austin

West Garfield Park

East Garfield Park

Near West Side

Loop

South Loop

Lower West Side

Near South Side

Chinatown

CHICAGO

South Lawndale

McKinley Park

Bridgeport

Douglas

Armour Square

Archer Heights

Brighton Park

New City

Fuller Park

Washington Park

Bronzeville

Oakland

Kenwood

Hyde Park

West Elsdon

Gage Park

Garfield Ridge

Clearing

Chicago Lawn

West Englewood

Englewood

Woodlawn

South Shore

West Lawn

Grand Crossing

Chatham

Avalon Park

South Chicago

Ashburn

Auburn Gresham

Burnside

Calumet Heights

MDW ✈

Washington Heights

Pullman

Beverly

Roseland

South Deering

Mount Greenwood

Morgan Park

Far Side

West Pullman

Riverdale

Hegewisch

0   5 km   0   2 mi

Contents

Post-Modern Chicago 8
Chicago Architects 16

100 Post-Modern Buildings:

1 **Loop and New Eastside** 33

2 **Near North Side** 75

3 **South Loop and Near South Side** 101

4 **Near West Side** 117

5 **Lincoln Park and Lake View** 133

6 **Chinatown, Bronzeville, and Bridgeport** 159

7 **Hyde Park, Woodlawn, and Grand Crossing** 173

8 **West Town** 193

9 **Irving Park, West Ridge, and Edgewater** 201

10 **Avondale and O'Hare** 211

11 **Northern Suburbs: Evanston, Wilmette, Glencoe, and Skokie** 219

12 **Far South Side: Brighton Park, West Lawn, and South Deering** 231

Interviews:

Stanley Tigerman 238
Helmut Jahn 242
Adrian Smith 246
Ralph Johnson 250
John Ronan 254
Jeanne Gang 258

Maps 264
Index 274
Author 278

View over Grant Park looking west toward Loop (to the right) and South Loop (to the left)

Post-Modern Chicago

Vladimir Belogolovsky

The desire to write this guide was sparked as soon as my previous book, *Architectural Guide New York: A Critic's Guide to 100 Iconic Buildings in New York from 1999 to 2020,* was published in March 2019 and came into my hands. I liked how it turned out, so my initial reaction was to gather a similar assemblage of iconic structures in another American city. A single guide is just one isolated case study, but two guides is a beginning of a potential series, which I hope it will grow into. It was also my attempt to identify local characteristics and compare them to those of other cities in the US and globally. Of course, the second book had to be about Chicago, a soaring metropolis that has amassed an unmatched collection of first-rate buildings in every possible style since late nineteenth-century industrialization. In fact, Stanley Tigerman (1930–2019), the late Chicago architect whose efforts influenced the course of architecture both nationally and internationally, used to say that 'being an architect in Chicago is like being born wealthy. It is an architectural city.' There are close to one hundred buildings built here by Frank Lloyd Wright and Mies van der Rohe alone, and at least as many important buildings by architects of the First Chicago School, which will be discussed in more detail in the introduction that follows this foreword.

It was Chicago's role as an essential industrial hub for the whole nation—the fastest-growing American city's commercial success—that has manifested into dozens of structures of note. Many of them have come to be recognized as undeniable masterpieces. They elevated Chicago's status to one of the world's most revered architectural capitals.

Speaking from his personal experience, another Chicago architect, Helmut Jahn (1940–2021), told me that young architects regarded a visit to Chicago as equal in importance to a pilgrimage to Rome or Athens. I can attest to that because as I have asked so many architects around the world what one building has influenced them the most, they have consistently preferred to name one city instead: Chicago. It is true, this city is home to the largest number of first-rate modern buildings. They are thoroughly original, particularly local, designed for their time, guided by real-life constraints and necessities, yet inspired by unbound boldness and innovation.

However, as in my New York guide, I wanted to focus on contemporary architecture and dedicate this guide to living architects. So, I was once again faced primarily with two questions: What buildings to include and where to begin? It was only after I signed the contract with DOM publishers and began gathering so-called iconic Chicago projects that I realized that even if I started counting from the time of Chicago's incorporation in 1837, selecting 100 *iconic* structures here would present an insurmountable challenge. It so happens that Chicago has far fewer explicit icons than New York City. The fact is that cities are not made up of iconic buildings, because they are rather rare, and most cities have none at all.

In my first guide, I assigned each of the selected building's nicknames such as Guillotine, Peacock, Shark's Fin, Turtle Shell, and so on. While some buildings put together in this collection could be described as glass egg, butterfly, fettuccine, wine glass, and Rolls Royce radiator grille, it would be much less convincing

'I adore Chicago. It is the pulse of America.'

Sarah Bernhardt (French Actress, 1844–1923)

to characterize all the buildings presented here as iconic. Architects in the City of Broad Shoulders do not set out to produce icons the way they do in the Big Apple. So, I selected buildings around a different theme.

As I analyzed what one significant event or project could be viewed as a watershed moment in local, recent architectural history, it became clear that it was necessary to address Chicago's structures through the prism of Post-Modernism—a period in architecture that is still very vaguely defined. While it is hard to pinpoint where and when Post-Modernism really started, many will agree with the late architectural critic Charles Jencks (1939–2019), who defined the symbolic death of modernist architecture as 3:32 p.m. (or thereabouts) on 15 July 1972 when the Minoru Yamasaki-designed Pruitt-Igoe public housing complex [a] in St. Louis (built less than 20 years earlier and praised by critics then) was spectacularly demolished with an explosive detonation on live TV. Should the same date be considered the birth of Post-Modernism? There are disputes about that. Other potential candidates include critical texts, unbuilt design projects, exhibitions, and buildings, some of which occurred some years before Jencks's date in 1972.

The most glaring examples include Robert Venturi's house for his mother, Vanna Venturi, completed in 1964 in the suburbs of Philadelphia, as well as his 1966 manifesto, *Complexity and Contradiction in Architecture.* Jencks's own 1975 essay, *The Rise of Post-Modern Architecture,* is another textual mark of architecture's shift from one paradigm to the next. Of course, this cultural transformation cannot possibly be reduced to one singular event. To

be sure, this transition was cumulative, and it lasted for over a decade before it became a fully-fledged movement in the 1980s. This fluid transition was accompanied by numerous ambiguous works that embodied both modern and Post-Modern features; they include early enigmatic works such as Ronchamp (1955) by Le Corbusier and Paul Rudolph's multi-referential Art & Architecture Building (1963) at Yale University.

Certainly, the most noticeable signal of the arrival of Post-Modernism was by now a seminal exhibition, *La Strada Novissima* [b] at the very first International Architecture Exhibition in Venice in 1980, directed by Paolo Portoghesi in line with the theme *The Presence of the Past*. It presented an impressive 230-foot-long (70-meter-long) sequence of 20 artistic facades—10 on each side of a wide street-like corridor in the Arsenale—designed by Japanese architect Arata Isozaki and Europeans Hans Hollein, Josef Paul Kleihues, Oswald Mathias Ungers, Ricardo Bofill, and Rem Koolhaas. American architects included Robert Venturi, Robert Stern, Charles Moore, Frank Gehry, Michael Graves, and Stanley Tigerman. A monumental entrance portal to this display of historicism was designed by Aldo Rossi. Among the key intentions of this action was to liberate architecture from the modernist orthodoxy largely manifested in its obsessiveness with functionalism, objectivism, universality, and reductivism. Post-Modernism returned to the most basic elements of architectural grammar, namely the classical language of architecture, by loosely relying on historical and pop-cultural quotations with a touch of irony. Even

a The Pruitt-Igoe projects being razed, St. Louis, 1972

though the term Post-Modern was not mentioned (Jencks was among the organizers), modernism was meant to be expanded, as was clearly expressed in the catalog's statement: 'The primary objective was to show how, without renouncing modernity, we could go on and try the road of heresy.'

Other important points that the show emphasized were the need to reinstate ornament, three-dimensionality, monumentality, playfulness, and the traditional street that was dismissed by Le Corbusier, whose proposed Plan Voisin (1922–1925) for Paris, strictly speaking, was the prototype of the failed Pruitt-Igoe. The show sent a strong message to the profession: modern architecture was allowed and even encouraged to be questioned. Young architects were asked to come up with alternative visions. There was a revolution in the making, no less. After Venice, the show went to Paris and San Francisco. In

b *La Strada Novissima* installation, Arsenale, 1st International Architecture Exhibition, Venice, 1980

my 2012 interview with Tigerman (included later in this book along with five other interviews with some of Chicago's leading architects), he described his participation in the Venice exhibition as a 'disaster', explaining that behind his flirtation with classical architecture, there was a need to experiment with the hybridization of very different architectural ideas, metaphors, and images. However, in retrospect, he saw his search for new means of expression in classicism as a dead end. It is important to mention that this attempt by young architects to return to the basics, to dig for new meanings, and to refuse to embrace Miesian modernism was not done spontaneously and in isolation from the rest of society and culture. In 1968 students protested around the world, often extremely violently, against authority and authoritarianism in general, and political and social injustice, bureaucracy, institutional rigidity, corruption, the violation of civil rights, dictatorships, pollution, and of course, the Vietnam War. The whole world order was being questioned.

Modernist architecture's authoritative methods and its visually hierarchical appearance were under attack; the modernists' vision of the future had to be redrawn. Think of *Playtime*, a 1967 film directed by Jacques Tati. The French filmmaker created an ultra-modern and impersonal Paris, a maze of nearly identical standardized glass and steel buildings and interiors filled with lookalike office cubicles. The film gives us a glimpse of a surreal urban world and modern life—all being celebrated, feared, and satirized at the same time. The turn to Post-Modernism was a clear indication that young people around the world did not want to inhabit a future that was sterile and devoid of life that so many modernist architects had achieved, of course, not intentionally so. Soon the ideas expressed in Venice started materializing in stone, brick, glass, and in student projects in many leading schools around the world. Among the most visible examples was Michael Graves's Portland Building (Portland, Oregon, 1982). It was an unyielding attack on the modern doctrine. Not everyone liked it, but everyone took notice. In the architect's words, the building became 'a symbolic gesture, an attempt to re-establish a language of architecture and values that are not a part of modernist homogeneity'. Of course, many thought it was pure pastiche. Then came the Neue Staatsgalerie (1984) in Stuttgart, Germany, where British architect James Stirling effectively and with great imagination combined traditional organization and historical elements with modern aesthetics, producing one of the most eclectic buildings in the twentieth century. Back in the US, the AT&T Building was completed the same year, authored by Philip Johnson, the inaugural recipient of the 1979 Pritzker Prize. Johnson appeared on the 8 January 1979 cover of *Time* magazine embracing the tower's model, as if he was Moses holding the Ten Commandments. The headline read: 'US Architects Doing Their Own Thing'. Where were Chicago architects in all this? For the most part, they were still at the front and center of the modernist movement. In fact, modern buildings designed by Mies and his imitators, particularly the large commercial firms that followed him in just about every way, dominated the city, particularly exemplified by the most visible and tallest buildings by SOM. Mies became a new Palladio, except that his principles were copied on a much larger scale and with less precision. No matter how handsomely, beautifully proportioned, and exquisitely detailed, the sheer accumulation of his buildings and knockoffs and their exhausting austerity soon caused many Chicagoans to become quite irritated.

Mies was still alive when Venturi's *Complexity and Contradiction* stated: 'Architects can no longer afford to be intimidated by the puritanically moral language of orthodox modern architecture. I like elements which are hybrid rather than "pure", compromising rather than "clear", distorted rather than "straightforward". I am for messy vitality over obvious unity ... I am for richness of meaning rather than clarity of meaning.' It was hard not to be drawn to these liberating ideas. His phrase 'less is a bore', a cheeky reversal of the Miesian dictum 'less is more', perfectly summarized the antipathy of leading young architects toward so many buildings that looked abstractly perfect, but were cold and impersonal glass boxes, regardless their appropriateness for their use and context. Venturi's ideas were initially viewed as too radical. The *New York Times* architecture critic Ada Louise Huxtable wrote at the time: 'The profession is split right down the middle—90 per cent against it.' Yet very soon a new generation of architects began to take them very seriously. Mies died in 1969 and by the mid-to-late 1970s, the profession started looking for opportunities to liberate itself from the straitjacket of modernism by contaminating it with diversity and pluralism.

Most relevant here is the formation of the Chicago Seven by the city's first generation of Post-Modernist architects. Along with Tigerman, the group included Larry Booth, Stuart Cohen, Ben Weese, James Ingo Freed (then dean at IIT's School of Architecture), Tom Beeby, and James L. Nagle. They were later joined by Helmut Jahn, and then expanded to 11 members when Gerald Horn, Kenneth Schroeder, and Cynthia Weese joined. They were reduced to 10 when Freed left for New York to join I. M. Pei and became a part of Pei Cobb Freed & Partners. These Chicago-based architects admitted from the outset that they had little in common except that they all stood united against the then total acceptance and domination of Miesian aesthetics that were often

c Helmut Jahn next to his townhouse model, *Exquisite Corpse* Exhibition, Graham Foundation, Chicago, 1978

applied blindly without the original rigor and clarity. They were not against Mies. In fact, they praised him, but they refused to follow in his footsteps without any space for interpretation. In my interview with Helmut Jahn, he spoke about his experience of having a love-hate relationship with Mies and his legacy that had quickly turned into a cult, which Jahn opposed. In 1976, the Chicago Seven combined their efforts to organize a series of exhibitions to challenge that year's other exhibition,

d From L to R: Helmut Jahn, Tom Beeby, Stanley Tigerman, Stuart Cohen, *Exquisite Corpse* Exhibition, Graham Foundation, Chicago, 1978

which was mounted by Chicago's Museum of Contemporary Art and called *100 Years of Architecture in Chicago: Continuity of Structure and Form*. The emphasis was on the First Chicago School and Second Chicago School, disproportionally celebrating the work of Mies. Tigerman and his group thought the show distorted the true story. They put together their own show, a sort of *Salon des Refusés*, called *Chicago Architects* and accompanied by a catalog in which the group described themselves and their ideals as '... the suppressed romanticism of Chicago's unknown architects'. Tigerman insisted that the alternative show was important, although no unified counter-style had emerged. The point was to be eclectic and that only by accepting both views could one fully grasp the rich Chicago architectural tradition. This is how these architects opened up the discussion beyond the descendants of the Miesian tradition and carved out space for themselves and other young architects that kept alive the tradition of Chicago as an international center for creative architecture. The same year, the Chicago Seven's *Exquisite Corpse* show premiered at Cooper Union in New York. For the next two years, it was shown in several galleries in Chicago, including at the Graham Foundation [c], and in Minneapolis. It explored variations of townhouse designs that flirted with historical styles in the most personified, romantic, and provocatively un-modern ways. Each scale model showcased a design on a 20-by-120-foot (6-by-37-meter) lot with a 15-foot (4.6-meter) front and a maximum height of 40 feet (12 meters). The point was to showcase the architects' abandonment of modernist rules and to broaden the local architectural culture. Lined up, the scale models [d] of the proposed townhouses looked suspiciously similar to *La Strada Novissima*, which occurred several years later on a much grander scale. Going over the variety of projects included in this new guide, it is safe to say that these pioneering, visionary Post-Modern architects were beginning to fulfil their mission.

Following these shows, Tigerman felt the need for a very special gesture: to declare his professional stance, a break with modernist traditions expressed in his 1978 conceptual collage. Daringly called *The Titanic* [e], it celebrated the sinking of the S. R. Crown Hall, the untouchable steel-and-glass temple of modernism, the heart and soul of the Illinois Institute of Technology, the mothership of mid-twentieth century architecture, and the home of the very school where one of the most authoritative fathers of modernism instructed generations of future architects in 'the correct way' of making architecture. That widely published image was meant to serve as the last nail hammered into the coffin of modernism. And if it was Venturi's book that was well timed in summarizing many of modernism's shortcomings and signaled the profession's readiness for the arrival of the new era, arguably Tigerman's *Titanic* gave the shift toward Post-Modernism an appropriate visual manifestation, capturing the no-longer relevant modernism right before its imminent demise. Ironically, much later Venturi refused to be even included in the Post-Modernists' camp.

Now that we have discussed the Chicago Seven's exhibitions and Tigerman's *Titanic*, it is apt to start this guide with one of the architect's earliest buildings: the 1978 Illinois Regional Library for the Blind and Physically Handicapped in the Near West Side [052]. In accordance with this building's function, Tigerman was

probing, somewhat experimentally, a new kind of architecture. This was a bold move at a time when so many modernist architects thought they had all the right answers. It is worth mentioning that just a few years earlier he was among those confidant architects, as unequivocally stated by his very first built-work, a residential high-rise at 4343 Clarendon Avenue. Completed in 1974 on the North Side, all-in-all it is a Miesean building. Over the years, Tigerman's library experienced abandonment, changes of ownership, and a 2005 conversion into a branch of Lakeside Bank. Although the building lost its original colors and function, it retains some of the Tigerman-designed features, including a 165-foot-long (50-meter-long) whimsical window—a kind of visual oath to his crusade against Mies's dogmatic right-angled buildings.

Following architectural guide conventions, this book is organized geographically. It features 100 buildings, representing close to 30 different programs, including 17 multi-family residential or hotel projects, 15 office buildings, 12 single-family houses, 10 university faculty buildings, seven libraries, six museums, five schools, four community centers, three theaters, three CTA stations, two galleries, two hospitals, two pavilions, an interior, adaptive reuse project, a fountain, and a sculpture. These projects were designed by 60 architects. Three-quarters of all entries were designed by local architects. Half of the outside architects are foreigners and half are from other American cities, with three-quarters of those coming from New York. Six local architects, who I interviewed especially for this book, cumulatively designed 36 buildings: Jeanne Gang (eight), Helmut Jahn (eight), Ralph Johnson (seven), John Ronan (five), Stanley Tigerman (four), and Adrian Smith of Adrian Smith + Gordon Gill Architecture (four). The one category that surprised me the most was the single-family house. If there were no issues with privacy, dozens more exemplary residences could have been added to this book. In fact, just about any residential block in Chicago will delight visitors with explicitly contemporary and innovative houses. This needs to be reiterated: just about any residential block in Chicago holds more design diversity than the residential blocks of all of New York City's boroughs put together. Such enviable devotion by Chicagoans to continue to create an architecture of its time is quite admirable.

Just one building in the book was completed in the 1970s. Thirteen were built in the 1980s, only six in the 1990s, 26 in the 2000s, a whopping 44 in the 2010s, seven since 2020, and three remain under construction: the CTA 'L' Station at State/Lake [005] by SOM is planned for completion by 2024, John Ronan's Chicago Park District Headquarters [098] in Brighton Park is expected to be completed by 2023, and the long-delayed Barack Obama Presidential Center [082] in Hyde Park by Tod Williams and Billie Tsien will be operational by 2025. Among my favorite buildings, I would include the Thompson Center [001] and the IIT Dormitory [072] both designed by Helmut Jahn, Wrightwood 659 [062] by Tadao Ando, and Rafael Viñoly's University of Chicago Booth School of Business [076]. I would also like to mention a new Chicago hybrid building type that has emerged in recent years. It is called co-location and comprises a community library on the street level and a housing block for seniors on the levels above. There are two such projects in the book: Independence Library and Apartments [089] by John Ronan and Northtown Library and Apartments [090] by Ralph Johnson, both on the North Side.

Now the reader may say: 'Very well, the buildings gathered in this book open Chicago's Post-Modern period that commenced in 1978. But why are all 100 projects identified here as Post-Modern? Now that we know when this period started, when did it end? There is a general belief that Post-Modernism ceased to exist sometime in the 1990s, but if that was the case, what is the name of the period we have been in since then?'

It is important that I clarify my position about this, which may not be shared by historians and other critics. I believe that Post-Modernism is still with us. History operates along a one-way street, no matter how winding it may be, and therefore modernism is a period that started sometime in the late nineteenth century and ended sometime in the twentieth. Whether it died in 1972, 1978, or 1980 is irrelevant. What is important is that it did indeed end and it cannot be reanimated, even if there are plenty of architects who are not exactly ready to give up their modernist aesthetics, which are often explained by economics rather than beliefs. There is no contradiction in such an approach, but with one condition—their creations should be classified as either late modern or neo-modern. And neo-modern, just like neo-classical, neo-Gothic, or any other style can happen in any period as a marginal occurrence that is out of sync with its time. It is a form of resistance of sorts, and when done well, it is a very admirable position, but nevertheless it is out of sync with its own time. Therefore, I believe that neo-modernism is a shade of Post-Modernism, an umbrella term describing a period that incorporates numerous other shades—classical or any historicist revivalism, high-tech, critical regionalism, new urbanism, deconstructivism, minimalism, parametricism, blobs, green architecture, iconic buildings, starchitecture, and so on. The same goes for modernism, which was not at all monolithic and comprised such shades as art nouveau, stripped classicism, futurism, art deco, De Stijl, Bauhaus modernism, constructivism, International Style, mid-century modern, brutalism, metabolism, Soviet modernism, and so on. All these styles started and ended, while often coexisting either entirely independently, fusing various characteristics, or in direct confrontation with one another. So, in a way, modernism cannot continue in the Post-Modern period without being nostalgic and utterly restraining. The key difference I see between modernism and Post-Modernism is in their relationship not even merely toward history and tradition, which was, of course, the starting point for both, but primarily to the pluralism of ideas and meanings.

While modernism was a reaction to historicist eclecticism, Post-Modernism was a reaction to the lack of eclecticism and pluralism. The key reason for blowing

e **Stanley Tigerman, *The Titanic*, 1978**

away modernist orthodoxy was to open up the discussion to new ideas, meanings, more personal experimentations, and to make the built environment more humanistic. The catalog of a remarkable exhibition, *Postmodernism—Style and Subversion 1970-1990*, that ran at the Victoria and Albert Museum in London from 2011 to 2012 stated: 'The modernists wanted to open a window onto a new world. Post-Modernism, by contrast, was more like a broken mirror, a reflecting surface made of many fragments. Its key principles were complexity and contradiction. It was meant to resist authority.' It also meant to push boundaries by asking such a seemingly silly but very important question as: 'Why not?' A search for a personal position and reflection is another important part of the movement. But perhaps the main reason for changes was the fact that a new generation of architects came of age and wanted to have their voices heard.

When many leading architects used history as their main source of inspiration in the 1980s, it seemed as if the movement focused on reviving historicist language was going to last for a long time. Yet this narrow theme turned out to be a blip. It survived barely a decade. In Chicago, buildings that were designed in classical or historical revival styles hardly left any

trace. This guide includes just three examples, two by outside architects: the 1987 U.S. Bank Building (formerly 190 South LaSalle Street) by New-York-based Philip Johnson [021], 1992's 77 West Wacker Drive by Spaniard Ricardo Bofill [004], and the 1991 Harold Washington Library by the Chicago firm Hammond, Beeby & Babka [024]. The latter is easily the most outrageous building in the city's history; it is quite literally overloaded with historical references, not much different from a picture book or a history lesson. When it was completed in 1991, the building was praised by American critics who hailed it as exemplary. It became perhaps the brightest flash of the entire Post-Modern movement in terms of its obsession with historical quotes and their wild distortions. Instead of becoming the trend's beacon, this grotesque structure extinguished it quite abruptly. That, of course, coincided with a very dry building period in the city and much of the world that lasted until the late 1990s. Nevertheless, architects used that break well to rethink their priorities and go beyond historical models, which enabled Post-Modernism to transition into other forms. Still, architecture never resorted to anything remotely modernist, remaining pluralist, discursive, and eclectic—the ideas this guide ultimately intends to celebrate.

Chicago Architects

Vladimir Belogolovsky

In this introduction, I would like to pay tribute to those architects who made significant contributions to the development of Chicago architecture in the years before 1978, prior to the period covered by this guide.

Chicagoans characterize their city as being much more driven by the pragmatism, sheer will, and determination of the locals than people do in the major coastal American cities such as New York, Miami, Los Angeles, and San Francisco. Yet it is Chicago that set the stage for harvesting much of what has become identified around the world as distinctly 'American'. Muddy Waters gave us the Chicago Blues. The aptly named rock band *Chicago* deftly blended jazz and rock. Al Capone and his violent gangsters made themselves household names by flaunting bootlegging laws during Prohibition. *Playboy* magazine helped usher in the sexual revolution. Perhaps Chicago's fundamental value was in being the country's largest meatpacking hub. In fact, there is no single innovation that transformed the American diet like the Chicago slaughterhouses. Because all the railroads from the south and west terminated in Chicago, millions and millions of hogs and cattle could be processed there and shipped east in refrigerated rail cars. For the first time, people could have fresh meat any day of the week, which was affordable to the masses. And then there is McDonald's. The McDonald brothers may have started their successful self-service drive-in restaurants in California, but it was a native Chicagoan, Ray Kroc, who opened the first restaurant for the McDonald's system in Des Plaines, Illinois, and eventually built the world's largest fast-food empire, headquartered in Chicago.

The kind of ingenuity and determination that characterize the innovations that Chicagoans have brought forth started early on. In Chicago's early days, its original street grid and buildings were built barely higher than the shoreline of Lake Michigan. That meant that initially, there was practically no naturally occurring drainage from the city, causing frequent epidemics, culminating in the 1854 outbreak of cholera that claimed the lives of six per cent of Chicago's population. The problem needed to be addressed urgently. Two years later, engineer Ellis S. Chesbrough (1813–1886) proposed a plan to install a citywide sewer system. It became the first comprehensive sewer system in the United States. The idea was to build it above ground and then raise all the city roads and buildings as much as 4 to 10 feet (1.2 to 3 meters) using an elaborate system of jacks [f]. More than 50 large masonry and brick buildings, along with the sidewalks attached to them, were raised already by 1858. Lifting and sometimes moving large buildings, some of which were up to six stories high, became common practice. During the lifting process, hotels, banks, offices, stores, and restaurants continued their business as usual. People were coming in at one address

f **Edward Mendel, Raising a block of buildings on Lake Street, Chicago, 1857**

and leaving at another. It was utterly dynamic. One city visitor reported with astonishment that he saw nine such moves on a single day. The process continued throughout the next decade. However, sewage still flowed into the lake and polluted the city's drinking water. A new tunnel was built deep under the lake to allow drinking water to be drawn farther from the shore, beneath the contaminated sewage, but eventually, the flow of the Chicago River was reversed in order to permanently carry Chicago's sewage away from the lake and into the rivers that feed the Mississippi River. So, before Chicago could become an arena for architects to design their progressive marvels here, its ground was quite literally completely re-engineered first.

The city's next watershed event was the Great Chicago Fire of 1871. Not only did it produce America's first building codes, but the tragedy changed the course of architectural history. The city had to be rebuilt practically from scratch and as quickly as possible. The genius of the Chicago architectural community yielded technology-driven modern architecture—frugal, rigorous, and proud skyscrapers clad in stone, brick, steel, and glass. It is a fact that no other American city can be compared to Chicago as far as cultivating a strong architectural culture, the backbone of which has been the world's most talented architects and engineers. For almost 150 years they have come and settled here while technology and industry were advancing as never before.

And unlike in other global cities, local architects tend to do their best work right here in Chicago. The city's relatively short history, even by American standards, is distinguished by an unprecedented succession of original architectural styles: First Chicago School, Second Chicago School, Prairie School Architecture, and the Chicago Seven are the most cited.

The First Chicago School, also known as the commercial style, refers to buildings built in the city from the early 1880s to the first decade of the twentieth century. It is easily identified by the three following principles.

First, these buildings, unusually tall for their time, were enabled by the use of new technology: steel-frame construction with masonry cladding. The façades are distinguished by large plate-glass windows. Second, these buildings' façades are divided into three parts, reflecting a classical column: the base (typically expressed with two lower sturdy floors), the shaft (a grid of repetitive windows), and the capital (a deeply projected cornice over a luxuriously decorated attic).

The third important feature of this style is in the design of the windows. They were also invented here and therefore are called Chicago windows. Each is composed of three parts that consist of a large, fixed center panel flanked by a small double-hung sash window on either side. These windows are either flat or configured into bays, and there are

g **William Le Baron Jenney, Home Insurance Building, Chicago, 1885. Top storys added in 1891. Demolished in 1931**

buildings that feature both, typically grouped into columns. Chicago buildings of this period are tough and very solidly put together, following efficient geometric order. They are gracefully clad in stone, brick, and terracotta, and shy away from displaying too much decoration.

Among the leading architects associated with the First Chicago School are William Le Baron Jenney, Henry Hobson Richardson, Dankmar Adler, Daniel Burnham, John Root, Solon Spencer Beman, and Louis Sullivan. Jenney (1832–1907), the oldest of the pack, went down in history as the Father of the American skyscraper. He was born and grew up in Massachusetts. After studying engineering and architecture at École Centrale Paris, where Gustave Eiffel was one of his classmates, Jenney returned to America and served as an engineer in the Union Army during the Civil War. After the war, he moved to Chicago in 1867 to start his architectural practice. Jenney's most important building was the Home Insurance Building [g]. This 10-story structure became the first fully steel-framed building and therefore is referred to as the first skyscraper. Built in 1885, two stories were added to the top in 1891. It was demolished in 1931.

Henry Hobson Richardson (1838–1886) was the first great American architect who developed his own style: Romanesque revival or Richardsonian Romanesque. Although he was not based in Chicago, one of the architect's most significant contributions was his Marshall Field Wholesale Store [h], a successful urban commercial prototype built a year after the architect's death. This seven-story building occupied the entire block and was clad in a rusticated stonework that gave it the appearance of an Italian Romanesque palazzo. The massive structure, one of the most emblematic examples of the First Chicago School and a model for subsequent commercial buildings throughout the United States, fell victim to its owner's consolidation plans and was unsentimentally demolished in 1930. The site is now a parking lot across South Franklin Street from the Willis Tower (originally the Sears Tower), once the tallest building in the world and still the tallest in Chicago.

Dankmar Adler (1844–1900) contributed greatly to rebuilding post-Great Fire Chicago. He hired talented draftsman Louis Sullivan in 1879, with Sullivan becoming a full partner after just two years with the firm. Adler's practice was renamed Adler & Sullivan in 1882. The partners were early employers and mentors of America's greatest architect—Frank Lloyd Wright—who came to work for them as an apprentice in 1888 and quickly grew to the position of head draftsman, only to be forced to leave in 1893 when his moonlighting was discovered. Adler was born in Germany and first came to Detroit

h **Henry Hobson Richardson, Marshall Field Wholesale Store, Chicago, 1887. Demolished in 1930**

in the US with his father at age 10. He went to Chicago to start his career and started his practice the year of the Great Fire. His best projects were designed in collaboration with Sullivan, particularly their Auditorium Building [i] with its 4,200-seat theater (1889), the Chicago Stock Exchange (1894; demolished in 1972), as well as numerous residences, theaters, clubs, hotels, and commercial buildings in Chicago and across the country. Yet their partnership was short-lived. It was dissolved in 1895 following the Panic of 1893.

Daniel Burnham (1846–1912) was born and raised in upstate New York and moved to Chicago at age eight. He tried his hand at various endeavors, including gold mining, politics, and business before finally establishing Burnham and Root with John Root (1850–1891) in Chicago in 1873. The successful partnership designed many great buildings, including the Rookery [j], the Monadnock Building [k], and the Marshall Field and Company Building (1892; now a Macy's).

Burnham's legacy, as the most prominent Beaux-Arts architect in America, was particularly solidified by the 1893 World's Columbian Exposition [l]. Root passed away two years before the exposition's opening and his original progressive design was radically transformed into what was nicknamed the White City, with splendid buildings in classical revival style. The city-in-miniature-like complex was built by some of America's finest architects in Jackson Park on the South Side, bordering Lake Michigan. The

k **Burnham and Root, Monadnock Building, Chicago, 1891. Photo: circa 1930**

organic lagoons and meadows were laid out by New York City's Central Park designer Frederick Law Olmsted (1822–1903). It was visited by more than 27 million people in just six months.

The Palace of Fine Arts, one of the grandest buildings at the exposition, was designed by Boston architect Charles Atwood (1849–1895), who is also credited with inventing the Chicago window in his design of the Reliance Building (1895), a skyscraper at 1 West Washington Street in the Loop. Atwood's Palace is the sole surviving structure from the fair. It was turned into the Museum of Science and Industry in 1933 and remains so to this day. Though little remained of the fair,

i **Adler & Sullivan, Auditorium Building, Chicago, 1889**

j **Burnham and Root, Rookery Building, Chicago, 1888. The lobby, remodeled by Frank Lloyd Wright, 1905**

⌐ **Daniel Burnham (Director of Works), World's Columbian Exposition, Chicago, 1893.
The Statue of the Republic and Administration Building**

the aesthetics of the White City gained traction and launched the city beautiful movement and neoclassical architecture became a preferred style in the US for many decades. Only in the 1940s and 1950s did modernism begin to win back important corporate, commercial, and educational commissions in America.

Meanwhile, the exposition's grounds, conceived as an ideal city, inspired Burnham to design his 1909 Plan of Chicago [m], which he envisioned as 'Paris on the Prairie' with wide diagonal boulevards culminating in noble fountains and sumptuous civic edifices. Even though much of his vision remained on paper, some of Chicago's most emblematic features came true, particularly in defining today's public parks along the shorefront of Lake Michigan, the Magnificent Mile, and the recreational Navy Pier. Even Frank Lloyd Wright, who opposed the nostalgic nature of neoclassicism, recognized Chicago as the most beautiful city in America, primarily due to Burnham's work. Apart from Burnham's buildings, it is his words that have become a familiar mantra to many an ambitious architect around the world: 'Make no little plans. They have no magic to stir men's blood and probably will not themselves be realized.'

Solon Spencer Beman (1853–1914) was born and grew up in Brooklyn. After

vacated and annexed by Chicago. It is now an Illinois state historic site on the far South Side. Beman was an eclectic architect and apart from some of his buildings designed in the First Chicago School style in Chicago and other cities in the eastern US, he designed many picturesque buildings in a variety of historicist styles, including Queen Anne, Gothic revival, and Romanesque revival. He also designed several temporary buildings for the exposition.

Louis Sullivan (1856–1924) was a Chicago-born architect who, together with Wright and Richardson, is considered to be one of the three greatest American architects. He is credited as being the creator of the modern, refined skyscraper. Before the Great Fire, he studied at MIT, worked briefly in Philadelphia with architect Frank Furness, and later apprenticed with Jenney for seven months after moving back to Chicago in 1873. From these functionalist architects, he developed an appreciation for all the key qualities that later would characterize his own architecture: boldness, originality, ornament, color, and most of all, a concern with the expression of structure and function.

Sullivan then studied for another year at the École des Beaux-Arts in Paris. While in Europe, the high point of his pilgrimage to Rome was Michelangelo's Sistine Chapel. He recalled staring at the frescoes for two straight days. He immediately identified with the Renaissance genius, realizing more clearly his own life's purpose. Quite immodestly, he saw himself as the next Michelangelo. He set out on developing his own art, a new architectural style. And, in fact, it is Sullivan who is widely regarded as the founding father of American architecture. He understood that a truly personal path should be discovered, not in the achievements of others, but within oneself.

Back in Chicago, Sullivan developed a theory about a new kind of architecture that would reflect rather than obscure the functions for which it was designed as was the case with the classical precedents. As we already know, Sullivan worked with Adler from 1879 until 1895. What was exciting about this productive

apprenticing for seven years, he started his own office in his hometown in 1877. Just two years later he received the most significant commission of his career, which prompted him to relocate to Chicago. He was hired by George Pullman, an American engineer, industrialist, and founder of the Pullman Car Company, which manufactured train cars, to design Pullman, Chicago, the first planned company town in the nation. The town grew into an enormous complex of more than 1,300 houses, a factory, administration building, water tower, theater, church, hotel, market, and schools. However, following the nationwide railroad Pullman Strike of 1894, the whole enterprise was

m **Daniel Burnham, 1909 Plan of Chicago. View looking west over the city, showing the proposed Civic Center, the Grand Axis, Grant Park, and the Harbor**

period in Chicago was that the city itself became a true laboratory for the construction industry, reflecting a remarkable population boom, exploding land values, and technological and industrial advancement. The changes were nothing short of revolutionary. The height limits of weight-bearing masonry buildings were a thing of the past. Modern technology was reflected in everyday living and architecture manifested itself as the most palpable confirmation of progress. In his 1896 essay *The Tall Office Building Artistically Considered*, Sullivan insisted: 'It is the pervading law of all things organic and inorganic, of all things physical and metaphysical, of all things human and all things superhuman, of all true manifestations of the head, of the heart, of the soul, that the life is recognizable in its expression, that form ever follows function. This is the law.' There was so much enthusiasm, a chance to build a completely new modern city. He noted: 'There can be no new New York, but there may be a new Chicago.'

By the mid-1890s it was the vision of Burnham's fairytale-like White City that captured the public's imagination, diverting attention from Sullivan's progressive stripping away of superfluous ornamentation from his architecture. As the architect accurately predicted, it would take 50 years before American architecture recovered. The 1909 Plan of Chicago solidified the detour, and the city was no longer a living laboratory. Instead, Chicago became immersed in modeling itself on Greco-Roman ideals. His early steps into what would one day evolve in time into modern architecture could not compete with a familiar, unchallenged, and genuinely likable image of the idealist past. Architects like Sullivan were no longer treated as prophets. His richly colored and ornamented Transportation Building, with large radiating golden arches marking its entrance, was a striking contrast to the other Beaux-Arts-style buildings at the fair. This memorable building was the only one to receive professional recognition and awards from abroad, while the public loved the totality and familiarity offered by the neoclassical edifices.

After his split with Adler, Sullivan struggled to win commissions. His last major work was the massive 12-story Carson, Pirie, Scott and Company Store designed and built in the Loop in stages from 1899 to 1904. The department store is now appropriately called the Sullivan Center. It distinguished itself with elaborate bronze-plated cast-iron florid ornamental work along with the two lower floors, particularly at the rounded corner entry at South State and East Madison streets. The store's huge windows—one per bay—are one of the earliest examples of Chicago windows. In the last 20 years of his life, Sullivan had only sporadic modest commissions such as banks, churches, residences, and façades, mostly outside of Chicago. Renowned for his uncompromising character and reluctance to make any concessions, he died in poverty in 1924, having survived on handouts from friends, including Wright. Both architects served as loose prototypes for Ayn Rand's 1943 novel *The Fountainhead*, with Wright as Howard Roark and Sullivan as his mentor, Henry Cameron.

Sullivan's protégé, Frank Lloyd Wright (1867–1959), was born and grew up in Wisconsin, just north of Chicago, and came to the city at the age of 20 for the same reason as many architects at the time: to build the new city. After his first year of working on small commissions for relatives and apprenticing at a couple of local firms, he was hired by Adler & Sullivan and worked with them for five years. During his second year at the firm, he settled with his first wife in the Chicago suburb of Oak Park, which is now home to the Frank Lloyd Wright Historic District where 25 of his houses still stand. They include his own Home and Studio (1889, 1898) on Chicago Avenue and his early masterpiece Unity Temple (1905), which pushed his work to a new level. After that, he said he 'ceased to be an architect of structure and became an architect of space'. The houses enabled Wright, who had practiced independently since 1893, to define a new style: the Prairie School. It emphasizes basic geometry and horizontal lines and planes to complement the land around Chicago. The direction was inspired by the arts and crafts movement as well as Sullivan's philosophy and details.

Wright lived a long productive life, practicing architecture for 72 years. He designed over 1,000 projects, of which more than half were realized. Some 270 of them were houses. Including those in Oak Park, about 40 houses can be found in Chicago today. His Robie House (1910), with its dramatically cantilevered roof, is now a part of the sprawling campus of the University of Chicago and a true masterpiece of Prairie School architecture. Apart from his houses, Wright was responsible for just one civic space in the city: the 1907 renovation of the lobbies and light court at the aforementioned Rookery. As the first decade of the twentieth century drew to a close, Wright focused on projects outside of Chicago.

In 1909, after 10 years of marriage, he abandoned his family and left for Europe with his mistress, Mamah Borthwick Cheney, the wife of Oak Park engineer Edwin Cheney, for whom Wright designed a house a few years earlier. After leaving his family, the architect spent most of his time creating masterpieces outside of Chicago. His futuristic Mile-High Illinois [n], a 528-story skyscraper designed in 1957 with the intention that it would be built in Chicago, never materialized. However, the one-kilometer-high Jeddah Tower, designed by Chicago firm Adrian Smith + Gordon Gill Architecture and currently under construction in Jeddah, Saudi Arabia, was undoubtedly modeled after Wright's daring and seemingly impossible vision.

After Burnham's exhibition, there were plenty of attractive buildings built in Chicago, but until the 1940s, most of

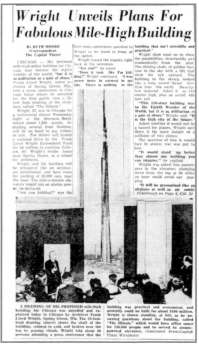

n Frank Lloyd Wright, The Mile-High Illinois (1.6 km), a visionary 528-story tower, Chicago, 1957. A newspaper article titled *Wright Unveils Plans For Fabulous Mile-High Building*

Tribune Tower:

o **John Mead Howells and Raymond Hood** p **Eliel Saarinen**

them were no longer uniquely local, nor were they representative of the times. As Sullivan had foreseen, making architecture modern was no longer the local architects' objective. And, as mentioned, even some of the key masterpieces of the First Chicago School were lost just a few decades after their creation due to their owners' relentless pursuit for greater profits. There was no architectural ambition for living up to Chicago's progressive past.

Even when the *Chicago Tribune*, the city's most popular daily newspaper, staged an international design competition to design 'the most beautiful and distinctive office building in the world' for its headquarters in 1922, it was yet another opportunity missed. This was despite the fact that it attracted the most talented international architects (263 entries from 23 countries). To be sure, the building that was ultimately built in 1925, and still proudly stands at the junction of Michigan Avenue and the Chicago River across from the Wrigley Building (1920–1924), fulfilled its promise: it

became the most beautiful office building in the world, at least in the eyes of the paper's owner and publisher Robert R. McCormick. The winning architects from New York, John Mead Howells and Raymond Hood, designed their 36-story tower in the neo-Gothic style [o]. Unfortunately, the jury of the twentieth century's most famous architectural competition failed to recognize other architects' pioneering attempts to manifest the spirit of the time and define a new look for the modern-age tower. Hood and Howells' building did not offer any particular innovation; it was just a refinement of earlier works such as the 1913 Woolworth Building in New York by Cass Gilbert. The second-prize project by Finnish architect Eliel Saarinen [p] was far more influential in the designs of the so-called art-deco-style skyscrapers that were built throughout the 1920s to 1930s, particularly in New York and including Hood's own RCA Building for Rockefeller Center. Numerous knockoffs followed, and it still serves as a model for architects all over the world. Walter

q Walter Gropius and Adolf Meyer

r Adolf Loos

Gropius and Adolf Meyer from Germany came up with another ground-breaking Bauhaus modern tower [q] devoid of any historical references. And yet another entry by Austrian Adolf Loos presented a multi-story Doric column [r] placed over a ziggurat; both forms seem to come straight from antiquity. In a strange, somewhat ironic or even provocative way, Loos's column predicts Post-Modern architecture by more than half a century. Nevertheless, there is something powerful in the phrase of an English critic Reyner Banham: 'Chicago has no tradition but modern.' It is so true. Once you think things have settled, something exciting happens here to stir up new energy and ideas. A constant influx of newcomers has a lot to do with it. Ludwig Mies van der Rohe became Chicago's next creative force. The architect came to the city with unmatched ambition. Suddenly, the almost-forgotten atmosphere of the nineteenth century Chicago First School style re-emerged in this pioneering architect's will to define a new kind of architecture that would be worthy of his

own century—the twentieth. His architecture would be referred to as the Chicago Second School style. Even after his death, Mies's 'less is more' motto would continue dominating the architectural scene in the city and it was embraced globally, at least for a while.

Ludwig Mies van der Rohe (1886–1969) was born in Aachen, Germany, and grew up in the family of a stonemason. He apprenticed at the office of Germany's most progressive architect, Peter Behrens, working alongside a young Le Corbusier and Walter Gropius. Strong criticism of buildings built in historical styles emerged in the years immediately following the First World War. Avant-garde architects viewed them as out of touch with the modern industrial age and new social order. There was an active search underway for lightness, greater transparency, and liberating means of assembling buildings. The projects that Mies succeeded in realizing in Europe before coming to America were small-scale undertakings.

Still, his German Pavilion for the 1929 Barcelona World's Fair, widely known as

Photo: Arthur Siegel (1954). Courtesy of Chicago History Museum

s **Ludwig Mies van der Rohe with a model of S. R. Crown Hall, College of Architecture, IIT, Chicago, 1956**

the Barcelona Pavilion, became one of the most revered and influential buildings of modern times. This petite, single-story ceremonial structure became a true manifesto that encapsulated Mies's early spatial and organizational principles, which would later be expressed on a much grander scale in Chicago. The building is a beautifully balanced composition of onyx, marble, and clear- and back-painted glass planes. It stands atop a gridded travertine plinth with two integrated reflecting pools, partially covered by a thin flat roof balanced over eight slender cruciform columns wrapped in chrome. Barcelona chairs and a bronze nude help bring the whole composition into graceful unity. The result, achieved through the use of only straight lines, rectangular shapes, and right angles, changed the idea of space and turned Mies's architecture into nothing but simplicity, clarity, and honesty. It was a total work of art or *Gesamtkunstwerk*, erasing all distinguishable boundaries between space and structure, indoor and outdoor, and architecture, furniture, and art.

Mies was the director of the Bauhaus when it was shut down by the Nazis in 1933. He was apolitical, but with few commissions in sight during those economically strapped years, he was looking for opportunities to align his progressive principles with the needs of the new Nazi government. The problem was Hitler's ambivalence about modernism's minimalist aesthetics, open plan designs, and insistence on revealing structure. Soon it would be Albert Speer's proposal for the megalomaniac city of Germania, with its splendid boulevards and pompous ministry palaces, that would preoccupy the attention of the delusional Führer.

There was no place for Mies's aesthetics and in 1938, he finally immigrated to America at the age of 52. He did not speak any English. He chose to come to Chicago because he was promised the position of head of the Department of Architecture at the Armour Institute of Technology on Chicago's near South Side. The planned merger of the Armour and Lewis Institutes resulted in the formation of the Illinois Institute of Technology (IIT) in 1940. So, the new IIT needed a new campus and Mies would get the commission, both for its master plan and all the individual buildings. For the next 20 years, he was preoccupied with heading the school and working on the campus project. A total of 20 buildings would be erected eventually, from the Minerals and Metals Research Building (1942) to the Metals Technology Building Extension (1958). The campus was the largest project in Mies's career.

t **Ludwig Mies van der Rohe, 860/880 and 900/910 Lake Shore Drive, Chicago, 1949 and 1951**

Today one can wander in dismay around IIT's crisp but bland matchbox-like buildings. However, we have to look at the context of the times in order to understand what these merely utilitarian and seemingly identical structures are all about and grasp all the intellectual gravitas that went into making them. The buildings, all exquisitely detailed and rendered in black-painted exposed structural steel, yellow-brown brick, bare concrete slabs, and large areas of clear and frosted glass were an attempt to create order out of the urban confusion all around them. Both Burnham's White City and IIT offered a new direction for architecture and urban planning. So much more so for IIT because it was the work of a single mind and architectural sensibility. In a way, it was the Barcelona Pavilion enhanced to city scale. In fact, it became a city within a city on a gridded carpet with rigorously placed volumes and spaces between them. The architect had total freedom not only in terms of geometry but even the organization of the program. After many trials, he established a modular system of 24-by-24-foot (7.3-by-7.3-meter) bays, each 12 feet (3.7 meters) high. All the dimensions utilized here fit into a larger system—horizontally, vertically, inside, and outside. Once you know

this, exploring the campus becomes a fascinating architectural and mathematical exercise. The 24-foot dimension was derived from the size of the standard American classroom of the time. The rationale of this disciplined approach was to achieve order, uniformity, and economy of construction.

Yet the project is more than just a kit of interrelated parts. One of the buildings, S. R. Crown Hall, College of Architecture [s], was conceived as the most important object on campus, clearly the architect's favorite. Even the 24-foot modular was tossed aside here to stretch every potential visual effect to the absolute maximum. The building is a gorgeous column-free single room, 120-by-220 feet, (36.5-by-67 meters) with a ceiling height of 28 feet (8.5 meters). The pure, prism-like volume has a flat roof supported by four external trusses, held six feet (1.8 meters) above the landscaping, to permit light into the basement through a continuous ribbon of clerestory windows. Crown Hall is a true masterpiece of large-span construction and is among the architect's greatest achievements.

Mies's inspirations ranged from Karl Friedrich Schinkel and Gerrit Rietveld to suprematism and De Stijl, but he was also greatly motivated by American skyscrapers, particularly those refined by

u **Ludwig Mies van der Rohe, Farnsworth House, Plano, Illinois, 1951**

Sullivan. Mies designed other projects in the city as work was underway on the IIT campus. One of his persistent interests was in creating fully glass-sheathed towers to express his 'skin and bones' concept, revealing buildings' underlying steel structure in the most uncompromising and optimistic ways. The idea was originally proposed in his early hypothetical projects in Berlin: the Friedrichstrasse Skyscraper (1921) and Glass Skyscraper (1922). In Chicago, Mies was able to realize more than a dozen glazed towers, most notably two pairs of residential blocks, 860/880 and 900/910 Lake Shore Drive [t], where he first employed exposed I-beams to dominate the exterior as symbolic decor accentuating verticality, thinness, and materiality of his buildings' structure within.

This very short excursion into Mies's career would be incomplete without at least mentioning another jewel from his genius: Farnsworth House [u] in Plano,

Illinois, about 56 miles (90 kilometers) from Chicago. This tiny glass house projects a sense of liberation from architecture's greatest challenge—gravity—although to achieve it, the architect liberated it from all kinds of life's pragmatics. The house's original owner is long gone, and it is no longer inhabited. It was turned into a museum that welcomes a constant stream of visitors who come in contact with what is truly one of the most poetic, even spiritual architectural creations of the twentieth century—a work of art first and a house second.

Mies died in 1969. His IIT campus is no longer as pure as it was originally conceived. Other architects—both those who followed his style to the letter and those who bring their own visions into the profession—have added to it. This guide features three of the most recent additions by Helmut Jahn, John Ronan, and the team of Rem Koolhaas and Jeanne Gang. Mies's last project, the IBM Building (now

AMA Plaza), a 52-story tower, was completed without him in downtown Chicago in 1973. Speaking of his intentions, Mies said that as an architect: 'You should express something other than yourself, if you really must express something. This something else is the essence, the spirit of civilization that architecture represents. This is what great buildings have done. They have said something about an epoch, not about a man. If a man must express himself, let him be a painter.'

Through the architect's rich body of work and long-held position of an admired educator, Mies created a methodology and architectural language that has attracted a global following. His 'universal' approach was carried on by his colleagues and students. In Chicago alone, Mies's students included Gene Summers of C.F. Murphy, Myron Goldsmith of SOM, David Haid, Bruno Conterato, Joseph Fujikawa of Fujikawa Johnson and Associates, and the architect's grandson, Dirk Lohan. All these architects created buildings in Chicago following their mentor's principles, collectively making a strong impact on the city. Perhaps Lake Point Tower (1965), a 70-story skyscraper situated at the bottom of Navy Pier, is the most imaginative interpretation of the Miesian modernist box. Shaped as a soft 'Y' in plan, the building was also designed by Mies's students George Schipporeit and John Heinrich to explore the potentials of curved geometry, mimicking Mies's own Glass Skyscraper that he envisioned back in Berlin in the early 1920s. By the mid-1970s, architecture by Mies's followers evolved into largely mass production of International Style modernism. It has become a noticeable presence in Chicago and in many cities around the world. To an untrained eye, these buildings are pretty much indistinguishable, if not just about the same. Both the public and professional communities have developed a degree of unhappiness with such anonymous architecture. Understandably, the new generation of architects felt that the time had come to express their own creative visions. One of them, Robert Venturi (1925–2018), a famous Philadelphia architect who brought our attention to the richness of the architectural environment around this time, which he eloquently expressed by turning Mies's 'Less is More' phrase around by declaring 'Less is a Bore'. This was a blatant assertion that

Photo: Ryan Guenther

v **Louis Sullivan, Getty Tomb, Graceland Cemetery, Chicago, 1890**

contemporary architects would no longer accept Mies's ideology as dominating and unquestioned. It should come as no surprise that it was in Chicago where this defiance was felt the strongest. As mentioned in my foreword, in 1976, the Chicago Seven group, the first generation of Post-Modernist architects, was established and started voicing alternative views, even though their own positions had little in common. It was that diversity that became their common goal.

Mies was buried at Graceland Cemetery, a large historic garden burial ground uptown on the North Side of Chicago that was established in 1860. He lies beneath a flat slab of black granite designed by Dirk Lohan. The cemetery is the final resting place of many prominent Chicagoans, particularly Chicago mayors, Illinois governors, lawyers, businessmen, philanthropists, and artists. We will also find here the graves of many great architects, as well as mausoleums, monuments, and tombstones designed by them for their clients and friends. The most famous architects buried at the cemetery include William Le Baron Jenney, who designed several expansions of the cemetery; Daniel Burnham, whose tombstone is situated on a tiny island in Lake Willowmere; Burnham's partner John Wellborn Root; Louis Sullivan, whose funeral expenses and modest tombstone were paid for by his friends; Marion Mahony Griffin (1871–1961), one of the first licensed female architects in the world and among the original members of the Prairie School; László Moholy-Nagy (1895–1946), the Bauhaus teacher, artist, and founder of the New Bauhaus (now IIT Institute of Design in Chicago); and Bruce Goff (1904–1982), an organic architect influenced by Sullivan and Wright, although his most representative projects were built in Oklahoma, some of his houses can be found on the streets of Chicago and across Illinois. There are also tombstones of three quintessential modern Chicago architects who worked at Skidmore, Owings & Merrill (SOM): Bruce Graham, Walter Netsch, and Fazlur Khan. Bruce Graham (1925–2010) was a Colombia-born architect and designer of two of the most iconic Chicago

towers: the John Hancock Center (1969) and Sears Tower (1973; now Willis Tower). Graham was called 'the Burnham of his generation' and a small alley in the shadow of his Hancock Center was named after him; it runs parallel with Mies van der Rohe Way. Walter Netsch (1920–2008) was the designer of Paul V. Galvin Library (1962) at IIT to match the iconic style of Mies's other buildings on campus and designed the Behavioral Sciences Building (1968) at the University of Illinois. Together with Graham, Netsch also designed Inland Steel Building (1957) with brushed stainless-steel cladding and flexible interior floor layouts with no interior columns. It was the first office building built in the Loop since the Great Depression. For more than 20 years, SOM was among the original tenants here. Fazlur Khan (1929–1982) was a Bangladeshi-American architect and the structural engineer behind both the John Hancock Center and Sears Tower. He is known as the Father of Tubular Design for high-rises.

Other distinguished monuments at Graceland Cemetery include two mausoleums designed by Sullivan: for lumber merchant Henry Harrison Getty [v] and his wife, and for Getty's partner, Martin Ryerson. Industrialist George Pullman's monument was designed by Solon Spencer Beman. Graceland Cemetery is in no way a complete tribute to those architects who practiced their art in Chicago, but it is a delightful city within a city and an apt place to reflect on the roles that people who are buried here played in building the great city of Chicago that we know today. Following the list of 100 entries, this book presents a group of interviews I have conducted with six leading Chicago-based contemporary architects: Stanley Tigerman (1930–2019), Helmut Jahn (1940–2021), Adrian Smith (b. 1944), Ralph Johnson (b. 1948), John Ronan (b. 1963), and Jeanne Gang (b. 1964). We discussed in detail their work, intentions, and inevitably, what they think of Chicago architecture. Four of these architects were born in the city and two came here because they believed that it would be the best place in the world to practice architecture.

1

001	James R. Thompson Center
002	333 West Wacker Drive
003	OneEleven
004	77 West Wacker Drive
005	CTA 'L' Station at State/Lake
006	Self Park
007	Chicago Architecture Center
008	Chicago Riverwalk
009	Illinois Center Sporting Club
	(now Lakeshore Sport & Fitness at Illinois Center)
010	Two Prudential Plaza (Pru Two)
011	Aqua Tower
012	St. Regis Chicago (formerly Wanda Vista Tower)
013	Blue Cross Blue Shield Tower
014	Crain Communications Building (formerly Associates Center)
015	Jay Pritzker Pavilion
016	Cloud Gate
017	Crown Fountain
018	Chicago Art Institute, The Modern Wing
019	Washington-Wabash Station
020	Xerox Center
021	U.S. Bank Building (formerly 190 South LaSalle Street)
022	71 South Wacker (formerly Hyatt Center)
023	Chicago Board of Trade Addition
024	Harold Washington Library

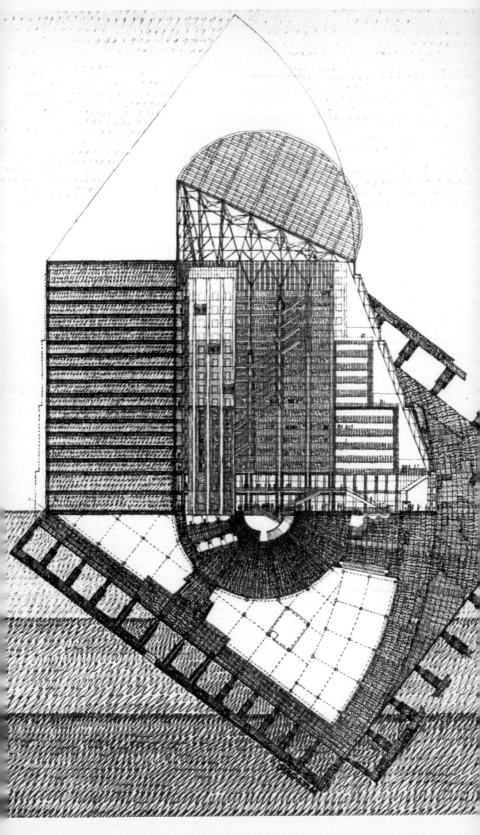

Juxtaposed axonometric views, plans, and section. Marker drawings by Helmut Jahn

James R. Thompson Center

100 West Randolph Street, Loop
Murphy/Jahn (since 2012, JAHN, Chicago)
1985

🚆🚆🚆🚆🚆🚆 To Clark/Lake
🚌 22, 24 to Clark & Lake; 134, 135, 136, 156 to LaSalle & Randolph

Every city has its odd building. Paris has the Centre Pompidou, London has Lloyd's, New York has the Guggenheim. Naturally, Chicago, the architectural capital of the world, has one too. Unquestionably it is the James R. Thompson Center, named for the four-term Illinois Republican governor (1977–1991) who was brave enough to get it built in 1985. Home to offices of the Illinois state government, the building is unlike anything you have ever seen. Unusually shaped and brightly clad in multi-colored glass panels, it occupies its entire city block and sits tightly across the street from City Hall in the central Loop area. You will not see anything remarkable on three sides, but come to the intersection of W Randolph and N Clark and you will be knocked off your feet by three sweeping tiers of conically-curved and angled setbacks. This surprising move generously freed up pricey urban land for a triangular public plaza. There are trees, benches, the child-like, colossal sculpture *Monument with Standing Beast* (fiberglass, 1984) by Jean Dubuffet, multiple options for shortcuts, and rare vantage points in the heart of the dense Chicago metropolis. // The glass-and-steel building may be nicknamed the 'Starship' for its futuristic shape, which seems to have landed from outer space in the shadows of Miesian boxes around it. However, according to its creator, German-born Helmut Jahn (1940–2021) who was one of Chicago's most charismatic architects, it is a symbolic structure, a contemporary take on a traditional state capital, and a domed government building. Topped with a sliced-off cylindrical crown, the center projects its iconic silhouette that serves as a central skylight over the immense 17-story, 160-foot-diameter (49-meter) rotunda below. This high-tech, cathedral-like, kaleidoscopic space is nothing short of breathtaking. It is invigorated by moving escalators and glass-enclosed elevators, constantly shifting sunlight and shadows and streams of people that come here for all sorts of reasons—meetings with bureaucrats, taking Chicago Transit Authority (CTA) trains, grabbing fast food at the basement-level cafeteria, and simply pausing to enjoy the exhilarating energy of the place itself. The whole building is hollowed out to celebrate the centrality and transparency of government. Symbolism extends to the choice of materials—toned down red, white, and blue glass panels arranged in bands that look more like salmon, silver, and baby blue. Not everyone agrees with this color palette, but these hues provide the building with a peculiar character that simultaneously evokes the 1980s and contemplates the sleek future. // Overall, the center's appearance is very impressive and perfectly civically minded. However, when it first opened, the press mainly paid attention to its environmental performance, which has never been 'high-architecture's' strongest suit. Most controversially, large expanses of glazing resulted in overheating in summer and cold drafts in winter. There are infamous photographs of office workers taking refuge under beach umbrellas on hot summer days, while ice would form on the interior wall panels in winter. Cooling towers had to be brought in to correct these issues. This all could have been avoided if the originally-specified curved, double-paned insulated glass panels were installed, but they were found to be prohibitively expensive. Flat, insulated glass panels were suggested, but that solution was dismissed by the architect as oversimplifying his building's design. That led to the use of single-paned (non-insulated), curved glass panels. The air conditioning system remains very costly to operate. // Apart from the great expense needed to maintain comfortable internal temperatures, the center shows many signs of wear and tear caused by years of deferred maintenance. Additionally, limited accessibility and hours of operation—it is open only during office hours and closed on weekends—never encouraged the public to embrace the building as a true civic space. Perhaps

Photo: Rainer Viertlböck

001 C

the center's ambition of creating a grand public space was a mismatch with its purpose as an office building from the outset. Reimagined, the structure could include a major IT company office, retail, restaurants, and why not condos and hotels to help pay for the building's operation? That is exactly what Jahn suggested in a speculative 2015 proposal: giving the building new life through adaptive reuse and a new 110-story tower to anchor the southwest corner. This may be the best way to save the Thompson Center because in 2019, Illinois Democratic Governor Jay Robert Pritzker signed a bill to begin the process of its sale. This initiative may lead to the building's demolition, which would be ironic, as the Governor's uncle, Jay Pritzker (1922–1999) and aunt Cindy Pritzker are revered by architects around the world for establishing the esteemed Pritzker Architecture Prize. // Chicago architects, historians, preservationists, and activists are now scrambling to save this most dazzling structure, although one would think that it would be enough to simply take a peek inside to see that it is a true architectural marvel. However, apparently seeing does not always translate into believing. Quite the opposite in fact. Few recognize the building's virtues and saving it will be an uphill battle. The demolish camp is much larger than the save camp. Those in favor of demolition tend to notice only what's in front of them: noise, dirt, a broken door here, a malfunctioning elevator there, the smell from the food court, too hot, too cold, too much glare, too much space wasted. Their lists mention nothing about wonder, awe, aura, and magic. Thankfully, the building has been listed among the most endangered historic places in Illinois in recent years, but the structure is not old enough to be awarded the landmark status urgently needed to save it from unjustified destruction. And so, as the fate of the Thompson Center remains unclear, here is a plea to the building itself: Starship Chicago, please don't go.

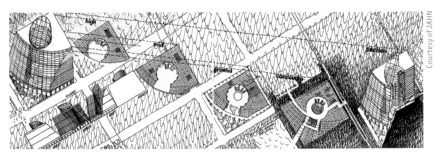

Courtesy of JAHN

333 West Wacker Drive

333 West Wacker Drive, Loop
Kohn Pedersen Fox Associates,
KPF (New York)
1983

002 C

🚇🚇🚇🚇🚇🚇 To Clark/Lake
🚌 37 to Franklin & Lake/W Wacker/Lake;
125 to Walker & Lake

Unlike the nearby Thompson Center [001], which is curved for reasons that are purely symbolic and conceptual, this building's dramatic, almost full-height curve is entirely a consequence of its strategic location at the junction of the Chicago River's three branches. The 36-story building could be described in just one word: reflection. However, it is more complicated than that. It is a reflection of the architectural currents of its time and of its diverse urban context. In plan, 333 West Wacker is shaped like a truncated triangle or a tall slice of pie with a large part of its tip already bitten off. The building's face, or one could say its chest, is its most impactful and memorable asset. If you take the popular Chicago Architecture River Cruise it will be pointed out that the building's sweeping curved blue-green glass façade matches the river's turn and color. That distinction alone helped the building top a list of the city's most respected structures. Readers of the *Chicago Tribune* voted it their 'Favorite Building' in 1995. The tower follows the hard lines of the surrounding structures on the Loop side. Completed in 1983, at the height of the Post-Modern period, the building tried to push itself as far away as possible from the restraint, rectilinearity, and severity of the universal Miesian modernist boxes that by then were viewed as boring and impersonal. Even the building's horizontal features such as its oversized, half-rounded mullions of stainless steel are emphasized here over the vertical ones, which are downplayed by painting them to match the color of the glass. This diversion from Miesian tradition is an attempt to relate the building to the horizontality of the river rather than expectedly celebrate the abstract notion of the verticality of the city. // 333 West Wacker is nuanced. For example, it is not all about glass. Instead, the base is articulated in gray granite and green marble. This choice of materials not only anchors the graceful structure by dressing the double-height lobby, but it also helps to hide another full floor above it, which is assigned to mechanical equipment and enables even the lower office floors to hover above the adjacent elevated train tracks. Another distinctive feature is the building's top. It is tastefully set back from the sweeping curve in a definitive straight line, which is a reminder to modernists that buildings used to make special gestures towards the sky instead of being cut abruptly in mid-air. // The tower was designed by the New York-based architectural giant Kohn Pedersen Fox. They are now among the most dominant corporate firms in the industry, but 333 West Wacker was one of their first major projects following the firm's founding in 1976. Back then, the success of this office building put KPF on the national map and secured the firm many subsequent commissions in Chicago. In fact, it also designed the two buildings on either side here: 225 West Wacker (1989) and 191 North Wacker (2002). This corner thereby serves as an enviable showcase for the company, reflecting not only the architects' talent for designing large commercial projects, but also their versatility. All three buildings represent very different design approaches, reflecting contrasting architectural fashions from different decades.

Photo: Kevin Dickert

OneEleven

111 West Wacker Drive, Loop
Handel Architects (New York)
2014

003 **C**

🚇🚇🚇🚇🚇🚇 To Clark/Lake
🚌 22, 24 to Clark & Lake; 134, 135, 136, 156 to LaSalle & Wacker/Lake; 36, 62 to Dearborn & Wacker/Lake

OneEleven, a 58-story luxury residential building on the Chicago River, was designed by Gary Handel, founder of the large corporate New York firm Handel Architects, as a retrofit for the abandoned Waterview Tower project. Originally designed as a 92-story (1,050 feet or 320 meters) hotel and condominium by Thomas Hoepf, who was with Teng & Associates at the time, the 2008 global financial crisis halted the project mid-construction. The 26-story structure was dormant for five years before Handel was commissioned to reprogram it as a less ambitious residential tower. The building's original stone façade was removed in favor of a highly reflective silver glass exterior with a deeply recessed, lit ribbon that runs up and across all four façades, breaking the building's mass into a series of interlocking blocks. These abstractly mimic the Chicago River's sharply-angled pathway below. Ascending the building, the ribbon creates opportunities for green spaces and terraces. At the 25th floor, it visually ties into the setback of its neighbor to the west, a classic art deco building at 121 West Wacker, and promptly marks the height of the unfinished structure of the original Waterview Tower. This all-amenities level features an indoor pool, sun deck, fire pit, and outdoor kitchens.

77 West Wacker Drive

004 C

77 West Wacker Drive, Loop
*Ricardo Bofill Taller de
Arquitectura (Barcelona, Spain)*
1992

🚇🚇🚇🚇🚇🚇 To Clark/Lake
🚌 134, 135, 136, 156 to LaSalle &
Wacker/Lake; 22, 36, 62 to Dearborn &
Wacker/Lake

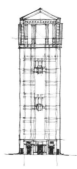

Courtesy of Ricardo Bofill Taller de Arquitectura

1

Standing on the Chicago River embankment diagonally across from the 65-story Marina City Towers (by architect Bertrand Goldberg; 1968), 77 West Wacker is an imposing, freestanding 50-story office tower. It was the corporate headquarters of United Airlines from 2007 to 2012. The building is the first Chicago project realized by Spain's most prolific architect, Barcelona-based Ricardo Bofill (1939–2022), who designed over 1,000 projects in over 50 countries during his hugely successful career. (The architect's second Chicago project was the 35-story Dearborn Center; 2003). 77 West Wacker, designed in the late 1980s and completed in 1992, is one of the most prominent examples of Post-Modernism in the city and a child of its time, especially following Philip Johnson's AT&T Building (1984) at 550 Madison in Manhattan. It became a beacon for numerous American architects and their clients, who saw dressing their buildings in pseudo-classical 'suits' as a way to 'legitimize' them. However, for Bofill, the design was not simply about following the period's fashion. The architect's tallest building became a logical climax of his prolonged, so-called French period during the 1970s and 1980s. Several of his large social-housing projects were built around Paris and in Montpellier during this time, with heavy displays of exaggerated precast concrete classical elements that make these buildings look like colonnaded and porticoed monuments. // In Chicago, the architect's 'modern classical'-styled high-rise is expressed in Portuguese Royal white granite and a silver-gray glass curtain wall. The building's straight-up form, extruded all the way to the top, culminates in a four-sided Greek portico inspired by Giotto's campanile at Florence Cathedral. The likeness is not stylistic, but in the way the building's façades are divided into various levels and linked by a grid of ornamented posts and lintels. In plan, the tower is a square with four cut-out corners—a smart solution for creating twice as many executive corner offices on each floor that take advantage of expansive all-around views. The ground floor, with three oversized gabled portals along either side of the building's northwest corner, is fully devoted to a monumental 59-foot (18-meter) high lobby dressed in gray and white marble. The lobby contains a mini Stonehenge-like sculpture called *Three Lawyers and a Judge* by Xavier Corberò, the Antonio Tapies painting *Big Eyelids*, and Bofill's own *Twisted Columns* sculpture rising over a black granite reflecting pool and lush plantings of bamboo trees. Both Corberò and Tapies are world-renowned Catalan artists.

Courtesy of Ricardo Bofill Taller de Arquitectura

CTA 'L' Station at State/Lake
Intersection of West Lake and
North State
Skidmore, Owings & Merrill,
SOM (Chicago)
To be completed in 2024

🚇🚇🚇🚇🚇 To State/Lake
🚇 To Lake
🚌 2, 6, 10, 29, 36, 62, 146, 148 to State/Lake

The new Chicago Transit Authority 'L' Station located at the intersection of West Lake and North State near the landmark Chicago Theater will replace the old one, built in 1895 as part of the Loop's original elevated train system. It aims to renew aging infrastructure, enhance transfers and the street-level experience, improve passenger and pedestrian accessibility and safety, and reduce intersection obstructions. The new station's single dominating design feature is its spanning canopy—a turtle shell-like glass marquee hovering gracefully over the street and just missing four building corners. The project was designed by Skidmore, Owings & Merrill (SOM), one of Chicago's most storied architectural firms, and will include almost theatrical, rim-like balconies along its north and south sides. Accessible via escalators, they will be open to the public free-of-charge and will be used as scenic platforms to overlook State in either direction. The second-busiest station on the Loop's 'L', the new structure will accommodate four elevators (one at each corner) and a flyover bridge with ADA access. Construction is expected to take about three years and the project is due to be completed by 2024. The benefits of this civic-minded undertaking are obvious. The only questionable aspect is its price tag, estimated to be a startling $180 million. The budget is comparable to some of the major cultural facilities around the world that surpass the size of this station many times over, even though it is not even a fully enclosed building and more like a pavilion.

Self Park ↗
60 East Lake Street, Lake
Stanley Tigerman & Associates
(Since 1986 Tigerman McCurry
Architects, Chicago)
1984–1986

🚇🚇🚇🚇🚇 To State/Lake
🚇 To Lake
🚌 3, 4, 26, 66, 143, 147, 151, 157 to Michigan & Lake/Randolph; 2, 6, 10, 29, 36, 62, 146, 148 to State/Lake

This mid-block parking garage screams its message loud and clear: 'I am a parking garage! Park your car here!' What you see is what you get—the front is a giant replica of

Photo: Barbara Karant

a Rolls Royce. The image is crude and exaggerated, but the resemblances to an old Rolls' grille, headlights, fenders, front bumper, and awnings stylized with half-tire treads, topped by a statue in full armor serving as a hood ornament, and even the second-floor 'Self Park' sign that looks like—you guessed it—a license plate, are all quite literal in their representation. The entire garage is a 12-story building-cum-billboard—an eye-catching example of a 'decorated shed', as defined by Robert Venturi, Denise Scott Brown, and Steven Izenour in their seminal 1972 book *Learning From Las Vegas*. The building's witty face makes any additional signage here quite unnecessary. Passing by this

humorously designed building may suggest that perhaps it was drawn by the client's own child. The project was in fact designed by Stanley Tigerman (1930–2019), one of the city's most prominent architects who was often referred to as the 'Dean of Chicago Architecture'. Self Park became one of the earliest and most outspoken manifestations of a revolt against Mies van der Rohe's famous dictum 'less is more' in support of Venturi's statement that 'less is a bore'. Despite being widely recognized as a classic example of Chicago's Post-Modern architecture, the building has become an old joke. Yet those who see Tigerman's creation for the first time will surely feel surprised or may even laugh.

Chicago Architecture Center

007 **C**

111 East Wacker Drive,
New Eastside
*Adrian Smith + Gordon Gill
Architecture (Chicago)*
2018

🚇🚇🚇🚇🚇 To State/Lake
🚇 To Lake
🚌 2, 3, 6, 10, 20, 26, 66, 120, 121, 151,
157 to Michigan & E Wacker; 134, 135,
136 to Wacker & Michigan; 4, 6 to Wacker
(Upper) & Stetson; 3, 20, 26, 66, 143,
146, 147, 148, 151, 157, 850, 851, 855 to
Michigan & South Water

The 20,000-square-foot (1,860-square-meter) Chicago Architecture Center, half of which is devoted to exhibiting highlights of local, national, and international architecture, is among the most popular attractions in Chicago and therefore cannot be overlooked by this guide, despite the fact that it focuses on buildings, not interiors. The center's unusual popularity has been achieved for two reasons. First, it is the home of the world-famous Chicago Architecture River Cruise, which uses a whole fleet of boats operated by Chicago's First Lady. Rated as Chicago's most popular tour, it is also the number one boat tour in North America. Second, the center houses a room-sized scale model of Chicago. Its footprint of 600 square feet (56 square meters) covers 3.3 by 2.3 miles (5.3 by 3.7 kilometers) of the city's central area. First built in 2009 for a temporary exhibition, the model attracted so much attention that no one dared dismantle it. It is regularly updated now and currently offers visitors a bird's-eye view of 4,250 miniature buildings, stylishly painted in a single light-gray color. The installation is accompanied by a video-storytelling feature on a day-night cycle. Formerly known as the Chicago Architecture Foundation, the Chicago Architecture Center is a nonprofit cultural organization that hosts dozens of daily boat, walking, bus, and 'L' train tours, as well as special temporary exhibitions, architecture-related programs, lectures, and events for all ages. It runs a free Open House Chicago festival every October. // The current space was designed by the local architectural duo Adrian Smith and Gordon Gill, founders of the firm that carries their names Adrian Smith + Gordon Gill Architecture (AS+GG) and opened in 2018. The largely see-through center was inserted into the base of the One Illinois Center (Mies van der Rohe; 1970). The architects lowered what used to be the tower's ground floor by dismantling its massive base to increase the original lobby to a dramatic space with 40-foot (12-meter) full-height windows overlooking the Chicago River and the Michigan Avenue Bridge. The original building, along with other neighboring towers, was built over the Illinois Central Railroad's subterranean yard, which stretched over 80 acres (32 hectares) that now compose the New East Side neighborhood built on top of it. The new interior space was also enlarged outwards all the way to the perimeter columns that used to be exposed. The center comprises the box office and orientation center, exhibition spaces, a bookstore, a lecture hall, and a large, mezzanine-level exhibition gallery with supersized architectural models, mostly skyscrapers from around the world. One of them, a replica of the AS+GG-designed Jeddah Tower (the world's future tallest building), stretches from the ground floor all the way to the upper gallery's ceiling.

1

Chicago Riverwalk

008 C

South Bank of the Main Stern of
the Chicago River between Lake
Michigan and the confluence of
the main, north, and south branches of
the Chicago River
Ross Barney Architects (Chicago)
Phase 1 (2009), Phase 2 (2015),
Phase 3 (2016)

🚇🚇🚇🚇🚇 To State/Lake or Clark/Lake
🚇 To Lake
🚌 2, 3, 6, 20, 26, 66, 120, 121, 151, 157
to Michigan & E Wacker; 2, 29 to State &
E Wacker; 134, 135, 136, 156 to LaSalle/
Wacker; 37 to Wells & Lake; 125 to Wacker
& Lake

The Chicago Riverwalk is a unique urban promenade skillfully woven out of what were once disjointed parking lots, docks, piers, and other unsightly leftover spaces along the Chicago River. It now constitutes the 1.25-mile(2-km)-long pedestrian path that meanders uninterrupted along the south bank of the river between Lake Michigan and the Y-shaped confluence of its three branches. The Riverwalk is one of those fortunate projects that could never have been designed so imaginatively from scratch. It was Carol Ross Barney, the founder of Ross Barney Architects and a native Chicagoan, who had the vision to join all the scattered pieces and reimagine them as a singular and gorgeous civic space with plenty of choices for both leisure and commerce. The project has been many years in the making and its expansion is likely to continue. What has been built so far is the result of three phases completed in 2009, 2015, and 2016. Every block stretches between Chicago's iconic bascule bridges and is designed to have a distinctive character. There are bench-lined walkways and ramps, river-level esplanades built out into the river to accommodate dining terraces, seating steps at the river's edge, jetties, marinas, and landscaped rest areas peppered with murals, sculptures, and banners. All are stitched together into an enjoyable borderless stroll with the help of a series of underbridge connections between the blocks. These links are spatially generous and sleek and accompanied by structurally independent neat canopies that shield passers-by from the open roadways above. // Highlights along the Riverwalk include the Vietnam War Memorial between North Wabash and North State, Marina Plaza with its high-backed teak benches, and the River Theater, a block-wide seating area between North Clark and North LaSalle with a fully-accessible path that connects the river with the city along West Wacker in several sweeping zigzags. There is also the Jetty, a series of piers and floating wetland gardens. Situated between North Wells and North Franklin, this is a perfect spot to view Art on theMART, the largest video-projection art installation in the world. It uses 34 30,000 lumen projectors to project contemporary artwork onto the 2.5-acre (1-hectare) river façade of theMART directly across the river. Situated right in the heart of downtown, the Riverwalk enjoys the most spectacular skyline views in the city. It can be accessed at numerous points along West and East Wacker and there are ADA compliant ramps on the east side of North State, the west side of North Clark, and west side of North Franklin. It is a remarkable example of how older cities can be reinvented by carefully examining what is already there, instead of endlessly expanding or building from scratch.

Chicago Riverwalk: the Jetty, a series of piers and floating wetland gardens between North Wells and North Franklin—the perfect location from which to view Art on theMART across the river

Illinois Center Sporting Club (now Lakeshore Sport & Fitness at Illinois Center)

009 C

211 North Stetson Avenue,
New Eastside
Kisho Kurokawa (Tokyo, Japan) with Fujikawa Johnson and Associates (Chicago) 1987–1990

Courtesy of Kisho Kurokawa architect & associates

🚇🚇🚇🚇🚇 To State/Lake
🚇 To Lake
🚇 To Clarke/Lake or Washington
🚌 3, 4, 26, 66, 120, 143, 147, 151, 157 to Michigan & Lake/Randolph

Advertised as the largest gym in the Loop with the best options for fitness classes and the tallest indoor climbing wall in North America, the Lakeshore Sport & Fitness at Illinois Center opened in 1990 as the Illinois Center Sporting Club (ICSC). The freestanding corner building is located diagonally across the intersection from the pencil-like 64-story Two Prudential Plaza building, built the same year and the next entry in this guide. Completely surrounded by very tall towers in the New East Side, this modestly scaled six-story building was designed as the only built work in the US by Kisho Kurokawa (1934–2007), a famous Japanese architect, one of the founders of metabolism (a movement based on principles of building urban megastructures similar to organic biological processes developed in post-war Japan), and the designer of the Nakagin Capsule Tower (1972) in Tokyo. In a way, the Sporting Club is a building within a building—a dark-glazed prism encased in a white-painted steel frame. The exoskeletal exterior is more decorative than structural and its multiple symbolic and historical references make the building a curious Post-Modernist work, strangely enough, expressed in a high-tech fashion. Here, however, the architect worked with Chicago's architectural history, paying tribute to two of the city's most prominent architects: Mies van der Rohe and Louis Sullivan. Mies is associated with the lower part of the center's steel frame, while the four roof-top turrets recall Sullivan's People's Savings Bank (Chicago; 1911). These closely-spaced elements look like the legs of an upturned table. They originally supported kinetic sculptures by Japanese artist Susumu Shingu, a whimsical nod to Chicago's famous nickname—the Windy City. At some point, the sculptures were removed for no apparent reason and their whereabouts remains a mystery. The two inverted-steel arches on the North Stetson side point to the building's entrance. Their mirror images evoke bridges over the nearby Chicago River. The concrete-frame interior is organized around a large, centrally-located atrium with an open connecting stair.

Photo: Valentino Matteis

Two Prudential Plaza (Pru Two)
010 C

180 North Stetson Avenue,
New Eastside
Loebl Schlossman & Hackl (Chicago)
1990

🚇🚇🚇🚇🚇 To State/Lake
🚇 To Lake
🚇 To Clarke/Lake or Washington
🚌 3, 4, 26, 66, 120, 143, 147, 151, 157 to
Michigan & Lake/Randolph

Framed by the Crain Communications Building [014] to the west and the AON Center (Edward Durell Stone; 1973) to the east, the 64-story Two Prudential Plaza is an attention-grabbing structure, particularly when seen at full height from Millennium Park. Together with the 41-story One Prudential Plaza, which became the tallest building in the city when it was completed in 1955, it makes up a huge office complex totaling 2.3 million square feet (210,000 square meters). It is now known by the cheeky name One Two Pru. The two buildings share a lobby and mezzanine level and feature a variety of community spaces and amenities, including a 7,000-square-foot (650-square-meter) roof terrace. One Two Pru occupies a full city block. It is linked to an underground maze of pedestrian walkways leading to nearby buildings and public transportation. In addition to its main entrance at 180 N Stetson, it faces a one-acre terraced and landscaped plaza with a fountain on the west side, a stone's throw away from Michigan Avenue. The tower's tenants include the *Chicago Tribune*, the Consulate General of Canada, and several radio stations. Upon completion in 1990 at a height of 995 feet (303 meters), it was the world's tallest reinforced-concrete building. It is the most striking design that its architect, local firm Loebl Schlossman & Hackl, has ever produced, before or since. The tower is dressed in gray granite and silver tinted glass to harmonize with the Indiana limestone-clad One Pru. The taller building is particularly distinguished by its pyramidal, multifaceted tip made up of four diamond-shaped slices, cut and rotated at 45-degree angles and topped by an 80-foot (24-meter) needle. Additionally, multiple chevron-pattern setbacks on the north and south sides give the building a dynamic presence and a likeness to a rocket ready to be launched on a mission into space. The building's angular design is a classic Post-Modern exercise, as it is based on numerous historical references—from the San Marco Campanile in Venice to Manhattan's art deco skyscrapers, particularly the Chrysler Building. The building also borrowed from much more recent examples—fellow Chicago architect Helmut Jahn's One and Two Liberty Place buildings completed in Philadelphia a few years earlier. Still, despite Two Prudential Plaza's derivative appearance, the result is quite striking and memorable, both during the day and at night when the building's pointy setbacks are generously lit in a variety of bright colors.

Photo: Victor Korchenko

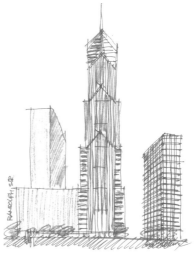

Courtesy of Rene Steevensz

Aqua Tower
225 North Columbus Drive,
New Eastside
Studio Gang (Chicago) &
Loewenberg Architects (Chicago)
2010

011 C

🚇🚇🚇🚇🚇 To State/Lake
🚇 To Lake
🚌 3, 4, 26, 66, 120, 143, 147, 151, 157 to
Michigan & Lake/Randolph

One of the most audacious and photo-genic high-rises in the city or anywhere, Aqua Tower, as its title implies, appears like a stream of rippling sea waves or hills and valleys of sand dunes. This new tower's morphology is a daring case study in how to successfully disrupt Chicago's love affair with the right angle. It was de-signed by the city's now most prominent living architect, Jeanne Gang (b. 1964), the founder of Studio Gang and a MacArthur Fellow in 2011. Reaching a height of 876 feet (267 meters) and con-taining 82 floors, this impressive mixed-use complex comprises a tower and two-story plinth that occupies the en-tire square city block in the center of New Eastside—one block south of the Chicago River and one block north of Millennium Park. This is one of the most advantageous positions in Chicago, with expansive views of the city, Lake

Michigan, and Millennium Park. The tower sits on the northwest quarter of its block and includes three programs: hotel rooms in the lower portion, rental apartments in the middle, and condominiums at the top. The podium includes offices, retail, restaurants, and amenities such as ballrooms, game rooms, conference rooms, a gym, and parking facilities. It is topped by an enormous 80,000-square-foot (7,500-square-meter) landscaped garden that incorporates winding pathways, strongly contrasting plants, a communal swimming pool, cabanas, and a fire pit. This hovering park was designed by local landscape architect Ted Wolff. // The building's unique appearance is achieved with a single-gesture approach. Floor slabs are extended beyond its rectangular glass envelope with wavy outlines, each slightly different from the next. The technique produces a gradual wavy pattern—a man-made landscape running vertically. The undulating balconies cantilever anywhere between just a few inches (10 centimeters) to 12 feet (3.7 meters), manifesting into sizable extensions to the tower's dwellings. The decision behind each balcony's configuration was determined through an elaborate study of the sightlines that must be navigated through gaps between the surrounding high rises. These overhangs, which become the deepest when situated next to living rooms, inevitably block some of the precious views, both when looking towards the sky and down the street. In exchange, they provide more optimal sun shading, which explains why the balconies are deeper on the south side than on the north side. // A chance to explore some of the building's apartments would show a visitor that the effect of the balconies' geometry is to make one perceive the entire interior as a fluid and visually stimulating space. In fact, those few apartments in the building that have no balconies and no floor extensions in front of them appear quite ordinary and boring in comparison. Note how metal pickets are pushed substantially away from the edges and are so thin that they almost fade from view, turning the balconies into entirely see-through ledges. This choice makes the slabs read very crisply, accentuating the purity and abstractness of the architect's original vision—to evoke a likeliness to limestone outcroppings that occur along the coasts of the Great Lakes. According to Gang, the uneven shapes help to 'confuse the wind'. This is intended to increase users' comfort, of course, but the scarcity of chairs, flowerpots, and people suggest that the wind may be confused, but it is still there. Nevertheless, Aqua Tower is an undeniably beautiful building—a delightfully gorgeous object to the point of being hypnotic.

St. Regis Chicago (formerly Wanda Vista Tower)

012 C

363 East Wacker Drive,
New Eastside
*Studio Gang, Chicago & bKL Architecture
(Chicago)*
2020

🚇🚇🚇🚇🚇 To State/Lake
🚇 To Lake
🚌 6, 20, 134, 135, 136 to Wacker &
Columbus

If nearby Aqua Tower [011] explores dynamic movement flowing vertically, here at St. Regis Chicago (formerly known as Wanda Vista Tower), Jeanne Gang, the architect of both, turned her attention to arranging geometric movements oriented vertically. Prominently sited on the Chicago River just west of Lake Michigan, this large residential complex is made up of 1.9 million square feet (175,000 square meters) of a hotel, condominium, restaurant, and amenity spaces. Shaped into three interconnected volumes of progressive heights, the tallest of which is the farthest from the lake, it reaches a commendable height of 101 stories or 1,196 feet (365 meters). This makes it the city's third-tallest building, behind only Willis Tower and Trump International Hotel & Tower. It is the tallest structure in the world designed by a woman—a distinction that used to belong to Aqua Tower. // The three-sister structure

Photos: Tom Harris Photography

1

evokes either totem poles or Constantin Brancuşi's famous *Endless Column* in three uneven parts. This is due to these towers' dynamic geometry, which is composed of truncated pyramids called frustums. These 12-story 'building blocks' are alternatively stacked, with a right-side-up unit over an upside-down unit. Each frustum is further subdivided into horizontal bands—one floor each with adjacent levels either stepping back or forward five inches. From a distance, this characteristic stepping pattern creates an illusion of gradual curves, giving the tower its graceful silhouette. The bands alternate in six different gradients of custom-coated, greenish-blue glass, each corresponding to solar exposure—the larger floor plates get less coating and the smaller ones get more tint. Together the three interlocking volumes produce additional corners, resulting in advantageous layouts in terms of views. Only the two side towers have elevator cores; the central one is held by them like a bridge that spans over a public pedestrian passage between Lakeshore East Park and the Riverwalk along Walker Drive. The central tower is aligned perfectly with both S Lake Shore and N Field. While the south and north façades are sleek at each level, there are inset balconies lined up along the east and west sides of each tower. The balconies close to the top of the building are the highest in the city. // There is a double-height slot on the 83rd floor, which occurs at the bottom part of the uppermost frustum. This so-called phantom or 'blow-through' floor is unoccupied. It was engineered to prevent excessive swaying in the wind. Still, this effort is not enough to stabilize the tallest of the three towers. To counteract the strong Chicago winds, there are six tanks filled with 400,000 gallons of water incorporated into the very top of the building. All the sophisticated engineering aside, it is important to recognize that this heroic complex succeeds in positively transforming Chicago's skyline. And its unusual geometry establishes a visual dialogue with two of Chicago's most iconic landmarks: Willis Tower and the John Hancock Center. While the former is also composed of stems or columns, the latter is known for its emblematic subtly tapering form. St. Regis Chicago and the neighboring Aqua Tower are arguably the two most original high-rises built in Chicago in recent decades.

View over New Eastside from Northeast with St. Regis Chicago
overlooking East Wacker Drive and the Chicago River

040

55

Loop and New Eastside

1

Blue Cross Blue Shield Tower

`013` `C`

300 East Randolph Street,
New Eastside
Goettsch Partners (Chicago)
2010

🚇🚇🚇🚇🚇 To State/Lake
🚇 To Lake
🚌 4, 60 to Randolph & Columbus

When the Blue Cross Blue Shield building at 300 E Randolph was chosen for this guide, it was on account of its see-through, airy structural bays that make up the full-height glazed atrium along its north side, as well as the swiftly moving, open elevators that are visible from the outside, especially at night. Unfortunately, the building's primary south façade at the front-row location overlooking Millennium Park is not particularly interesting. Nevertheless, it is the story of how this edifice was planned, constructed, and spatially organized that is fascinating. Serving as the dual headquarters for rapidly expanding Health Care Service Corporation (HCSC) and its Blue Cross and Blue Shield of Illinois division, the tower was designed in such a way that it could be extended vertically when needed. Phase one, finished in 1997, measured 33 stories and included three levels underground. In addition to workspaces, it included a conference and training center and a 900-seat cafeteria. The initial foundation and structure were designed to support the fully expanded building. Phase two, completed 13 years later, added 24 additional stories, bringing the total area to 2.2 million square feet (204,000 square meters). Over 4,000 office workers continued with their day-to-day activities during the three-year expansion process. Additional spaces introduced by the second phase included new workspaces—enough to double the companies' workforces—a conference center, a satellite cafeteria, a fitness and wellness center, various conference and training facilities, and a partial green roof. Half of the new floors are to be leased to outside tenants and could eventually be appropriated for future expansion. // The aforementioned full-height atrium, adjacent to the north façade and designed as an exposed grid across five 40-by-30 foot (12-by-9 meter) open structural bays, is the most striking visual feature. While the central bay is reserved for an open high-tech stair to facilitate inter-floor circulation, it is also utilized as meeting spaces every three floors. Other bays hold glazed elevator cabins. // The building's architect, Goettsch Partners, traces its history to the office of Mies van der Rohe, founded in the city in 1938. At various times the firm has been known as Fujikawa Conterato Lohan Associates (Dirk Lohan [b.1938] is the grandson of Mies), Lohan Associates, Lohan Caprile Goettsch Architects, and since 2005, Goettsch Partners. Two other large projects designed by the firm are included in this guide: the Viceroy Hotel [035] and 150 N Riverside [045].

Crain Communications Building (formerly Associates Center)

014 C

150 North Michigan Avenue, Loop
Epstein & Sons (Chicago)
1984

🚇🚇🚇🚇🚇 To State/Lake or Washington/Wabash
🚇 To Lake
🚌 3, 4, 26, 66, 143, 147, 151, 157 to Michigan & Lake/Randolph

Originally opened as the Associates Center in 1984 and since renamed more than once, the Crain Communications Building, as it has officially been called since 2012, occupies one of the most prominent spots in the city: the intersection of North Michigan and East Randolph diagonally across from the northwest corner of Millennium Park. It is this building's unique location that explains its eye-catching geometry. The high-rise's plan is a rectangle of squarish proportions with its southeast and northwest corners precisely cut, giving its otherwise chunky shaft a handsome profile. However, the 39-story building's most striking feature is its diagonally-sliced, diamond-shaped slanted top, directly facing the park. Furthermore, the diamond is split into left and right triangles, pulled apart and separated by an indent at the very top. In fact, there are two tops, each reserved for five levels of mechanical rooms for HVAC equipment. // On the inside, the building's service core is rotated 45 degrees from the street grid to produce diagonally-oriented office floorplans and take full advantage of the expansive southeast views. The tower's façades are clad in a horizontal zebra-stripe pattern of alternating bands of narrow tinted glass and wide white aluminum and stainless-steel panels. Apart from two lower floors slightly set back along N Michigan, the office floors follow the same footprint until reaching the 31st story. This is where the tower's slant starts, progressively reducing the area of each subsequent floor. The diamond could be inspired by any number of things—a sail, a face with pointy ears, or body parts, none of which the building's designer, Sheldon Schlegman of A. Epstein & Sons (now Epstein Global) would confirm. Whatever one sees in this architectural Rorschach test, these crystalline forms are quite telling, especially at night when the diamond is crisply outlined with white lights, distinguishing its presence on the Chicago's skyline on a typical night and accentuated with colored lights on holidays. What's more, on special occasions, short illuminated messages may say 'GO' on the left and 'CUBS' on the right in support of one of Chicago's favorite baseball teams, aptly playing at Soldier Field Stadium [041] diagonally across Grant Park.

View from Tribune Tower towards the Loop with Chicago's finest buildings from Art Deco and French Renaissance style to modern and twenty-first-century Post-Modern skyscrapers along the Chicago River

014

Jay Pritzker Pavilion
201 E Randolph Street,
Millennium Park
Frank Gehry (Los Angeles)
2004

`015` `C`

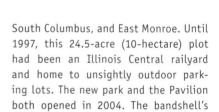

🚇🚇🚇🚇🚇 To State/Lake or
Washington/Wabash
🚇 To Lake
🚌 3, 4, 26, 66, 143, 147, 151, 157 to
Michigan & Lake/Randolph

Technically a bandshell for outdoor concerts, the Jay Pritzker Pavilion is much more than that. This heroic structure is the only piece of architecture in Chicago designed by Frank Gehry, arguably the most celebrated living architect. Gehry was specifically sought out for this commission by Cindy Pritzker, the widow of Jay Pritzker (1922–1999) whose prominent Chicago-based family owns Hyatt Hotels, among other businesses. The couple is widely known in the architectural world for establishing the Pritzker Architecture Prize in 1979, the profession's most prestigious honor. They made a significant donation towards the construction of Millennium Park, and it was Cindy Pritzker who insisted on choosing the architect. Gehry is the 1989 recipient of the Pritzker. Curiously, the architect's unique but expectedly sculptural design is officially designated by the City of Chicago as ... 'a work of art'. // However, let's start with its location. The Pavilion is the centerpiece of Millennium Park—the northwest portion of Grant Park that lies within the rectangle defined by North Michigan, East Randolph,

South Columbus, and East Monroe. Until 1997, this 24.5-acre (10-hectare) plot had been an Illinois Central railyard and home to unsightly outdoor parking lots. The new park and the Pavilion both opened in 2004. The bandshell's

substantial presence attracted a potential lawsuit since it exceeded the permitted height limitations for structures inside Grant Park. As in the case of the nearby 1927 Buckingham Fountain, the city avoided this conflict by classifying the bandshell as a work of art rather than a structure. The ongoing polemic about what is the difference between architecture and art is infinitely interesting, however, in this case, the status is official! // The Gehry piece is just a small portion of the overall project, and in fact, is an extension of the Harris Theater for Music and Dance, the park's indoor and largely underground performing arts venue at 205 East Randolph. The two structures (Harris is a building and not included in this guide) share a loading dock, rehearsal rooms, and back-of-house facilities. The bandshell is firmly built on top of an underground parking garage that can accommodate 4,000 cars. The proscenium's curly ribbons of brushed stainless-steel clad aluminum panels evoke a hairdo with an upswept, back-twisted look. Some of these lightweight-looking panels weigh up to 20,000 pounds (9,000 kilos). Their design brings to mind Gehry's most iconic works: the Guggenheim Museum Bilbao, the Disney Concert Hall in Los Angeles, and the floating forms inside the Issey Miyake flagship store in New York City. In all these examples, titanium and steel panels are sculpted so smoothly that it would be fitting to describe their curves and twists as the visual manifestation of the sound of music. The stage area is clad in Douglas fir and can accommodate an orchestra of up to 120 musicians. A choral terrace has space for a choir of up to 150 members. The amphitheater for the spectators is no less delightful. It is defined by the giant oval-shaped trellis of steel piping hovering overhead. This luscious system distributes speakers and accent lighting over the Great Lawn, which can comfortably welcome 11,000 people, including 4,000 in fixed seating. The Pavilion is home to the Grant Park Symphony Orchestra and Chorus and the Grant Park Music Festival. It also hosts a wide range of annual performing arts events including the Chicago Jazz Festival, the Chicago Gospel Music Festival, and more than 100 free concerts, films, and programs each year. The last important design element is the BP Bridge—a snake-like 925-foot (280-meter) pedestrian bridge linking Millennium Park with Maggie Daley Park across S Columbus, whose design was orchestrated by Gehry. It is named after the energy giant British Petroleum and due to its low-profile posture is not officially designated as ... a work of art.

Photo: Diego Delso

Cloud Gate

Millennium Park
Anish Kapoor (London, UK)
2006

 016 **C**

🚇🚇🚇🚇🚇 To State/Lake or
Washington/Wabash
🚇 To Lake
🚌 3, 4, 26, 66, 143, 147, 151, 157 to
Michigan & Lake/Randolph

Cloud Gate, also affectionately dubbed 'the Bean' due to its curved shapes, is a design competition-winning, mercury-drop-inspired sculpture and one of only two non-building projects in this guide (the other is the next entry, Crown Fountain). Its scale, hovering form, and the complex engineering that went into building it all contribute to one's overall experience, which is thoroughly architectural. The sculpture was designed by the India-born British conceptual artist Anish Kapoor, who has realized spectacular sculptures at urban plazas all over the world, but *Cloud Gate* is arguably his most famous. In fact, this centerpiece of AT&T Plaza at Millennium Park is said to be the most photographed attraction in Chicago. It must be so for several reasons at once: its size, shape, surface, and highly central location. Measuring 33-by-66-by-42 feet (10-by-20-by-13 meters) the sculpture weighs 110 tons and is shaped into an arch with a 12-foot (3.7-meter) high, spoon-like underbelly, enabling crowds of people to pass under it and, in a way, enter its 'naval'. It is surely the Bean's unique, mirror-finished, continuous surface that

warps, flips, and twists into myriad funhouse reflections of street fronts and the city's skyline, transforming the view with every step, that wins everyone's heart. // These photogenic effects were achieved by welding together 168 stainless steel plates that were ground, sanded, and polished by a 24-person crew for months to achieve the seemingly perfect mirror-like finish to a point that none of the seams can be either seen or felt. Kapoor's sculpture plays with such dualities as perfection-distortion, reality-reflection, limited-limitless, material-immaterial, heavy-light, solid-empty, and interior-exterior. It continues the artist's captivating series of concave-convex stainless-steel sculptures that deal with distorted perception, ambiguity, and the state of 'in-betweenness'. The sculpture also illustrates the idea of removing the artist's signature from his works and all traces of their fabrication to heighten viewers' fascination with art that seemingly 'dropped from the sky'. When the sculpture was first presented, many of the experts did not believe that the artist's call for a seamless surface on such an enormous scale could be achieved. The outer shell rests on two steel rings, independent of each other, to allow for the expansion and contraction caused by Chicago's extreme temperature swings. The 3/8-inch (10-mm) thick panels of the shell were fabricated in Oakland and brought to Chicago by trucks to be assembled on-site. Special supports that held the two rings in place were removed. The piece took two years to complete at a final cost of $23 million.

Crown Fountain

Millennium Park
Jaume Plensa, Krueck + Sexton Architects (Chicago)
2004

017 C

🚇🚇🚇🚇🚇 To State/Lake or Washington/Wabash
🚇 To Lake
🚌 3, 4, 26, 66, 143, 147, 151, 157 to Michigan & Lake/Randolph

Situated at Millennium Park along S Michigan near Anish Kapoor's *Cloud Gate* and across E Monroe from the Art Institute of Chicago, Crown Fountain is a unique meeting point and space for reflection that has become a popular spectacle. Constructed over two levels of underground car parking, it is a piece of art and a work of architecture, engineering, and technology all at once. It was designed by Barcelona-based artist Jaume Plensa (b. 1955) in collaboration with local firm Krueck + Sexton Architects. Plensa's proposal was selected after a shortlisted competition that included designs by Maya Lin and Robert Venturi. The competition was overseen by Lester Crown, a local billionaire whose family donated $10 million towards the project. The fountain's total cost amounted to $17 million, all from private donations. Opened in the summer of 2004, this deceptively simple structure comprises a pair of freestanding 50-by-23-by-16-foot (15.2-by-7-by-5-meter) towers clad in 22,000 10-pound, custom-made white glass blocks inset into stainless steel T-frames and illuminated from within. The towers rise from either end of a long rectangular basin of water made of black granite and measuring 230-by-46 feet (70-by-14 meters). The water's surface is aligned with the surrounding plaza level and is a mere 1/8-inch (3-millimeters) deep. // Designed as an informal meeting space and playground for all ages, the fountain serves as a kind of public stage. It is not an object to look at, but an environment to be experienced and to engage others. Composed of contrasted dualities, such as its geometries (horizontal and vertical) and materials (stone and water, as well as light and water), the area is further enriched by the ongoing dialogue between video transitions of the faces of 1,000 Chicagoans. The 5-minute clips play forwards and backwards at various speeds based on original 80-second videos recorded using a high-definition camera turned on its side. The clips are shown in random sequences on two behind-the-glass LED screens that match each tower's front face. Interaction and conversation are provoked as these images look straight at each other and spout water from their mouths—15 seconds at a time—as if they were twenty-first-century gargoyles. Moreover, the glass block towers act as cascading waterfalls, inviting people to come around them by literally walking on water. The fountain operates from mid-spring to mid-fall, with the images on view year-round. The *Chicago Tribune* reported that surveillance cameras were installed atop each tower in 2006, however, they were removed following public outcry.

Photo: Nic Lehoux

Chicago Art Institute, The Modern Wing

018 **C**

111 South Michigan Avenue
(Monroe Street entrance),
Grant Park
Renzo Piano Building Workshop
(Genoa, Italy; Paris, France)
2009

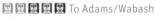 🚇🚇🚇🚇🚇 To Adams/Wabash
🚇🚇 To Monroe
🚌 3, 4, 6, 26, 143, J14 to Michigan &
Monroe; 3, 4, 26, 143, 147, 850, 851, 855,
J14 to Michigan/Jackson

The high-tech style is particularly well represented in Chicago by the work of local architect Helmut Jahn. The most outstanding examples are his Thompson Center (1985) and South Campus Boiler Plant at the University of Chicago (2010), both featured in this guide. Yet these buildings, however brilliant, are somewhat derivative, as they are rooted in the aesthetics of a truly seminal work designed by Renzo Piano and Richard Rogers at the very beginning of their careers: the Centre Pompidou in Paris (1970–1977). Thankfully, Piano, a Pritzker Prize-winning architect who has become the go-to master when it comes to planning world-class museums, has built one of his best works in the very heart of Chicago.

Opened in 2009, his Modern Wing of the Art Institute, a 264,000-square-foot (24,500-square-meter) expansion, made the museum one of the largest in the world. The Modern Wing unifies and completes the cultural and urban campus of the Art Institute. Sitting in Grant Park on a site between S Michigan and S Columbus that is bisected by railroad tracks, the new building stretches to the north reaching E Monroe, where a new point of access to the museum is provided. This side is distinguished by large expanses of glass (its panels are so big that they could not be manufactured in the United States and had to be ordered from Germany). These alternate with vertical slivers of solid limestone walls to pay tribute to the architecture of the original 1893 Art Institute building to the south.// The glass building is topped by a floating lightweight metal roof. This thin, luminous sunshade does not appear to touch the upper floor galleries underneath and is nicknamed 'the flying carpet'. The new building faces Millennium Park to the north where it is directly aligned with Frank Gehry's Jay Pritzker Pavilion [015]. Despite hewing to a highly-disciplined orthogonal geometry, the building can be explored in a variety of playful ways. For example, there are two distinct options for getting inside the

1

Modern Wing—those in a hurry can enter swiftly from E Monroe at the ground floor level, but those who want a special treat can enter the building via a 625-foot (190.5-meter) elegant pedestrian bridge, the Nichols Bridgeway, that carries people from Millennium Park over E Monroe all the way to the wing's third floor, which has a fine restaurant cleverly named Terzo Piano. Note that both ends of the bridge, diagonally cut, recall the stern of a boat—a nod to Piano's love for sailboats. Next to the restaurant is an open-roof sculpture terrace with regularly changing exhibitions. It overlooks the forest of iconic skyscrapers lined up along Millennium Park's western and northern edges. As a bonus, both the terrace and restaurant are accessible to visitors without a ticket. // The Modern Wing brings a visit to the Art Institute to a whole new level. Once inside, you will immediately appreciate the architect's renowned sense of order and clarity, his ability to pick and assemble beautiful materials and colors, intricate details, and handle daylight in the most awesome ways possible. The naturally-lit double-height foyer and the central circulation area are known as Griffin Court. On the way into the museum, visitors will pass the Ryan Learning Center on the left and the gift shop to the right, both sitting within the free-of-charge zone. The museum's highlights include the contemplative Pritzker Garden on the east side. It features the only work commissioned for the Modern Wing, Ellsworth Kelly's *White Curve* (2009). The exquisitely-designed stair in the middle of Griffin Court that leads to the second floor seems to be put together out of elements that barely touch each other. It is as powerful as any sculpture in the galleries and accompanied by a continuous skylight; its structural filigree is delightful and can be enjoyed from the mezzanine level Balcony Café over a leisurely snack.

Washington-Wabash Station 019 C

North Wabash Street between
East Madison Street and East
Washington Street
Thomas Hoepf of EXP (Chicago)
2017

🚃🚃🚃🚃🚃 To Washington-Wabash

Located in the Jewelers Row historic district in the East Loop, the new Washington-Wabash elevated station on the Brown, Purple, Orange, Green, and Pink lines serves as the premier celebratory public transportation gateway to downtown's Millennium Park. It was the Loop's first new 'L' stop in 20 years. Opened in 2017 at a cost of $75 million, it replaced two now-demolished stations at Madison and Wabash and at Randolph and Wabash. The station provides state-of-the-art amenities including new elevators, street-to-mezzanine escalators, and much wider platforms. However, what is particularly appealing here is the station's uncompromisingly contemporary and positively uplifting look. Designed by the Chicago-based architecture and engineering firm EXP, the station's new image is expressed in a wavy pattern of laser-cut, white-painted guardrails along the second and third floors topped by two mirrored steel-and glass canopies that undulate over two block-long passenger platforms. Each of the two canopies is placed over a single row of steel columns, elliptical in section. The canopies constitute asymmetrical V-shaped assemblies of steel ribs and narrow rectangular glass panels. Equally spaced, these ribs and glass panels vary in length, and despite all these elements being flat and straight, they create an

illusion that the canopies curve and twist in every direction. While the glass panels incorporate geometric fritted patterns to provide shade underneath, the ribs reach much further, extending their LED tips and accentuating their cumulative dynamic form. This handsome high-tech structure assumes a spiky look that can be likened to a rhythmic skeleton— a strong but graceful contrast to the muscular, stone-clad buildings located all around. Additionally, the north and south lobbies at the mezzanine-level entrance pavilion greet passengers with two luminous glass murals titled *Cosmic Wanderlust 1 & 2*. They reproduce fictional narratives of oil paintings by Chicago artist Michiko Itatani.

Xerox Center ↗

55 West Monroe Street, Loop
C. F. Murphy Associates
(since 2012, JAHN, Chicago)
1980

020 **C**

🚇🚇 To Monroe
🚇🚇🚇🚇🚇 To Adams/Wabash or State/Van Buren
🚌 22, 24, 36, 62, 151 to Dearborn & Monroe; 1, 7, 28, 126, 130, 151 to Adams & State

The Xerox Center, a 41-story office tower at 55 West Monroe, is an elegant solution to a classic architectural problem: how to turn a corner. And, in fact, this 1980 tower's most memorable and proudest possession is its rounded corner, which is so seamlessly engaged with the rest of the structure that it could be defined as the 'round-corner building'. Apart from its oversimplified form, the tower is distinguished by its minimalist surface, a flush curtainwall of alternating horizontal bands of white-painted aluminum and reflective glass. At the double-height ground floor, the curved bands are set back to form two entrances, one on each side. As you raise your eyes, the bands' repetitive ascent culminates in a rounded mechanical penthouse. Occupying a quarter of its block at the corner of W Monroe and S Dearborn, the tower faces Marc Chagall's *Four Seasons* mosaic at the base of the Chase Tower Plaza

to the north and is diagonally sited across the street from the Inland Steel Building (SOM; 1957). // The Xerox Center was designed by Helmut Jahn, then the leading designer at C. F. Murphy Associates, which was renamed Murphy/Jahn just one year later and has simply been known as JAHN since 2012. The Xerox Center was Jahn's first true skyscraper and a real breakthrough for him, leading to a whole series of distinctive towers that followed that decade in Chicago, New York, and Philadelphia, culminating in his most iconic skyscraper of that period: the 63-story Messeturm (Frankfurt; 1991). Jahn added many more audacious towers to skylines across Europe, Asia, and the US. The gesture was mimicked in subsequent structures in Chicago, including 333 West Wacker (KPF; 1983), 71 South Wacker (Pei Cobb Freed & Partners; 2005), and Jahn's own sweeping James R. Thompson Center (1985) a few blocks north (all three examples are cited in this guide). Other historical precedents that surely must have served as inspirations to Jahn would include Louis Sullivan's Carson, Pirie, Scott and Company department store (now Sullivan Center; 1899) with its famous rounded northwest corner, located just two blocks away. The other precedent is no less exemplary: the Schocken Department Store (1926; demolished 1960) by Erich Mendelsohn that was located in Stuttgart, Germany, Jahn's country of birth.

U.S. Bank Building (formerly 190 South LaSalle Street)

190 South LaSalle Street, Loop
Johnson/Burgee Architects
(New York)
1987

🚇🚇🚇🚇 To Quincy
🚇 To Monroe
🚌 134, 135, 136, 156 to LaSalle & Adams;
1, 7, 28, 126, 130, 151 to Adams & Clark;
37 to Wells & Adams

Completed in 1987, the U.S. Bank Building is a massive office skyscraper in the financial heart of Chicago. It was originally identified by its street address, 190 South LaSalle. The structure is the only building in Chicago designed by New York starchitect Philip Johnson (1906–2005), then of Johnson/Burgee Architects (1967–1991). This fact alone is a good enough reason to include it in this guide. Johnson was the inaugural Pritzker Architecture Prize winner in 1979. As a prolific designer who has often been referred to as the Dean of American Architecture, he altered the skylines of many cities around the world and was an influential curator at the Museum of Modern Art. His 1932 *Modern Architecture: International Exhibition* introduced the International Style to America, and it eventually became the bedrock of corporate architecture. Yet Johnson's influence goes far beyond popularizing the glass-box International Style. For Johnson, designing modernist icons such as his Glass House in New Canaan, Connecticut, or the twin, sleek, trapezoidal Pennzoil Place towers in Houston was not enough. He switched styles as often as he saw fit. As a result, his building on LaSalle has little to do with the modernist ideology he was bored with by the 1980s. // The building's design feeds on numerous references to historicism, making it one of the most in-your-face examples of Post-Modernism in Chicago. The corner structure was built a few years after Johnson's Chippendale-top AT&T Building (550 Madison Avenue, 1984) in Manhattan, so his Chicago foray into historicist pastiche was not entirely shocking. The 40-story U.S. Bank Building is an eye-catching structure thanks to its ornate summit of multi-gabled, mint-green colored roof sections, which are peppered with fairy-tale-like finials. Interestingly, this design is not at all frivolous, but rather an abstracted quotation of a Burnham & Root-designed building: the 1892 Masonic Temple that stood a few blocks away at Randolph and State and was unfortunately demolished in 1939. Another feature of the architect's playful contextualism is the building's reddish-brown granite overcoat that mimics its famous neighbor, the Rookery Building (1886)—another masterpiece designed by Burnham & Root diagonally across the street. The Rookery is also occupied by U.S. Bank. // Inside Johnson's creation, you will discover a generous civic gesture—a grand marble and gold-leaf barrel-vaulted lobby with a 28-foot (8.5-meter) shockingly modern bronze sculpture entitled *Chicago Fugue* by English abstract sculptor Anthony Caro in the alcove at the north end. Due to its immense size, the work, which alludes to various elements of musical instruments and was specially commissioned for this building, had to be constructed on-site inside the lobby. When the building opened, *Chicago Tribune* architecture critic Paul Gapp was not impressed. He called it 'a cartoonish echo of the Masonic Temple' and 'a pallid, wishy-washy piece of Post-Modernism that cannot be taken seriously'. Of course, Johnson was the last person who would take himself seriously. His career went on and his preferences changed many times. Trying different styles and attitudes was the name of his game. The Minneapolis-based bank is the building's largest tenant. According to the terms of the renewed 2013 lease, the naming rights will remain valid through to 2026.

Photo: Marshall Gerometta

71 South Wacker (formerly Hyatt Center)

022 C

71 South Wacker Drive, Loop
*Henry North Cobb of Pei Cobb
Freed & Partners (New York)*
2005

🚇🚇🚇🚇 To Quincy or Washington/Wells
🚌 37 to Wells & Monroe; 1, 7, 28, 126, 130, 151, 156 to Adams & S Wacker; 20, 56, 60, 124, 157, J14 to Madison & Franklin

Photo: Steve Hall

Conceived as the Hyatt Center and now straightforwardly named after its street address, 71 South Wacker was built by the same Chicago-based Pritzker family behind the esteemed Pritzker Prize. The 48-story building two blocks north of the Willis Tower is distinguished by its two handsome curved façades that face north and south and are clad in alternating sleek bands of steel and glass panels. The project was originally envisioned as the 60-story Pritzker Tower and was to have been designed by the 1999 Pritzker Prize-winning celebrity architect Norman Foster. However, the plans for a costly trophy skyscraper to house a corporate headquarters were scrapped following the terrorist attacks on 11 September 2001. The client reportedly telephoned Foster to inform him of the decision on 12 September. The current, more marketable version of that project was designed as a downgraded speculative office building. It was the first tower planned in post-9/11 Chicago, which is the reason for the many new, but now standard, high-tech security measures integrated into the design. Yet the tower appears like a graceful vessel meandering in a sea of blocky buildings and right through some of the low-hanging clouds, overturning the common impression of a corporate headquarters as an impenetrable fortress. // The project's design was undertaken by Henry Cobb (1926–2020) of the New York firm Pei Cobb Freed & Partners. It was Cobb who decided to mold the building in the shape of an eye in plan, reminiscent of the elliptical design of his steel-and-glass Tour EDF (2001), a striking skyscraper at La Defense in Paris. The Chicago solution was inspired by an unusually narrow site densely surrounded by office towers, and the client's request for column-free

Typical office plan: floors 22–33

Courtesy of Pei Cobb Freed & Partners

floors of at least 33,000 square feet (3,065 square meters) each. The opposite ends of the tower feature broad, sheltering canopies that invite visitors into grand, gently curved, and fully-glazed spaces that culminate in a 50-foot-high (15-meter-high) ceiling. The lobbies showcase art panels by Keith Tyson and a *trompe-l'œil* ('eye-deceiving') mural by Ricci Albenda. There is extensive landscaping both inside and outside, shaped by the building's footprint on the block-long south side. The tower's two opposite ends are clad in floor-to-ceiling stainless steel panels. This appears to be a missed opportunity for creating unique panoramic highpoints, which would have been possible if they had been fully glazed instead. Cobb explained his design solution by saying that corner offices were not required by the prospective tenants, which led to the decision to curve the building to avoid a typical orthogonal floor plate in the first place.

Chicago Board of Trade Addition 023 C

140 West Van Buren Street, Loop
Murphy/Jahn (since 2012, JAHN, Chicago)
1983

🚇🚇🚇🚇 To LaSalle/Van Buren
🚇 To Jackson
🚉 JG to Van Buren & Financial Place;
134, 135, 136, 156 to LaSalle & Quincy;
1, 7, 28, 126, 130, 151, 156 to Jackson &
Franklin

Photo: Rainer Viertlböck

This bulky black-and-silver glass building on West Van Buren right next to the LaSalle/Van Buren stop of the Loop 'L' train is one of the earliest realizations of a design by Helmut Jahn. Completed in 1983, the 23-story structure recalls the radiator grille of a 1930s-era car. This likeness is due to the building's pyramidal-shaped skylight roof, topped by the Board of Trade logo. The building is a southern addition to the Chicago Board of Trade (Holabird & Root; 1930) at 141 West Jackson, an imposing 45-story, limestone-clad art deco skyscraper distinguished by its own pyramidal roof that is crowned by a 31-foot aluminum sculpture of Ceres, the Roman goddess of agriculture. The sculpture is best seen from LaSalle. The addition derives its formal characteristics from an abstracted duplication of the existing building. The relationship between old and new is used here as a generator of both form and décor—a typical technique for Post-Modern buildings that prioritized symbolism and ornamentation over modernism's focus on expressing function and technology. // The addition's spectacular skylit atrium, which occupies the upper 12 floors, is distinguished by its art deco-inspired streamlined curves. They are repeated in marble flooring and faceted glazing. The space culminates in expressive filigreed steel roof trusses painted in a striking green. The atrium's northern end is the limestone wall of the original Board of Trade building. There is a central tower with exposed glass elevators on either side—a dynamic feature Jahn realized on a much grander scale a couple of years later inside his Thompson Center [001]. The tower of elevators is counterbalanced by another element: a freestanding steel lattice that holds John Warner Norton's *Ceres*, a three-story tall mural over a symbolic portal. This historic artifact used to be displayed on the original trading floor and now serves as a visual link to the new building's roots. The old Chicago Board of Trade and the new addition on Van Buren are connected by a two-story central passageway open to the public. Unfortunately, the atrium with the *Ceres* mural is not.

Drawing: Helmut Jahn

Photo: Judith Bromley

Harold Washington Library
400 South State Street, Loop
Hammond, Beeby & Babka
(Chicago)
1991

 024 C

🚇🚇🚇🚇🚇 To Harold Washington
Library-State/Van Buren
🚇 To Jackson or Harrison
🚇 To Jackson or LaSalle
🚌 2, 10, 29, 130, 146, 147, 148 to State
& Van Buren; 22, 24, 36, 62 to Dearborn &
Ida B Wells Drive

Named after Chicago's first African American mayor, who supported its construction, the Harold Washington Library is the main branch of Chicago's public library system. It stands heroically just south of the Loop 'L' at 400 South State, occupying the entire city block. Opened in 1991 when little was being built anywhere, this strangely familiar building, which is striking in its scale and detailing, instantly became one of the most talked-about architectural wonders in America. Criticism of the building was mostly spoken, not expressed in print, as many prominent critics approved and praised it as exemplary. Architectural critic Paul Goldberger, still among the most quoted and revered critics in America, wrote in the *New York Times:* 'No building erected in our time has demonstrated more

clearly a total commitment to the notion of the public realm. This building is of the city and for the city.' Norman Ross, chair of the jury that selected this project as the winner of a design competition, said: 'This looks like a library. This is a building that you can trust.' And it is true; there is nothing ambiguous about it. The building works like an open book or the way ancient temples and medieval cathedrals used to be built: pictorially. // The building's façades can literally be read as an homage (in the form of a collage) to Chicago's built history. Its rusticated base quotes the Rookery (1888), the thick sloping base refers to the Monadnock Building (1893), and the swirling guilloche terracotta design comes from the Marquette Building (1895). The multi-story arched windows recall the Auditorium Building (1898), and to top it all, the triangular pediments of the two-story gabled structure belong to the Art Institute of Chicago (1893). All of these famous landmarks are within a few blocks of the library. The resulting jumble of historical references is stylized as a sumptuous Beaux Arts edifice dressed in granite and red brick over a reinforced concrete base and shaft, with an excessively decorated glass-and-aluminum crown over a steel-frame top. However, the building's design strategy goes much deeper than merely quoting familiar landmarks in the city. Its abundance of symbolic detailing includes seven giant metal ornaments, called acroteria in classical architecture. They are positioned at four corners, and three pediment apexes feature giant owl figures perched in foliage to symbolize knowledge to be obtained within. There are terracotta wall medallions connected with garlands, including the face of Ceres, the Roman goddess of agriculture generously decorated with corncobs; Windy City Man whose cheeks are puffed out so as to blow the observer away; and Y-symbols referring to the shape of the Chicago River. // The building was designed by Thomas Beeby (b. 1941) of Hammond, Beeby & Babka (now HBRA) who was Dean of the Yale School of Architecture when the building was designed and a prominent proponent of the new urbanism and the new classical architecture movements. The library remains Beeby's most outstanding design, and it is no coincidence that he was elected to the College of Fellows of the American Institute of Architects the same year the building was finished. He was also a member of the Chicago Seven, an informal group of architects that included Stanley Tigerman and James Ingo Freed. They had little in common except that they all stood united against the total acceptance and domination of Miesian aesthetics, which by the mid-1970s were often applied quite blindly without Mies's original rigor and clarity. Nowhere was this need for change felt more acutely than in Chicago. The alternative architecture these young rebels were advocating for soon became widely referred to as Post-Modern, which found its inspiration in historical references. // By the time Beeby's library came along, historically-inspired buildings had been built for at least a decade, particularly in America. In fact, the library became the apotheosis of Post-Modernist architecture, which had included Michael Graves's Portland Building (1982) and Philip Johnson's AT&T Building in Manhattan (1984). Post-Modernism was on its way out, and it is hard to find history-inspired buildings built on such a scale and so passionately detailed after this library's completion. The economy was sluggish and by the late 1990s, particularly after

Frank Gehry's Guggenheim in Bilbao, architects began to shift toward expressing their own identities rather than historical precedents. The library's image is an oddity of its time—a moment in a short-lived fascination within the long history of a profession that constantly embraces new ideas and constantly gets tired of them. // Still, the building remains equivocal: it attracts and repels at the same time. For example, the library was included on 'America's Favorite Architecture' list in 2007. Just a couple of years later, it featured on a list of the 15 ugliest buildings in the world prepared by *Travel & Leisure* magazine. Aesthetics and popular opinion aside, the most disappointing part of the building is its interior. The building's solidity and lack of open space are disconcerting. The ground floor has a smallish central reception space. The lack of a grand atrium or even a decent-size dome is particularly disgraceful. The building is missing civic grandeur entirely and cannot match even that of several nearby department stores, hotels, and office building lobbies. The reading spaces are squeezed under flat low ceilings and even the top event space, lined with glass walls and crowned by a large central skylight, is far from generously proportioned, let alone spectacular. None of the monumentality and grandiosity on the library's façades translate into the interior of the building. Of course, it is easy to criticize Harold Washington Library in the context of the many inventive libraries that have been built around the world over the last three decades. Perhaps no other building type has been reinvented as dramatically as the library in that time. However picturesque the Chicago's main library is with its façades, not providing a generous, let alone imaginative, civic space within it was a missed opportunity.

Photo: Timothy Hursley

2

025   Trump International Hotel & Tower
026   Apple Michigan Avenue
027   Yard Shakespeare Theater
028   Anti-Cruelty Society
029   Contemporaine
030   Poetry Foundation
031   Erie on the Park
032   Museum of Contemporary Art (MCA)
033   Sofitel Hotel
034   Fourth Presbyterian Church, Gratz Center
035   Viceroy Hotel
036   Tower House

Trump International Hotel & Tower
025 C

401 North Wabash Avenue, River North
Adrian Smith, Design Partner at SOM (Chicago)
2009

🚇🚇🚇🚇🚇 To State/Lake
🚇 To Lake or Grand
🚌 29 to State & Kinzie; 2, 3, 26, 66, 120 to Michigan & Hubbard

Slightly taller than the nearby John Hancock Center, the Trump International Hotel & Tower is a sparkling, soaring skyscraper that sits almost flush against the northern edge of the main branch of the Chicago River. It is currently Chicago's second tallest building after the Willis Tower (formerly the Sears Tower), which itself was the tallest building in the world for nearly a quarter of a century. The 98-story Trump Tower is uniquely situated on a boomerang-shaped site outlined by two streets—East Kinzie to the north and North Wabash to the west—and the Chicago River to the southeast. Together with Marina City and 330 North Wabash to the west and the Wrigley Building to the east, the proud tower aligns itself with the riverfront row of buildings, forming one of Chicago's most iconic scenes. The building rises in several irregularly shaped and spaced setbacks, as it reaches a height of 1,171 feet (357 meters), or 1,388 feet (423 meters) if you include its spire. Its strategic location—dead-centered on the Loop's Wabash and the Chicago River to the east—makes it among the most visible landmarks in the city. It occupies a portion of the site of the undistinguished mid-1950s seven-story Sun-Times Building—the now-demolished former headquarters of the city's second-largest paper. // As its name suggests, the tower was developed by Donald Trump. It was completed in 2009, years before his presidency. Its design went through multiple iterations. When it was proposed back in 1999, it was to be no less than 150-stories and would reach a height of 2,000 feet (610 meters), which would easily have made it

the tallest building in the world. By the summer of 2001, the project was lowered by 25 percent, still making it the world's tallest building. However, those plans were scrapped after the September 11 attacks. // The tower was designed by Adrian Smith, who was then a design partner at SOM Chicago and later left the firm in 2006 to start his own practice, Adrian Smith + Gordon Gill Architecture. Surely Trump Tower's most appreciated civic gesture is its generous 1.2-acre (0.5-hectare) terraced riverfront park and the pleasant river walk that conveniently provides a covered shortcut between Michigan and Wabash. Despite its immense size, the building is a curious case study in contextualism, as its setbacks correspond both to the heights of some of the most prominent buildings immediately around it and to the programs within—from a parking garage, retail spaces, a restaurant, health club and spa, and executive lounges at the base to its five-star hotel in the middle. The upper stack contains spacious condominiums, topped by a luxurious 14,260-square-foot (1,325-square-meter) 89th-floor penthouse with 16-foot (4.9-meter) ceilings. The whole package culminates in a cylinder for mechanical equipment, and finally, a skimpy needle on top. // The use of circular geometry helps to diminish the skyscraper's bulk and is reiterated in multiple rounded corners and massive round columns that vary in height from three to five stories along the perimeter of the inset lower levels. Still, breaking the mass of the building, which is a whopping 2.6 million square feet (240,000 square meters) in size, into smaller, skinnier, and rounded volumes does not succeed in shaping it into an elegant structure. Its appearance is quite hefty despite the use of floor-to-ceiling reflective, silvery light-catching glass bands that alternate with brushed stainless-steel and clear-anodized aluminum spandrel panels. The setbacks accentuated by broad horizontal bands of double-floor-height louvered panels do not help express the building's verticality either. A polished and deeply projected stainless-steel mullion system adds glitz but does

not help correct the overall stumpiness. Blair Kamin, the *Chicago Tribune's* long-time architectural critic (1993–2021), described Trump Tower as 'exhilaratingly thin from some angles and unpardonably fat from others'. He concluded: 'This sky-scraper is at its most convincing when it is viewed in fragments rather than as a whole, or from angles that conceal its bulk.' Finally, the building's sign—stainless steel letters backlit with white LED lighting spelling out TRUMP—is placed directly below the first setback. Its excessive size—141 feet (43 meters) by 20 feet (6.1 meters)—makes it quite invasive, although, of course, that was intentional. The architect distanced himself from this 2014 afterthought, which for purely aesthetic reasons one only hopes will not be long-lasting.

Apple Michigan Avenue `026` `C`
401 North Michigan Avenue, Streeterville
Foster + Partners (London, UK)
2017

🚉🚉🚉🚉🚉 To State/Lake
🚉 To Lake or Grand
🚌 2, 3, 26, 66, 120, 121, 143, 146, 147, 148, 151, 157 to Michigan & Hubbard

The Apple Michigan Avenue store at the intersection of the Chicago River and North Michigan's Magnificent Mile has urban aspirations despite its modest scale. It turned the almost cliff-edged boundary between Pioneer Court plaza and the Chicago River's north bank into a public promenade of gently cascading granite steps with built-in wooden benches.

This pleasant tiered form appears to flow seamlessly from outside to inside, as they are separated by huge clear sheets of laminated glass—up to 32 feet (9.8 meters) high with rounded corners and no mullions. The pavilion-like building's ultra-thin roof of lightweight carbon fiber with continuous curved edges and corners is held up by four columns—two firmly encased in stone and two in steel-cladding so slender that the flat slatted ceilings of stained American white oak appear to float. The roof's design evokes an oversized, horizontal iPhone or iPad. It serves to discreetly advertise what have become some of the most iconic 'must-have' objects of our times. Under it, the airy single-room event space, or 'town hall' as touted by Apple, holds plenty of seating for presentations or just lingering, where folks enjoy both protected views of boats passing by and free wifi. The architecture here dissolves into 'almost nothingness', as Mies van der Rohe used to say. It is barely noticeable for its precision and refinement in its attempt to echo Apple's products. The store is London-based Foster + Partners only built project in Chicago. However, the firm also designed the Apple Park campus in Cupertino as well as unique Apple stores in New York, Singapore, Tokyo, London, Paris, Milan, and other cities around the world. The firm's founder, British architect Norman Foster and the 1999 Laureate of the Pritzker Prize, is known for iconic buildings such as the Hong Kong and Shanghai Bank Headquarters in Hong Kong, the Reichstag in Berlin, and the Great Court at the British Museum in London.

Ingeniously sited into a gently cascading stepped public promenade right over the Chicago River's north bank, Apple Michigan Avenue store is a see-through single-room pavilion with an ultra-thin flat roof that evokes the ultimate consumerist icon: an oversized iPhone or iPad.

Photo: Nigel Young/Foster+Partners

Yard Shakespeare Theater

027 C

800 East Grand Avenue at Navy Pier, Streeterville

Adrian Smith + Gordon Gill Architecture (Chicago), Charcoalblue (London)

2017

🚉 To Grand
🚌 29 to Navy Pier Terminal

sides of the stage, facing each other), and traditional proscenium. Seating capacity can vary from 150 to 850 seats. // Adrian Smith + Gordon Gill Architecture designed the two-level, steel-and-concrete lobby connecting CST's existing building to the Yard. Audiences are welcomed with expansive views of the city and lakefront as they walk through the dramatic 170-foot-long lobby with its curving curtain wall glazed

Yard Shakespeare Theater, the year-round, flexible performance venue, was built in 2017 as an extension to the existing Chicago Shakespeare Theater (CST), which has operated on Navy Pier in Streeterville on the Near North Side since 1999. The CST has become one of the largest theater companies in Chicago. Apart from Shakespeare's plays, it is known for presenting large-scale musicals, newly commissioned works, programs for children, and premiering international productions. The Yard is an adaptive-reuse project. The new space is tucked beneath the existing 1994 tent structure and over an existing parking garage. An existing stage box and backstage were also incorporated into the new building. The Yard consists of nine movable seating towers designed by the London-based theater consultancy Charcoalblue to address mobility, transformational space, and flexibility concerns. The three-story structures can be placed in multiple configurations to best suit a specific production, including in-the-round, traverse (audience on two

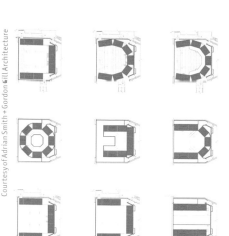

Nine of twelve seating and stage configurations

with electrochromic material that mitigates both glare and heat. The computer and sensor-controlled glass, manufactured by SageGlass, is transformational. It tints during the day, turning the exterior into a mirror reflecting the Chicago skyline, and goes clear in the evening, as the sun sets and performances begin. // Navy Pier measures 3,300 feet (1,010 meters) in length and encompasses over 50 acres (20 hectares) of parks and family-oriented attractions. It originally opened to the public in 1916 as the Municipal Pier according to the 1909 Plan of Chicago designed by Daniel Burnham and Edward H. Bennett to serve as a dock for freighters, passenger traffic, and indoor and outdoor recreation. Navy Pier was re-envisioned as a mixed-use venue in 1995 to incorporate retail, dining, entertainment, and cultural spaces. The current plan is based on the 2012 competition-winning design by Field Operations, a New York-based landscape architecture firm led by James Corner. The firm reimagined the historic pier as a waterfront promenade. Implemented in 2016, the Pier or 'pierscape' acts as a green spine connecting the city and Lake Michigan. The landscape architects conceived it as a series of thematic 'rooms' of engaging social spaces, contemporary architecture, water features, atmospheric lighting, and seasonal plantings throughout. Top attractions include a botanical garden, Chicago Children's Museum, *Amazing Chicago's Funhouse Maze*, a drop tower, the wave swinger fountain, a Ferris wheel, a carousel, and much more.

Photo: Howard N. Kaplan

Anti-Cruelty Society

510 North LaSalle Street
Stanley Tigerman & Associates
(Since 1986 Tigerman McCurry
Architects, Chicago)
1981
Remodelling, Interactive Design Architects
(Chicago)
2011

028 **C**

🚇🚇 To Merchandise Mart
🚇 To Grand
🚌 22, 156 to LaSalle & Grand; 65 to
Grand & Clark

This modestly-scaled, billboard-like building designed by Stanley Tigerman communicates its mission right on its North LaSalle façade. It depicts a cute puppy dog-like face that one could imagine saying: 'Come on in and adopt me!' Founded in 1898 to provide compassionate care for animals in need, the Anti-Cruelty Society is Chicago's oldest and largest not-for-profit animal shelter, which grew over the years to a campus of several buildings. It houses an animal-receiving area, a veterinary clinic, a rehabilitation facility, a training center, classrooms, offices, and lounges, and the society provide services such as cat and dog adoptions, education programs and pet-related workshops, cruelty investigation and rescue, a free helpline, group sessions, euthanasia, and cremation. The building's symbolic gesture is one of the early examples of Post-Modern iconography, but with a twist. Instead of turning to history for its inspiration, here, the façade is a humorous cartoon, as is the case with Tigerman's Self Park [006], which was

Sketch: Stanley Tigerman

built a few years later. The 1981 addition was built to replace a 1950s modernist structure and is focused on re-educating the public about the center's pet adoption services. The façade's original inexpensive aluminum siding, leaky windows, and lack of sunlight protection proved to be short-lived. After being repeatedly damaged, the center had to be remodeled in 2011 by another local firm, Interactive Design Architects. The façade was replaced and upgraded with improved energy efficiency and durability, but the whimsical face remained. The new terracotta rainscreen wall and sunscreen systems were detailed to replicate the horizontality of the original design. A landscaped, green-screen trellis was added on the roof to conceal the unsightly mechanical units from street view. Tigerman's building was cheaply executed and may well be remodeled beyond recognition, but his strong, image-driven façade survived and will likely continue carrying its quirkiness into the future.

Photo: James Steinkamp

Contemporaine ↗
516 North Wells Street,
River North
Perkins&Will (Chicago)
2004

029 C

🚇🚇 To Merchandise Mart
🚇 To Grand
🚌 65 to Grand & Franklin; 37, 125 to Wells & Grand

Contemporaine is a strikingly confident-looking 15-story condo tower of exposed concrete and floor-to-ceiling glass. It marks the intersection of N Wells and W Grand in the heart of the River North neighborhood a few blocks north of the Chicago River. Opened in 2004, it stands out among similarly scaled but less expressive concrete-and-glass towers built in recent years because of its bold sculptural form, and it contrasts greatly with older low-rise brick buildings that still dominate the area. Assembled as an urban collage of crisp geometric prisms, the building's L-shaped residential floors sit over the four-story square base. The ground-floor commercial space is topped by the three-story garage entirely glazed

and brightly lit at night. The building is animated by vertically-aligned, narrow balconies projected over sidewalks below that effectively break down the building's overall mass. The N Wells side of the building is particularly arresting for its corner alignment of balconies, which evoke diving boards, as well as a powerful east-west concrete wall that rises above the base and turns into a canopy at the very top, and two round columns—one supporting the corner balconies and the other holding the floating canopy. // The tower was designed by Ralph Johnson, Global Design Director at Perkins&Will. He was hired by Colin Kihnke, the developer and president of CMK Companies. The decision was based on projects Kihnke saw published in Johnson's monograph, which he came across at a local bookstore. Contemporaine won regional and national awards for its outstanding architecture and led to further collaborations between the architect and developer. The building's amenities include a swimming pool, gym, rooftop lounge, theater, grill and patio, not to mention sweeping views of the downtown skyline to the south and east.

Photo: James Florio Photography

Poetry Foundation
61 West Superior Street,
River North
John Ronan Architects (Chicago)
2011

030 C

To Chicago
To Chicago
22 to Dearborn & Huron; 66 to Chicago & Clark

Seductively screened along two unequal sides of the L-shaped corner site at the crossing of Superior Street and Dearborn Avenue, the Poetry Foundation is not an ordinary building. It is rather a sequence of unfolding and interconnected spaces, veiled and layered much like the lines and words of a poem—a metaphor the project's architect John Ronan used in his international competition-winning design. He called his construct a 'spatial narrative'. The two-story structure is the enviable home of the Poetry Foundation, a non-profit charitable organization with a singular mission: to celebrate the finest poetry and promote its presence in our culture. The institution was formed in 1941 by the Modern Poetry Association, which was the publisher of *Poetry* magazine, founded in 1912 by Harriet Monroe. Monroe was also the sister-in-law of John Wellborn Root, who was among the founders of the Chicago School style and the co-founder of Burnham and Root with Daniel Burnham. The Association was reformed and renamed the Poetry Foundation in 2003 thanks to a gift of $200 million from philanthropist Ruth Lilly (1915–2009). // The new building's perimeter screen is assembled out of a combination of solid and perforated corrugated panels made of pre-oxidized zinc. They bring sophistication to the street and veil the interior of the contemplative courtyard inside. The space can be accessed at any time and is entered through the missing corner section. The entry door is tucked deep into this 'room' under the open sky to avoid anything that would

Photo: Steve Hall /Hedrich Blessing

Photo: Steve Hall /Hedrich Blessing

suggest a shortcut. Going inside is more like a journey through slowly peeling opaque, see-through, and reflected planes and surfaces. It is a discovery, one step at a time. The interiors, wrapped in intricately assembled panels of concrete, glass, steel, and birch are a fluid array of interlocked spaces for seminars, readings, exhibitions, a poetry library of 30,000 volumes, and private listening booths. The acoustics of the 125-seat room for readings were designed so that poets can read without a microphone. The Poetry Foundation Library is the Midwest's only library dedicated to poetry. The concrete pavement in the garden spills freely inside, blurring the boundaries between interior and exterior, and from every part of the open plan, visitors never lose sight of the courtyard garden, which is complemented by bamboo stalks in the stairwell. No matter where you stand, it is not possible to see the whole space at once, just as you cannot read a poem all in one glance. The spaces, their limits, and edges are expanded, compressed, and juxtaposed; they are perceived and experienced in fragments casually, gradually, and joyfully.

diagonal façades. A series of almost chaotic angled setbacks and open framing towards the building's pinnacle may suggest its construction is still ongoing. In fact, the structure looks like it was deliberately left unclad. Surely this unusual, rugged dynamism comes from the area itself, particularly the old steel truss bridges over W Grand and W Kinzie to the south. There is something daring about this building that evokes dynamic projects by Russian constructivists in the 1920s. Erie on the Park was finished in 2002 and it represents a rare example of the steel-and-glass residential high-rise types built in Chicago since buildings by Mies van der Rohe. // The building has a sibling called Kingsbury on the Park that is situated diagonally across from the park. It is slightly taller but contains fewer apartments and is not as expressive formally and structurally. Kingsbury was built one year after Erie and designed by the same architect for the same client, Smithfield Properties. Both towers are a testament to the architect's refreshing experiment, inspired by site-specific industrial language for residential architecture. Although based on Lucien Lagrange's subsequent projects—predominantly dressed in stone and concrete forms that are covered in historically inspired décor and topped by mansard roofs—this experiment was short-lived.

Erie on the Park ↘
510 West Erie Street, River North
Lucien Lagrange Studio (Chicago)
2002

031 C

🚇🚇 To Chicago
🚌 37 to Orleans & Erie, 65 to Grand & Kingsbury, 66 to Chicago & Larrabee

Lucien Lagrange Studio designed Erie on the Park, an idiosyncratic 24-story asymmetrical assemblage of 195 loft-style condominiums. Situated mid-block among low-rise residential and commercial buildings, Erie on the Park overlooks the modest Ward (A. Montgomery) Park and unsightly parking lots on the northern branch of the Chicago River. This robust building is perfectly aligned with the diagonal portion of N Kingsbury Street, which approaches it from the south and is the best direction from which to approach and view it. The tower is distinguished by the exposed, white-painted steel cross-bracing on its long

Courtesy of Lucien Lagrange Studio

Museum of Contemporary Art (MCA) 032 C

220 East Chicago Avenue, Streeterville

Josef Paul Kleihues (Berlin, Germany)
1996

To Chicago

3, 26, 66 to Chicago & Mies van der Rohe; 125, 157 to Mies van der Rohe & Pearson; 143, 146, 147, 148, and 151 to Michigan & Chestnut

'In its thoughtfulness and integrity, [the museum's] design evokes the golden age of Chicago architecture. But it makes no attempt to reach forward with the fumbling, restless desire of contemporary life.' This assessment by the late *New York Times* critic Herbert Muschamp sums up the essence of the Museum of Contemporary Art (MCA), which opened in 1996 in the middle of an elongated corridor of city parkland in the tony Magnificent Mile district. There is an unequivocal sign of disappointment in Muschamp's unsympathetic remarks, concluding that: '[The building] puts art back in a box, at the top of a Parnassian staircase that undoubtedly flatters artists even as it undermines contemporary art.' It is hard to disagree with the critic at a time when exuberance, not restraint, was beginning to be celebrated in architecture. After years of economic stagnation, the profession was coming alive and there was an expectation of new exciting projects. By the following year, two major buildings—the colossal Getty Center in Los Angeles by Richard Meier and Frank Gehry's flamboyant Guggenheim Bilbao—already sparked everyone's imagination and pointed to new possibilities. The MCA paled in comparison and seemed like an opportunity missed, especially since the project was selected out of more than 200 entries in an international architectural competition. // Nevertheless, the building has quietly stood the test of time, as it is much more than what meets the eye. Far from other sensational works of architecture, in its own subtle way the MCA is a quintessential case study of what constitutes a true Post-Modernist building. In a way, it is an intellectual construct, a multireferential response to its complex context—physical, cultural, and historical, both local and international. The museum replaced the 1917 Chicago Avenue National Guard Armory, a hulking steel-frame and masonry building that was demolished in 1993. The new building was designed by a Berlin architect Josef Paul Kleihues (1933–2004), who defined its immediate site as being in the middle of 'an artificial canyon in which the towering walls of the surrounding buildings represent a cross-section of Chicago's history'. And it was the city and its history that inspired the architect's design decisions. // Two themes that Kleihues pursued obsessively here are symmetry and the endless application of square grids and shapes. The five-story, boxy building's perfectly symmetrical front evokes a likeness to the Propylaea, the gateway to the Acropolis. This ceremonially grand entry leads to a full-height, recessed-glass front set within a square grid and accessed through two flights of broad stairs that bring visitors to the top of a 16-foot (5-meter) base of Indiana limestone. Here the second-level entry lobby opens onto a narrow, all-white, four-story central atrium topped by two square skylights. This photogenic space overlooks the towering skyline towards Michigan Avenue and the museum's one-acre sculpture garden looks towards Lake Michigan. // The building's setbacks, its geometry, and the employment of a two-foot (60 cm) grid in the designs of the chessboard-like plaza, façades, and interiors is an ode to squares and rectangles. All dimensions are related to a two-foot module and rigorously determine the placement of all details. For example, the base limestone tiles are all 2-by-2 feet (60-by-60 cm), while the upper floors' cast aluminum panels are 6-by-6 feet (1.8-by-1.8 m) set within a two-foot-wide grid. Squares are applied to floor plans, ceiling grids, entryways, windows, mullion patterns, skylights, column and beam dimensions, and even details such as garden railings and air conditioning grille patterns. This logic is a nod to Chicago's original square street plan, the squarish grid façades of

its modern buildings, and the city's most famous modernist architect, Mies van der Rohe, whose buildings were quite literally three-dimensional grids. Curiously, for almost three decades Mies lived right across the street from here, in a six-story 1916 Italian Palazzo-inspired building at the corner of East Pearson Street and the former Seneca Street that runs in front of the museum. Seneca was renamed Mies van der Rohe Way to mark the German architect's 100th birthday in 1986. The way the museum's mass is handled is a strong reference to Karl Friedrich Schinkel, the nineteenth-century Prussian neoclassical architect, who both Mies and Kleihues admired. // There is a rationale behind the choice of each material and even their colors—nothing is random or inconsequential. For example, the light yellow limestone tiles refer both to the design of Frank Lloyd Wright's 1892 Charnley House for the Adler and Sullivan office in North Chicago and the color of the historic Water Tower and Pumping Station one block to the west. Both of these

Courtesy of Kleihues + Kleihues

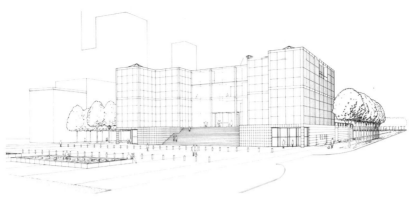

neighboring structures are centered on the museum's central axis. Note that the limestone tiles and aluminum panels are fastened by countersunk screws, either at the four corners or in the center. These shiny aluminum medallions allude to an inventive façade articulation first utilized in the 1906 Austrian Postal Savings Bank building by Otto Wagner in Vienna. Such details make dialogues between architects and their buildings possible. // The building's two corners on the main façade are designed exactly the same way, but while the left corner opens to the single-level education center, library, and 300-seat auditorium, the right one leads to a bookstore that extends to the second floor, spilling into the museum's lobby. The spectacular eye-shaped stair on the left, which rises to the exhibition floors, is designed around a fountain. Its ellipsoidal shape evokes the ground floor fountain at Wright's Guggenheim Museum in New York. The stair's shape is carried over to the look of light fixtures and elevator button panels, both designed by Kleihues. Despite such zealous attention to every detail, the galleries are autonomous and neutral. There is no competition between architecture and the artworks on view. These spacious rooms are flexible thanks to the use of temporary partitions. The top floor features four

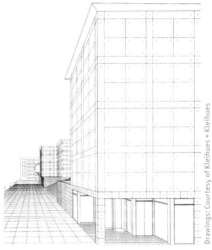

2

Drawings: Courtesy of Kleihues + Kleihues

parallel naves of exhibition galleries lit by skylights, with natural light dispersed through barrel-vaulted false ceilings in translucent glass tiles. // The MCA was the architect's only commission in America, where he was teaching. Kleihues built all over Germany and throughout western Europe and is most notable for his contributions to the reconstruction of Berlin. He was also planning director of the International Building Exhibition Berlin (1979–1987). One of the architect's most celebrated buildings is the Hamburger Bahnhof Museum of Contemporary Art in Berlin, which opened in 1996—the same year as the MCA.

The top fourth-floor galleries with high vaulted ceilings

Sofitel Hotel

20 East Chestnut Street, Rush & Division

Jean-Paul Viguier (Paris, France)

2002

  033 C

To Chicago

22 to Dearborn & Delaware; 36 to State & Delaware; 143, 146, 147, 148, 151 to Michigan & Chestnut

The 33-story Sofitel Chicago Magnificent Mile situated on North Michigan one block due west of the John Hancock Center is one of the most striking towers in Chicago. Its unconventional geometry is a result of the merging of three basic forms: a low rectangular podium at the corner of North Wabash and East Chestnut, topped by a 30-story prism with a right triangular plan whose acute angle points to the intersection, and a conical void inscribed into the southeast corners of both the podium and the triangular prism. While the first two forms are largely clad in white screen-printed glass, the scooped-away surfaces of the imaginary cone that constitutes the building's face are entirely glazed. From this spectacular corner, the building looks like the prow of a huge ship. This likeness is accentuated by the building's knife-like diagonal edge, which is angled so dramatically that the upper floors cantilever over the sidewalk. This leaning gesture over the street creates unparalleled views and leaves the most memorable impressions on passers-by. The tower's triangular floor plates and its diagonally-cut façade mimic the triangular footprint of the small Connors (William) Park directly across from North Wabash. Carrying this geometry into the sky makes the city's street grid visually integral to its buildings. Note the tower's southern tip—its diagonal cut gets skinnier as it rises—practically turns into a point at the very top. The irregular patterns of aligned square and rectangular windows on the tower's two broad façades are evocative of punched cards. // The building was designed by French architect Jean-Paul Viguier (b. 1946) who won an international competition for this building in 1998. Built in 2002, the tower was named 'Best New Building in the last 10 years in Chicago' by the American Institute of Architects in 2004. Two of the tower's original drawings by Viguier are now a part of the Chicago Art Institute's permanent collection. The base platform, with a sweeping curved glass front leaning outwards contains the lobby, conference rooms, and restaurants that open onto a small elliptical and canopied plaza. The hotel was the first building realized by this Paris-based architect in America. He has since designed a lovely addition to the McNay Art Museum, built in San Antonio in 2008. His firm is also known for emblematic projects such as the competition-winning Parc André Citroën on the left bank of the river Seine in Paris (1992), the French Pavilion at the Seville Expo '92, and office and residential towers built more recently in La Défense, west of Paris.

Fourth Presbyterian Church, Gratz Center
126 East Chestnut Street, Streeterville
Gensler (Chicago)
2012

🚇 To Chicago
🚌 143, 146, 147, 148, 151 to Michigan & Chestnut

The Genevieve and Wayne Gratz Center is a narrow five-story, mid-block building stretched from its formal entrance at East Chestnut to its rear at East Delaware. The building takes on the shape of its site—an elongated parallelogram aligned with the neighboring properties, the diagonal of North Rush to the west, and angled orthogonally to the buildings to the east. The structure completes the Fourth Church campus built almost a century earlier. It is an accessory to the main sanctuary, a profusely detailed limestone building in Gothic revival style at the corner of North Michigan and East Delaware, and the Tudor-style parish house with its cloister and clergy house south of the sanctuary. // Both of the new building's ends are distinctly wrapped in attention-grabbing patinated blue-green-colored copper, making them the most striking and memorable features on their respective blocks. The weathered copper skin complements the original church's copper detailing such as dormers, roof flashing, gutters, and downspouts. Both block-spanning interior walls are glazed to bring maximum natural light to the center's classrooms, library, preschool

facility, gathering spaces, dining room, and kitchen facilities. The building's south façade cantilevers out over the deeply inset, glazed ground floor to symbolize community outreach. A versatile double-height chapel for up to 350 people sits in the lower half of the cantilever. The chapel's backdrop wall is wrapped in a warm, dirty-penny patina—a conscientious contrast to the exterior treatment to avoid eventual color discrepancies between the interior and exterior copper. This side's stark, mostly opaque façade is cut by a single 38-foot (11.6-meter) slender rectangular window, sculpturally recessed on the right side. The façade's minimalist detailing and crisply angled copper-cladding folds around the window and is pleasant to the eye. The center's cantilever is accentuated by the copper cladding that continues on the underside. The roof over this end is partially green, and so is the building's setback to the east over the entry hall. // The Gratz Center was designed by the Chicago office of Gensler, a global design and architecture firm with nearly 50 offices and over 6,000 employees. The Fourth Church's sanctuary, built in 1914, was designed by Ralph Adams Cram, America's leading Gothic revival architect. He was designing the Cathedral of St. John the Divine in New York City at the same time. Curiously, the Fourth Presbyterian

Church was organized in early 1871 as a consolidation of various congregations. Its original church was dedicated a few blocks away on 8 October that same year; later that day it was destroyed by the Great Chicago Fire. It was soon rebuilt and 40 years later the congregation built this much grander building. Today, it is the oldest building on Michigan Avenue north of the Chicago River, combining the best elements of the English and French Gothic styles.

Photos: Richard Barnes

Viceroy Hotel
1118 North State Street, Rush &
Division
Goettsch Partners (Chicago)
2017

035 C

🚇 To Clark/Division
🚌 36 to State & Maple or State & Elm;
70 to Dearborn & Maple

The Viceroy Hotel is located in the heart
of the Gold Coast neighborhood, where a
diagonal part of North State Street splits
into three branches. North State continues north, North Rush joins diagonally from the south, and East Cedar begins and goes off to the east. The new
hotel is a hybrid project; it is a redevelopment of the former Cedar Hotel from
the 1920s and the ground-up addition of
an 18-story building behind it. The building was designed by Goettsch Partners,
a Chicago-based architectural firm with
additional offices in Shanghai and Abu
Dhabi. The interior design was the work
of TAL Studio, a Las Vegas-based firm
that has since merged with Wynn Design
and Development of Wynn Resorts. The
four-story, brick-and-terracotta façade
of the original Cedar Hotel was preserved, rebuilt, and given fresh life. The
hotel's new tower, wrapped in a highly reflective and irregularly folded glass curtain wall, seems to grow right out of the
older building's roof. This project exemplifies an inventive reuse of a historical
structure that can no longer satisfy the
full potential of its site with a new program. Of note is a 30-foot (9.1-meter)
art wall with inscribed quotes from
Marcel Proust—the design centerpiece
of the hotel's 'living room' lobby. Pushed
back on three sides, the tower's symmetrical façade is inspired by the argyle-like
pattern of the brickwork on the old building's façade below. // East Cedar Street offers the best head-on view of the building. Behind the period façade, visitors

Photo: James Steinkamp Photography

will find a three-story lobby space with an adjacent restaurant that features the original neon Cedar Hotel sign. In addition to a restaurant with outdoor dining, spaces include a lounge, meeting rooms, a large ballroom with a terrace extending to the original building's roof, and a rooftop landscaped terrace with an outdoor swimming pool and views over the skyline to the south. Surely it is inevitable that this type of architecture will become more common over time. Such juxtapositions of old and new result in unique synergies and feel quite appropriate in this case, despite exceeding the original building's scale several times. It may be too early to call it a trend, but there are some interesting precedents for such adaptive reuse around the world, including Tadao Ando's Wrightwood 659 [062].

2

Tower House
1306 North Cleveland Avenue,
Old Town
Frederick Phillips & Associates
(Mettawa, Illinois)
2001

🚇 To Clark/Division
🚌 37 to Sedgwick & Scott; 70 to Division & Clybourn

One of the smallest projects in this guide, Tower House is a freestanding residence near the southern border of the Old Town neighborhood, a short distance from North Clybourn. The structure occupies the central portion of what appears to be a leftover space—a small equilateral triangle—a hinge of sorts, where buildings to the south are misaligned with

buildings to the north. The robust miniature urban villa is tacked between two multi-family buildings of similar heights. The spot offers compelling slivers of city views in the southeast direction, even from the ground level. It was this adventitious position that inspired local architect Frederick Phillips to erect his own house here. In fact, the site's superior diagonal views toward the city became the key strategy for the building's vertical design. These views are uninterrupted from the upper levels. // The building features a blue-colored, six-legged steel framework on a module of 13-by-13-by-10 feet (4-by-4-by-3 meters), which makes each of the four floors twice that area—13-by-26 feet (4-by-8 meters)—and results in a total height of 40 feet (12 meters). Only two of these floors are

enclosed. The ground level serves as a carport and is entirely open. The second floor is split between two bedrooms and a shared bathroom. The next floor up has a single, open-plan space with a kitchen, dining, and living room. And the top level is an open roof terrace. This high-tech tower is accompanied by a solid 10-by-10-foot (3-by-3-meter) masonry stair tower standing a few feet away. It bridges over to the main structure at every level. Additionally, there is an exterior spiral staircase that connects to the stair tower. Painted screaming red, it provides a second means of egress (a requirement by the city). The second and third floors are clad in shiny corrugated steel panels and red-painted steel windows—full-height

toward the city views and ribbon ones at eye level on the side of the stairs. Both of the short ends on these two floors are windowless. Retractable translucent awnings provide optional sun protection over the roof terrace. // After living in what seems like an early career built manifesto for a few years, Phillips sold the house to another architect who 'treats it with respect', which shows. His practice, Frederick Phillips & Associates is based in Mettawa, a village north of Chicago. From there he has been working to realize various site-built and manufactured houses in the US and abroad and has been teaching a design studio at the College of Architecture at the Illinois Institute of Technology.

1 Parking Area
2 Entry
3 Bedroom
4 Bath

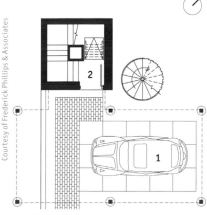

First floor plan

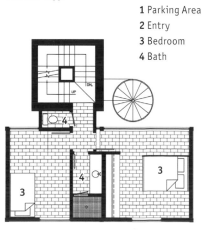

Second floor plan

037   Spertus Institute
038   William Jones College Preparatory High School
039   Columbia College Chicago Student Center
040   NEMA Chicago
041   Soldier Field Stadium
042   Chicago Horizon Pavilion
043   River City

Spertus Institute 037 C
610 South Michigan Avenue,
South Loop
*Krueck + Sexton Architects (now
Krueck Sexton Partners, Chicago)*
2007

🚋🚋🚋🚋 To Harold Washington Library-
State/Van Buren
🚋 To Harrison
🚌 1, 3, 4, 26, 28, 147 to Michigan &
Harrison; 2, 6, 26, 28 to Balbo & Michigan

The crystal-like multifaceted glass façade of the Spertus Institute for Jewish Learning & Leadership on South Michigan, which with the exception of the glass-clad Columbia College building next door, stands in striking contrast to its neighbors—a perfect line of shoulder-to-shoulder nineteenth- and twentieth-century masonry-dressed buildings with squarish windows, invariably grouped in aligned columns and rows. The institute's origami-like glass folds attract attention to their non-stop act of reflecting, retracting, and transforming the sky and clouds above, the trees of Grant Park opposite it, and passing vehicles and pedestrians below. The 10-story façade is made up of some three dozen parallelogram- and triangular-shaped milky glass planes with a frit pattern of tiny dots. They tilt in every direction and are further fractured into 726 individual glass panels of 556 different shapes. // The institute was built in 2007 on the only vacant lot along South Michigan in this area, immediately north of 618 South Michigan, the institute's home since its founding in 1924. Apart from administrative offices and classrooms, the institute features an airy atrium with a faceted south wall, a 400-seat multi-use auditorium behind it, a museum, a library and archives, a children's center, a gift shop, and a kosher café. When the original design by the Chicago-based Krueck Sexton Partners (then known as Krueck + Sexton Architects) was presented to the client, the response was reportedly that its straight roofline did not represent 'a Jewish building'. Therefore, the rationale behind the building's open, irregular top is to reflect the idea that the process of learning is a limitless journey. This explains why the building's apex is fragmented like a rock formation. At night, the glowing building echoes the Spertus logo, a flame accompanied by the biblical phrase in Hebrew that stands for 'let there be light'—the light of learning. The building's green roof manages stormwater and absorbs air pollution and heat. Note that the lower central part of the façade splits into the second skirt-like fold over the entrance, forming a sleek canopy element. After Spertus moved, its original building was acquired by Columbia College Chicago in 2012. Its stone front was replaced with a generic glass façade designed by Gensler, which somewhat diminishes the contrasting presence of Spertus' reflecting folded skin.

William Jones College
Preparatory High School
700 South State Street,
South Loop
Perkins&Will (Chicago)
2013

038 C

🚇 To Harrison
🚌 2, 6 to Balbo & State; 29, 62, 146 to
State & Polk

William Jones College Preparatory High School (commonly known as Jones College Prep) is an important prototype of a vertically-organized school in a dense urban neighborhood. It is a new approach to planning and a smart alternative to a sprawling campus that would not be possible in the heart of the South Loop. The seven-story edifice is situated on a long narrow lot along S State. Designed by Ralph Johnson of Perkins&Will, it resembles an oversized bookcase and constitutes an assembly of open and closed volumes constructed of precast concrete panels on round concrete columns. Placed on a grid they appear and disappear as they ascend on their way to the top. // The current building was built in place of the original Perkins&Will-designed school structure that had stood here since 1967 and was demolished to make room for it. A three-story grand lobby in the middle of the building is prominently positioned right at the center of a T intersection directly facing E Balbo. The space is used as a commons and serves as a pre-function space to support a 500-seat auditorium behind the solid wall to the north. The theater can be shared with the public during after-school hours. There are administration offices on the south end of the ground floor, with a spacious cafeteria directly above and a media center on the third floor. Classrooms run the length of the building on the fourth and fifth floors. There are more collaboration spaces and facilities on the next floor up, and a swimming pool and gymnasium top the vertical campus on level seven. There are large windows throughout and outdoor terraces at the summit with views of Grant Park a few blocks away and glimpses of Lake Michigan to the east. Stairways were widened to support student interaction. They have abundant natural light, views out, and encourage chance encounters between students and faculty on their way to classes. The interiors are efficiently planned and allow for great flexibility.

Columbia College Chicago Student Center
754 South Wabash Avenue,
South Loop
Gensler (Chicago)
2019

039 C

🚇🚇🚇 To Roosevelt
🚌 29, 62, 146 to State & Polk, 2, 6 to Balbo & State; 1, 3, 4 to Michigan & 8th Street

From your very first glimpse of this welcoming, engaging see-through structure, you get an instant sense that there is something creative and exciting going on inside. The block-wide, five-story building is the new Student Center for Columbia College Chicago (no affiliation with Columbia University or any other Columbia Colleges in the US), a private, non-profit university in the South Loop and Near South Side that specializes in the arts and media. Close to 6,000 students are currently enrolled in more than 60 undergraduate and graduate degree programs here. The center was designed as a large solid cube surrounded by airy, interconnected multi-floor volumes expressed in glazed horizontal strips stacked along its south and east sides, elevated over the ground floor along Wabash. It has everything students could want: a large event center, lounges and meeting rooms, activity spaces, a game room, performance and presentation spaces, music practice rooms, a film screening room, a fitness center, a food court, a coffee shop, and outdoor terraces with downtown views. These programs open onto a sleek atrium visible from the street. They spill seamlessly outdoors, merging with the sidewalk that doubles as a landscaped park. The center acts as a stage—a true hub for innovation, creativity, collaboration, and chance encounters. In the absence of a traditional campus, it is located amid the college's some 20 buildings and spaces scattered across the neighborhood. It is an indispensable place for students to meet between classes or for specific meetings and events. Gensler, the building's architect, worked directly with some 200 students to achieve not just a handsome look, but also a space capable of bringing students together. This collaborative approach is evident in the resulting character of the structure—a layered environment rather than the defined form of a singular building. Full-height glazing, a bright neon 'Columbia' sign, as well as dramatic ceiling lights and a large colorful mural on the third floor all contribute to the building's energetic presence, particularly at night when it quite literally lights up the neighborhood.

Photo: Tom Harris

NEMA Chicago
1210 South Indiana Avenue,
South Loop
Rafael Viñoly Architects (New York)
2019

040 C

🚇🚇🚇 To Roosevelt
🚌 12, 146 to Roosevelt &
Michigan/Indiana; 1, 3, 4, 18 to Michigan
& Roosevelt

NEMA Chicago—a lifestyle brand with sister buildings in San Francisco and Boston—was originally designed as a twin-tower development at the southwest corner of Grant Park, however, only the shorter of the two towers was built. The building's developer, Crescent Heights, still intends to complete the second tower one day. The 76-story residential rental tower occupies the one-acre (0.4-hectare) eastern half of its block at the corner of E Roosevelt and S Indiana, while the western half that stretches to S Michigan remains empty. The tower is the tallest in the South Loop and is one of the most iconic structures among the front-row buildings along Grant Park. While New York City architect Rafael Viñoly's original vision was most likely inspired by graceful Art Deco twin towers along Central Park West in Manhattan, NEMA Chicago's distinctive massing of multiple step-like square columns evokes the bundled-tube design of the Willis Tower (formerly the Sears Tower), Chicago's tallest building. According to the architect, these interesting references make the building 'not just an architectural idea, but an urban design idea'. // Viñoly is famous for projects such as a much-publicized 432 Park Avenue tower in New York and the Tokyo Forum. His Booth School of Business on the campus of the University of Chicago is also included in this guide [076]. The tower's interiors were designed by another New Yorker, Chicago-born architect David Rockwell, who is well-known for his spectacular hotels, theaters, and restaurants around the world. // The tower sits on the 16-story base of a parking garage, retail, and a fitness center that includes a basketball court, indoor swimming pool, spa and is topped by a landscaped pool deck on the south side. Additional amenities are housed on the 48th floor. The tower is best viewed towards its northeast corner along South Indiana towards the park, where it appears to rise dramatically like a compact city of square towers. The building's floor-to-ceiling glass windows offer unparalleled views of Grant Park, Lake Michigan, and the skyline to the northwest.

Photos: Courtesy of Rafael Viñoly Architects

View looking south toward South Loop (to the right) and
Museum Campus (to the left) over Grant Park

040

Soldier Field Stadium **041** **C**
1410 Special Olympics Drive,
Museum Campus
Wood + Zapata (Boston), Lohan
Caprile Goettsch Architects (Chicago)
2003

Metra To 18th Street
🚆🚆🚆 To Roosevelt
🚌 2, 6, 26, 28 to 1100 South Columbus;
146 to Soldier Field & Field Museum

Soldier Field Stadium is located on Museum Campus in the company of the Field Museum, Shedd Aquarium, Adler Planetarium, Burnham Park Yacht Club, and Northerly Island Park—all tightly packed and dotted with gardens, pavilions, memorials, and monuments—between South Lake Shore and Lake Michigan. Home to the Chicago Bears since 1971, this municipal stadium originally opened in 1924. Its name changed the following year as a memorial to US soldiers killed in combat. The stadium sits immediately south of and on an axis with the Field Museum, an imposing 1921 building with Greek temple-like porticos and oversized Ionic columns. It was designed as a visual extension of the museum with two Doric stoas defining its east and west façades, with their colonnades perched above the arena. These Neoclassical features invariably remained as the stadium's most prominent symbol as

it underwent numerous renovations to enhance its ability to host a variety of events—from track and field and football games to auto racing and public assemblies. When Soldier Field hosted the 1994 FIFA World Cup, its capacity was nearly 67,000 seats, and its look still resembled its original appearance, mainly due to the presence of the iconic stoas. It was the 2003 renovation that changed the stadium's appearance beyond recognition and cost Soldier Field its designation as a National Historic Landmark. // A lot of controversy surrounds this project. It is loved by some and passionately loathed by others. However, when you delve into the reasons for the disapproval of this reincarnation, it turns out there are just two: it is too big and too modern. While the first point may be valid, the alternative would be to find another site for a new stadium, which was not an option. As for the second point, the project was a joint venture of two firms: Wood + Zapata (they since have split into two firms, Carlos Zapata Studio in New York and Studio Shanghai led by Ben Wood) and Lohan Caprile Goettsch Architects (now Goettsch Partners). The architects chose not to package new programs in a pseudo-historicist style to mimic the original building, which would have been dubious. Interestingly, while the building's critics call it 'the spaceship that landed in the stadium', those who love it

describe it using the exact same words. // In any event, despite increasing in bulk, the new building's number of seats was actually reduced to 61,500 to allow for the modernization of the team's training and dressing rooms, improved sightlines, the addition of 133 luxury skybox suites, three club lounges, and other amenities without which a modern stadium would be unthinkable. As a result, the new stadium now rises dramatically and without much regard for its original appearance or even of Classical architecture's basic principles such as symmetry. Yet the way the uncompromisingly modern steel-and-glass forms now leap over the historical colonnades, juxtaposing contrasting materials and styles, is surprisingly engaging, intriguing, and at times delightful. The area around the stadium was also transformed from ugly disjointed parking lots to appealing extensive parkland with striking downtown and lake views over a multi-level underground garage.

Photo: Pygmalion Karatzas Photography

Chicago Horizon Pavilion
Grant Park, Museum Campus
Ultramoderne (Providence, Rhode Island)
2015

042 C

🚇🚇🚇 To Roosevelt
🚌 2, 6, 26, 28 to 1100 South Columbus;
146 to Soldier Field & Field Museum

The Horizon Pavilion, sitting in the southeast corner of Grant Park on the Lakefront Trail and the northern tip of Museum Campus, is an open, square pavilion originally built for the inaugural 2015 Chicago Architecture Biennial to host talks, films, and workshops. It won the BP Prize in the Chicago Lakefront Kiosk Competition organized for the event. The kiosk was designed by Aaron Forrest and Yasmin Vobis, architects, university professors, and founders of Ultramoderne, an experimental architectural practice in Providence, Rhode Island. They are particularly focused on the innovative use of mass timber technologies, such as cross-laminated timber (CTL), as a sustainable replacement for steel and concrete. Specific inspirations for this project were found in the long-span structures of Mies van der Rohe and the classic 1977 documentary film *Powers of Ten* (filmed in this area) about the cosmos and the microcosmic and made by the legendary husband-and-wife design duo Charles and Ray Eames. The key objective here was to construct the largest flat wood roof possible. Designed and built in just 10 weeks, the project is the result of close collaboration between architects, engineers, and fabricators. // The architects used CLT to build their 56-foot (17-meter) square pavilion—a planar roof 8.25-inch (21-cm) thick, supported by 13 columns at a height of 8 feet (2.4 meters). These columns, rectangular in section, coming out of a square concrete floor of a slightly larger footprint, are distributed in a radial pattern in response to lateral loads and wind uplift, while also directing visitors' views outwards. Apart from the columns and a few scattered benches, the roof engages two see-through volumes. Both are tacked under it, each in its own corner and each wrapped in chain-link fencing stretched between the roof and the ground. The smaller volume houses bookshelves—it functioned as an architectural library during the Biennial. The other volume, slightly angled, sits under a rectangular cut-out and houses a staircase used as a viewing platform, allowing visitors to look around over the roof that acts as an artificial horizon. It shuts out the foreground and accentuates the presence of the vertical skyline to the north and uninterrupted views toward the lake to the east. The Chicago Park District is the steward of the pavilion; it oversees its maintenance and occasional programming. The Horizon Pavilion is essentially a playful viewing device that frames the city, lake, and sky in a variety of abstract settings that visitors can control based entirely on the power of their imagination. Otherwise, it provides summertime shade and serves as a pleasant umbrella protecting park goers from precipitation.

River City
800 South Wells Street,
South Loop
*Bertrand Goldberg Associates
(Chicago)*
1986

🚇 To Harrison
🚋 To LaSalle
🚌 24 to Clark/Polk

River City is a large, curvaceous mixed-use development built of cast-in-place concrete that hovers in places over the south branch of the Chicago River. It is one of the most unusual Chicago structures that people call home. It is best viewed from the Chicago Architecture River Cruise. In fact, the boat turns around right in front of the building before heading back downtown. The structure appears to be stationary, just momentarily, before seeming ready to disembark for its own adventurous voyage. Harvard and Bauhaus-trained Chicago modernist architect Bertrand Goldberg (1913–1997) conceived and designed the complex as a city within a city where one could live, work, shop, learn, and play all in one place. // Goldberg acted not only as its original architect and promoter but also as co-developer. He became internationally renowned almost 20 years earlier for another project, Marina City, with its iconic 60-story twin 'corn cob' towers built over a marina on the main branch of the Chicago River. River City, though, is a small portion of what was originally proposed as a huge high-density urbanist vision, which was supposed to contain everything from schools to shopping centers as well as residential towers reaching 72-stories grouped in trios and linked by skybridges with various communal services. Snaking along the

river, there was to be a lengthy mid-rise housing complex, of which the present complex is but a small section. // As built in 1986, it is a reverse S-shaped, 10-story residential building on top of a four-story podium that contains 250,000 square feet (23,225 square meters) of offices, co-working spaces, common areas, multiple lounges, shops, a conference center, restaurants, a health club, educational facilities, kindergartens, a 70-boat marina on the opposite riverside, and a one-acre (0.4-hectare) private landscaped outdoor park over its roof. // The atrium, an interior street dubbed the 'River Road', soars up to 12 stories, undulating along the building's central spine. It sits over townhouses, entered from their top floors. The apartments above, from studios to four-bedroom duplex penthouses with terraces, are accessed through linear open balconies acting as corridors on either side of the interior street, which is reached by tower elevators and bridges. There are clerestories on the apartments' 'inner side' to gain light from the atrium, which is topped by a continuous skylight made of glass blocks held in thin concrete ribbing. The River Road evokes European shopping arcades and some of the hotel atriums designed by the late Atlanta architect John Portman. // Originally envisioned as rental housing, the complex of 449-units was later converted into condominiums. The units were purchased back in 2019 and converted into rentals following extensive renovations. The latest redevelopment saw the original textured gray tone of exposed concrete, which was meant to be beautifully rendered by daylight, painted a stark white. Local preservationists criticized the choice. Very few of the apartments have balconies or terraces and all have either river or city views or both through narrow windows with rounded corners that recall cruise ship windows. Despite low ceilings and tight layouts, there is a feeling of abundant shared space that fosters a sense of community and the pride of living in a building that has a rich history and distinctive design character. // The complex has become more integrated with the rest of the city in recent years as more residential towers are built to its

043 C

north and east. There are also plans to connect it to the Southbank Riverwalk. So, this once desolate part of the South Loop is beginning to acquire a more residential feel, although an unsightly electrical substation and a postal service distribution center directly across the river are unlikely to be relocated any time soon. // Bertrand Goldberg was also known for designing a rear-engine automobile, prefabricated and canvas houses, unique furniture, mobile vaccine labs, and even easily convertible ice cream shops supported by tension wires from a single column. He was famous for designing unconventional, often circular forms, made of mundane materials such as plywood and concrete. Most importantly, he ceaselessly tried to propose new models for people to live together, whether on the scale of a house or a city.

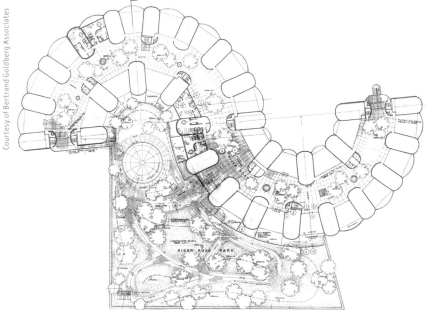

Plan at a typical floor and private landscaped park over a four-story podium

Near West Side

4

044   Accenture Tower (formerly Citigroup Center)
045   150 North Riverside
046   River Point
047   River Cottages
048   CTA Morgan Street Station
049   800 Fulton Market
050   Skybridge
051   Rush University Campus Transformation Project
052   Illinois Regional Library for the Blind and Physically Handicapped
         (now Lakeside Bank)
053   SOS Children's Villages Illinois
054   Legacy Charter School

Accenture Tower (formerly Citigroup Center) ←
500 West Madison Avenue, West Loop
Murphy/Jahn (since 2012, JAHN, Chicago)
1987

044 **C**

🚆🚆🚆🚆 To Washington/Wells
🚆🚆 To Clinton
🚌 60, 124, 125, 157 to Canal & Madison

Located one short block west of the south branch of the Chicago River, Citigroup Center is a 42-story structurally expressive office tower facing W Madison. It was designed as a gateway into the city, as it sits directly over Ogilvie Transportation Center, the terminus of all the trains from the northern and western suburbs. It replaced the 1911 Chicago and North Western Terminal, which was built in the Renaissance Revival style with a barrel-vaulted ceiling. Occupying the entire width of the block, the building seems to pick up all the energy and movement carried by the arriving trains and convert it vertically into a series of cascading wave-like curves clad in dark greenish reflective glass. The composition evokes the image of a bursting fountain. The metaphor works well with both the nearby river and the trains that once inspired architects with their steel wheels, speed, and progressive, streamlined look, particularly when Art Deco skyscrapers were going up in America in the 1920s and 1930s. A continuous arcade along W Madison Avenue and a sequence of multi-story atria enhance commuter traffic flow to the platforms. The spacious block-long retail gallery is topped by curved skylights at heights of up to 80 feet (24.5 meters). Ground-floor escalators connect to an even higher train-level atrium. // The building was designed by the late Helmut Jahn at a time when his high-tech inspired towers were rising in Manhattan and Philadelphia as well as his iconic United Airlines Terminal 1, dubbed 'The Terminal for Tomorrow', at O'Hare International Airport [093]. Note the skybridge over N Canal into the neighboring building to the east. The building's original name was changed to Northwestern Atrium Center and most recently to Accenture Tower.

150 North Riverside →
150 North Riverside Plaza, West Loop
Goettsch Partners (Chicago)
2017

045 **C**

🚆🚆 To Clinton
🚌 620, 56 to Washington & Canal; 120, 125 to Canal & Randolph/Washington

150 North Riverside, a 54-story tower that locals refer to as 'the champagne flute', stands prominently at the confluence of the three branches of the Chicago River. It sits boldly on a two-acre site on the Chicago River's west bank. Before this unusual building could rise, it was necessary to construct a platform to bring the new structure's lobby to the level of the adjacent streets. Only a portion of this platform could hold a building—the area between the tracks that carry Metra and Amtrak trains into Chicago Union Station and the river. Additionally, the city's building codes stipulated that any new construction along the riverbank had to leave at least 30 feet (10 meters) of space in front of it for a public riverwalk. Architecture firm Goettsch Partners came up with a clever solution—to mount the tower on a thin base that occupies only a quarter of the building's site and constitutes the tower's core. This trick allowed the upper floors to cantilever over the riverwalk on one side and the train tracks on the other. Within the platform between the tracks and the river, there is an underground conference center with an auditorium and a restaurant with a terrace overlooking the river. // The site around the building was turned into a public park, with its western half raised over a single-story parking garage. While the underside of the building's cantilever next to the river is left open, the opposite side is glazed and turned into a spacious lobby that reaches nearly 100 feet (30 meters) at its peak. Inside there is a 150-by-22-foot-long (46-by-6.7-meter-long) multimedia wall: a digital light sculpture that comprises 89 LED vertical blades. Integrated into the building's design, the installation was created by McCann Systems. The content is being commissioned from artists and students.

045 C

Curiously, the building's likeliness to a champagne flute is further justified by the fact that there is liquid in it: 12 rooftop tanks contain 1,000 tons of water to counterbalance heavy wind loads and keep the building from swaying. What is disappointing about this building is the fact that the architects already used the exact same form in another one of their projects—a mixed-use development built several years earlier for the same developer client, The John Buck Company, in Abu Dhabi in the United Arab Emirates. There the architects designed four champagne flutes—towers rising from much thinner core-size bases scattered on a large site and seemingly unrestrained by any site conditions.

River Point

444 West Lake Street,
West Loop
*Pickard Chilton (New Haven,
Connecticut)*
2017

 **046** **C**

🚆🚆 To Clinton
🚌 125 to Wacker & Lake

River Point is one of Chicago's most eye-catching new buildings. It is distinguished by its graceful curves, rising dramatically over the emblematic 'Y' intersection where three Chicago River branches meet. An arresting edifice for this spot was long in the making. The 52-story tower sits diagonally along a large triangular site at the corner of North Canal and West Lake on the edge of the West Loop neighborhood and directly faces the main branch of the river. The building's bulging east and west—and entirely glazed—façades are symmetrically sliced on an angle at the very top to produce a distinctive U-shaped pinnacle. These parabolic curves are mirrored at the building's foot, but more subtly, almost as a graphic device outlining spacious lobbies; the main lobby that faces the river is three stories. The building's location on its fully engineered site is conditioned by the existing Amtrak and Metra tracks that curve around it. This explains why the tower is pushed away from the river and occupies only a small portion of the

046 C

site, which is transformed into an expansive 1.5-acre (0.6-hectare) terraced park with the pre-existing riverwalk passing in front of it. The park and plaza, which cover a three-level parking garage, employ curves similar to those that define the geometry of the building. // The New Haven-based global firm Pickard Chilton designed the tower. As you would expect, the designers rationalized their use of curves as a response to the river and the train tracks running below and around the building, as well as the desire to communicate with another curved building—333 West Wacker—on the other side of the river's 'Y' intersection. The truth is: Pickard Chilton has been testing similar geometries for many years, as the firm has designed a whole series of curved buildings in cities around the world from nearby Milwaukee, Houston, and Atlanta to Dubai and Riyadh in the Middle East. This modern-day tower provides large column-free floor plates with floor-to-ceiling glazing that offers expansive views over downtown, the Chicago River, and Lake Michigan from its upper floors. Its amenities include fitness and conference centers, retail, and restaurants. As a special bonus, there is a 29-foot (8.8-meter) steel sculpture designed by Spanish architect Santiago Calatrava on the riverside of the building. *Constellation* is a fractured bright red spiral that evokes a dancing firebird, however abstract its intentions.

River Cottages ↘

047 C

357–365 North Canal Street, West Loop
Harry Weese (Chicago)
1988

🚇🚇 To Merchandise Mart
🚇🚇 To Clinton
🚌 37, 125 to Orleans & Merchandise Mart; 56 to Desplaines & Fulton/Milwaukee/Kinzie

Perched on the west bank of the Chicago River's north branch, the River Cottages— four townhouses with private boat docks—are best viewed from aboard a sightseeing cruise or water taxi or from the West Kinzie Street Bridge immediately to the north. This compact and whimsical complex, packaged into two unequal buildings, was designed by modernist architect Harry Weese (1915–1998), a Chicago native. There are two five-level and two six-level residences, with units ranging from 2,200-square-feet (205-square-meters) to 4,200-square-feet (390-square-meters) and all forming a distinctive triangular silhouette. The slopes echo the 1908 Chicago and North Western Railway's Kinzie Street Bridge across the river. A designated Chicago landmark, this single-leaf bascule bridge has been unused since 2000 and is permanently raised in the open position. The building's profile also recalls a sail, which is not only an apt reference to the river location, but also a reflection of the architect's hobby as a sailor. To emphasize this point, Weese peppered his project with numerous nautical elements, such as steel spiral staircases, pipe parapets and railings, portholes, open decks, and a plethora of triangles and diamonds. Thankfully, internal elevators make climbing multiple and ever-shifting stairs optional. // Like River City's architect Bertrand Goldberg, Weese saw the downtown riverfront as an underused asset and proposed a residential development of 1,000 apartments and townhouses to be built over a marina. He even acquired a site large enough for this project in 1976. However, the River Cottages complex and the conversion of a neighboring existing warehouse into condominiums are the only remnants of that original vision. This is the only Weese project included in this guide, as his most representative works predate the book's focus on projects built since 1978. Weese's most celebrated masterpieces are Washington D.C.'s metro system (1976), with its strikingly beautiful brutalist concrete vaults, and the Metropolitan Correctional Center (1975), a robust, modernist building. In that regard, the River Cottages complex is a true Post-Modernist project—an oddity in Weese's oeuvre. Interestingly, the architect's younger brother, Ben (b. 1929), who worked at Harry's large office shortly before opening his own practice, was an original member of the Chicago Seven, the first generation Post-Modern group of architects in Chicago. // All four cottages belonged to their original owners until recently. One of the larger three-bedroom, 2.5-bath units went on the market for the first time in 2015 and sold for $2.25 million. The interior photo of the vacant space provides a glimpse into what it is like to live under the slanted roof.

Photos: Andrea Bauer

4

Photo: Kate Joyce Studios

CTA Morgan Street Station
958 West Lake Street, West Loop
Ross Barney Architects (Chicago)
2012

  048 C

🚉🚉 To Morgan

The Morgan Street 'L' Station is housed in a pair of towering steel-and-glass rectangular prisms built on either side of the CTA's Green and Pink lines. The twin volumes are linked by a fully glass-enclosed bridge that allows passengers to switch to the opposite platform without leaving the paid zone. The station sits in a recently gentrified area known as Fulton Market (short for Fulton-Randolph Market District) in the West Loop that served as a meatpacking, warehouse, and industrial zone for much of the nineteenth and

twentieth centuries. The station was originally built in 1893, but later demolished in 1948 due to the area's decreasing population, leaving the neighborhood without a quick and convenient connection to the central business district for more than 60 years. However, after 2000, corporate headquarters, tech companies, hotels, bars, restaurants, and retail started coming to what has become one of the hottest submarkets for commercial real estate and the most dynamic neighborhood in Chicago. This made the need to reopen the station apparent and even urgent. // The new reincarnation opened in 2012 with a design by Chicago-based Ross Barney Architects, the designers behind Chicago's Riverwalk [008], several other CTA stations, and Searle Visitors Center [060]. The two towers that form a symbolic gateway to the neighborhood are assembled out of perforated stainless steel and glass panels. They are brightly lit from within at night and identified by the oversized 'cta' sign. The new platforms are made of concrete and covered by translucent polycarbonate canopies. There are young trees, landscaping, and artist-designed bicycle racks at street level along West Lake. The glazed bridge offers stunning nearby views of downtown Chicago as well as serving as a means of conveyance. The design anticipates the potential extension of both platforms and canopies should the current passenger flow increase.

Photo: Kate Joyce Studios

800 Fulton Market
800 West Fulton Market,
West Loop
SOM (Chicago)
2021

049 C

🚇🚇 To Morgan
🚇 To Grand
🚌 8 to Halsted & Fulton Market; 9 to
Halsted & Lake

Situated near the intersection where the Amtrak and Metra tracks cross the Kennedy Expressway in the West Loop, 800 Fulton Market is a mixed-use creative office building. Occupying its own block, the 18-story glass-and-brick-building rises incrementally in a series of landscaped setbacks—straight and angled—to carefully negotiate the appropriate scale with its much lower residential neighbors to the south. The new development is designed to enliven the neighborhood's streetscape with retail and restaurants in the three-story podium to match the existing scale of the already vibrant restaurant scene along West Fulton Market Street. Its public amenities include a spacious lobby, fitness center, penthouse lounge, roof deck, and below-ground parking. The building's east and west façades are distinguished by external steel cross-bracing designed as a reference to the neighborhood's industrial character, to ease the structure's thermal expansion and contraction, and withstand Chicago's fierce wind loads. Together with an offset core, this structural system enables large, open floor plates and flexible, light-filled workspaces. The building was designed by SOM. The firm is responsible for some of Chicago's most iconic buildings, including the Sears Tower (now Willis Tower) and the John Hancock Center (875 North Michigan Avenue). This guide includes three other recent projects by SOM: the Chinatown Branch of the Chicago Public Library [067], the Trump International Hotel & Tower [025] and the planned CTA 'L' Station at State/Lake [005].

4

Photo: Dave Burk/SOM

Skybridge

737 West Washington Boulevard,
West Loop
Perkins&Will (Chicago)
2003

🚌 8 to Halsted & Madison; 20 to
Washington & Halsted

Although this 39-story residential tower directly faces Chicago's busiest highway—the 10-lane Kennedy Expressway—it rewards residents of apartments on the building's east façade with sweeping views of downtown Chicago and distant glimpses of Lake Michigan. All other apartments face the quieter side where they enjoy front-row, unobscured views of sunsets over the low-rise western suburbs. The building sits on its own block and is composed of two basic parts—a podium with a parking garage and a large Whole Foods Market that serves the Greektown and neighboring communities in the West Loop and a tower with apartments that start from the 6th floor. The four-story podium is by and large unremarkable: a solid wall, interrupted by narrow ribbons of grilles on the highway side and mostly glass panels tinted in several shades of gray on the opposite side, all topped by roof parking. It is the tower that rises both from the podium and street level on the West Washington side that makes this building quite special. The intention of this competition-winning project designed by Ralph Johnson of Perkins&Will was to break the visual monotony and dullness of a typical residential high-rise by introducing spatially compelling voids, notches, shifts, alternating balconies' patterns, and an array of concrete treatments—from exposed to brightly painted—all to create a seemingly random, ad hoc village-like character. // The Skybridge name comes from the topmost structure bridging a 30-foot (9.1-meter) wide split that starts at the 14th floor and runs all the way up between the masses of two unequal halves of the tower. This steel structure then turns into an open trellis resting on a four-story round column and ends precariously in mid-air, pointing due north. The split doubles the number of corner apartments and links the tower's two sides by a stack of fully glazed linking walkways measuring just seven feet (2.1 meters) in width. They provide required access to the south side apartments since only the north side is equipped with elevators, although there are interior fire stairs in both towers. Contemporaine [029], Johnson's much smaller residential building and a sibling of Skybridge, was built one year later in the River North neighborhood on the Near North Side and relies on many similar design strategies and features. Both buildings can be credited with reviving the use of exposed concrete in residential construction in Chicago.

Rush University Campus Transformation Project

1653 West Congress Parkway, Near West Side
Perkins&Will (Chicago)
2012

🚇 To Illinois Medical District
🚇 To Polk
🚌 7, 126 to Harrison & Ashland

The striking four-winged butterfly-like form that hovers a couple of floors over a massive, glazed podium cannot be missed by motorists driving in both directions along the Dwight D. Eisenhauer Expressway that directly links Chicago's downtown with its western suburbs. The two-part building, referred to as 'the tower', is an addition to the Rush University Medical Center. It is a part of a campus-wide transformation project that also includes an orthopedic building, a parking garage, and new loading and delivery systems. The new rectangular podium comprises seven floors of new diagnostic and treatment facilities and connects to existing diagnostic treatment facilities and a garage. The butterfly—the project's most distinctive feature—is a five-story tower for patient beds. The building's designer, Ralph

4

Johnson of Perkins&Will, rationalized his unique solution as the direct result of an 'inside-out' design approach, which, in fact, was realized in close collaboration with doctors, nurses, and administrators to the point of building full-scale mock-ups in order to test and streamline adequate distances and the overall performance by staff. // The resulting form maximizes views and natural light in patient rooms, which are distributed along the outlines of the four wings, while the caregivers are placed at the core to enable more convenient and faster care for patients. While the building's north side, which faces the highway, is split into the lower base and the upper butterfly top, its south side scales down the building by bringing the tower's curvilinear geometry down to the ground. This is where the building's public elements, including lounges and waiting areas, are located. There is a multi-story entrance pavilion at the junction of the new and old areas with a landscaped roof and garden at level four. There are skylights that pop up through the garden and act as sculptural elements, one of which dips all the way down to the ground and encloses a terrarium. There are green roofs at the top of the podium and the top of the butterfly. It would have been logical to provide a heliport on the butterfly's rooftop, but the landing zone is situated on the ground at the west end of the campus.

Illinois Regional Library for the Blind and Physically Handicapped (now Lakeside Bank)

052 C

1055 West Roosevelt Road, Near West Side
Stanley Tigerman & Associates (Since 1986 Tigerman McCurry Architects, Chicago)
1975–1978, 2005 remodelling

🚌 12 to Roosevelt & Blue Island

The original Illinois Regional Library for the Blind and Physically Handicapped has served as a Lakeside Bank branch since its 2005 remodel. The two-story triangular structure sits at the obtuse-triangle corner where West Roosevelt Road and South Blue Island Avenue cross. Unfortunately, it is a mere shadow of what was once a small but important building—one of the finest works by Stanley Tigerman (1930–2019). It is arguably the very first example of Post-Modernist architecture in the city and Tigerman is referred to as the local 'Godfather of Post-Modernism' whose whimsical projects voiced the architect's disagreement with the austerity of the often dogmatic right-angled buildings by Mies van der Rohe. The 1978 building predates all other entries in this guide. Many of its features have changed dramatically so they cannot be fully appreciated today. Nevertheless, it remains meaningful and valuable due to the fact that its original shell is largely intact. //

Before falling into disuse, the original library welcomed primarily blind patrons. The architect insisted that a 'barrier-free' environment was not enough. His design suggested that blind people are as entitled to metaphorical symbolism as the sighted. The building was color-coded—perimeter: bright orange; structure: yellow; and mechanical equipment: blue. It has now been repainted in the bank's corporate colors: blue and white. // The lightweight metal-clad steel skin is opaque, while the dense concrete hypotenuse wall along South Blue Island Avenue is pierced by a 165-foot (50-meter) undulating window—a tribute to Tigerman's close friend, the New York architect and educator John Hejduk (1929–2000). It recalls a window profile in Hejduk's Barbar House (1972). The feature also evokes a stretched drawing of an elephant eaten by a boa constrictor in *The Little Prince*. Inside, the window's profile is mimicked in elevation of a service counter stretched along the window with sections dipping down to allow customers in wheelchairs to come in direct contact with staff. Many of the design features were meant to help guide blind people to navigate the space.

Hard-surface materials such as metal panels and concrete walls accentuated the blind customers' heightened perception of sound. The architect avoided employing hard corners and all objects were anchored down, not hung, so that their positions could be easily noted. Unfortunately, many major changes in the design of the original building that were made when it was remodeled into a bank now lessen its value as an architectural artifact. Still, it is preserved in photos, drawings, and the architect's intentions that must be referenced on a visit to this important structure.

4

SOS Children's Villages Illinois `053` `C`
1133 West 13th Street,
Near West Side
JGMA (Chicago)
2020

🚌 60 to Racine & 13th Street

The new Roosevelt Square Community Center was created by and is operated by SOS Children's Villages Illinois, a foster care organization. It sits on a prominent corner site along active S Blue Island in the Roosevelt Square neighborhood in the Near West Side. The single-story, skewed, L-shaped building houses various community programs, group study areas, an event space, an educational kitchen, and administrative and counselling offices. Despite its modest scale, the pavilion draws attention due to its unusual façades with slightly rising corners. They are wrapped in glass panels and steel sidings in three different colors—black and two shades of blue—and corrugation widths that come down from the roof at various angles and fold gracefully into a continuous narrow canopy that marks the entry at the elbow-like obtuse bend along

West 13th. As the building's skin transitions from one side to the next, it engages the eye, which wants to follow the intriguing structure that reveals new turns and slopes with every step. The interior is entirely visible from the outside. It is assembled out of cross-laminated timber members that bring warmth to the space. The steel panel colors are carried inside and expressed in walls, flooring, and furniture. All materials are exposed and durable, and the space is open-ended with various zones intertwined. There is a small triangular plaza before the entry and a community garden and playground in the back. A variety of angles, both in plan and on the elevations of this sleek tiny building, produce an unusually dynamic effect, provoking the curiosity of passers-by. // Designed by Juan Gabriel Moreno, a Colombia-born architect and founder of JGMA in Chicago in 2010, the center represents a family of visually connected projects due to their characteristic dynamic organization. This guide includes two other works by this active studio: El Centro [092] and the Daley College Manufacturing, Technology & Engineering Center [099].

Photos: Tom Rossiter

Photos: Karant+Associates, Inc.

4

Legacy Charter School
3318 West Ogden Avenue,
Lawndale
*Lothan Van Hook DeStefano
Architecture, LVDA (Chicago)*
2017

054 A

🚇 To Kedzie
🚌 157 to Ogden & Spaulding; 18 to 16th
Street & Spaulding

The Legacy Charter School is a colorful, three-story freestanding building west of Douglas Park in North Lawndale on Chicago's West Side. It occupies a tight trapezoidal site on West Ogden Avenue, which is also part of the historic Route 66, one of the original US highways that runs from Chicago to Santa Monica. It cuts through Lawndale diagonally from southwest to northeast. This tuition-free, independent K-8 public school used to share space with another local public school. The new facility caters for pre-kindergarten through eighth grade and is organized into grade clusters that allow for appropriate accommodations

and furnishings for each floor. The first floor supports grades pre-K through second grade, while the second floor houses grades three through five, and the third floor has grades six through eight. Students call their new home the 'big crayon' because of its colorful geometric layout. The building, which angles slightly from West Ogden Avenue to form a small triangular plaza, is constructed of brightly colored pre-cast structural concrete and is handsomely wrapped in layers of perforated metal screens that beautifully engage with sunlight from dawn to dusk throughout the year. Despite the use of inexpensive industrial materials, the result is playful and attractive. Additionally, the school's designers, Lothan Van Hook DeStefano Architecture, turned their building into a platform for teaching students about sustainability. They created an instructional unit to educate students about their building's performance. For example, they will learn that photovoltaic panels assembled on their rooftop provide 13 percent of the building's total electricity use.

Lincoln Park and Lake View

5

055   Steppenwolf Theatre
056   Mohawk House
057   Glass and Steel House
058   Orchard East
059   Education Pavilion and Nature Boardwalk at Lincoln Park Zoo
060   Searle Visitors Center at Lincoln Park Zoo
061   Peggy Notebaert Nature Museum
062   Wrightwood 659
063   Lake Shore Drive
064   House Etch
065   Claremont House
066   WMS Boathouse at Clark Park

Steppenwolf Theatre
1650 North Halsted Street
Adrian Smith + Gordon Gill, AS+GG
(Chicago)
2021

055 B

🚇 To North/Clybourn
🚌 8 to 1700 N Halsted

The Steppenwolf Theatre is a Chicago theater company. Its campus has three adjoining low-rise buildings lined up along the west side of North Halsted Street in Lincoln Park. Architecturally, it is the 2021 addition—a state-of-the-art ensemble theater in the round, an education center, and two new bars—that attracts everyone's attention. Designed by Adrian Smith + Gordon Gill, the four-story building is a contorted structure—an assortment of setbacks, projections, cavilies, and opaque and glazed walls that simultaneously allow glimpses inside a cave-like dynamic lobby and reflect the brick and brownstone buildings across the street. The lobby varies in height from two to three stories and is flooded with natural light thanks to the generous façade glazing and skylights above. Despite all its formal complexity, the building's spatial organization is clearly expressed around the solid object-like body of the theater, which bursts through the roof at an angle and manifests itself like a bold, solid rock. Its mass is prominently visible and theatrically lit at night. // The Loft is Steppenwolf's arts and education center and it encompasses the new building's entire fourth floor. It has several learning spaces, gallery walls featuring works by young visual artists, and an outdoor terrace. The 400-seat in-the-round performance space, designed by the UK theater consultant Charcoalblue,

is the only such auditorium found in a major Chicago theater. It is only six rows deep, always placing the actor no more than 20 feet from spectators in order to establish a dynamic and intimate spatial relationship with the audience. There is a modular staging system held in place by crisscrossed walkways assembled out of steel gratings directly above the stage that allows designers and directors to control scenography, adjust seating capacity, and explore different stage footprints. // Apart from the new in-the-round theater, the Steppenwolf Theatre campus features the 515-seat Downstairs Theatre for world premiere productions and fresh interpretations of classic and contemporary plays, and the flexible 80-seat cabaret-style 1700 Theatre can be used for a wide variety of genres and shows. The wall at the southern end features a large, vibrantly colorful mural entitled *Night and Day in the Garden of All Other Ecstasies* by the celebrated Chicago-based artist and actor Tony Fitzpatrick. Beneath the mural, there is a sidewalk lounge with brightly colored street furniture. // The theater was founded by a small group of aspiring Highland Park high school actors in 1974. The name Steppenwolf came from the namesake 1927 novel by German-Swiss poet and novelist Hermann Hesse. It was this book that one of the theater's founders had been reading at the time. The title translates as 'the steppe wolf'. The company was originally housed in a church in Deerfield, Illinois, and moved several times before settling at its current location in 1991. The company collaborates with internationally-acclaimed playwrights. It has received multiple prestigious grants and awards, and its productions are performed on Broadway and world-renowned stages.

5

Photos: James Steinkamp Photography

Mohawk House
1712 North Mohawk Street,
Old Town
UrbanLab (Chicago)
2015

 056 B

🚊🚊 To Sedgwick
🚌 9, 72 to North Ave & Cleveland

Mohawk House in the Old Town part of Lincoln Park is a striking contrast to all the other residential properties on its block, which is populated almost entirely by single-family houses. The house stands out on just about all accounts—its imposing size, abstract and spare appearance, and the choice of materials, predominantly the unusually dark brick as well as the mullion-free, clear glass picture windows. These inset into concealed steel frames. What appears to be a three-story house from the street is in fact a four-level dwelling on the side of the sunken garden. The 8,000-square-foot (743-square-meter) house sits comfortably on two lots. Compared to its tiny neighbor immediately to the north, it could be mistaken for a compact apartment building. Designed by Chicago-based UrbanLab duo Sarah Dunn and Martin Felsen, the project is an appealing minimalist structure. Its almost cubic form is a result of a series of geometric moves that finetune this austere building to its immediate surroundings. The west-facing backside is sliced at an angle in plan and is entirely glazed to maximize the afternoon sun and open the house to its garden. A sleek, elegantly terraced and folded landscape brings the terrain up high and entirely covers the garage on the opposite end of the site. A square area is removed from the master bedroom on the top floor to create an outdoor landscaped courtyard. The front is minimalist yet nuanced. Its brick pattern is a Flemish stretcher bond with extruded headers that cast a dense array of stumpy shadows that make the façade appear highly textured. Its checkerboard pattern is echoed in the low front wall

with every other brick removed. The three rows of tall windows appear to be the only elements that are almost randomly arranged. Yet there are only three widths and they are very carefully aligned along their edges, and although they avoid any symmetry, their composition is well calculated and balanced. The front entry is particularly inconspicuous—a single door made of black, solid steel under a perfectly flat rectangular steel canopy, smaller than its shadow. The first floor is designed as an open-plan family room. The interior staircase is assembled out of steel panels. Their perforated risers mimic the checkerboard pattern design strategy throughout. Curiously, the house sits right across from a service alley, making it possible to appreciate its large façade from a distance without the risk of being invasive.

Photo: Hedrich Blessing

Glass and Steel House
1949 North Larrabee Street,
Old Town
*Krueck + Sexton Architects (now
Krueck Sexton Partners, Chicago)*
1981

057 B

🚇🚇 To Armitage
🚌 73 to Armitage & Larrabee

The Glass and Steel House is situated close to the northern end of its predominantly residential block in the center of Lincoln Park, just below W Armitage. The large double-lot house is the very first project of Ron Krueck, one of the leading Chicago architects and the founder of Krueck Sexton Partners. He is a graduate of IIT, a studio professor at his alma mater, and visiting professor at the Harvard Graduate School of Design. Historian Kenneth Frampton described this house as 'the neo-Miesian architecture of the latter-day Chicago School at its most sophisticated'. It was designed in the early 1980s, so it is not surprising that it was also influenced by Post-Modernism, then just on the rise in popularity. The influence is most visible on the house's vibrant and wide-ranging color palettes, both inside and outside. It is also heavily influenced by some early examples of high-tech architecture by British masters such as Norman Foster and Richard Rogers. The 1932 Parisian house, Maison de Verre, designed by Pierre Chareau (1883–1950) no doubt served as another reference for this Chicago house when its client, who also acted as a contractor, asked the architect to employ industrial materials and use factory aesthetics as the chief inspiration. // The house is a C-shape in plan—three double-height rectangular pavilions joined together—with a garden on its open south side to let in as much sunshine as possible. The main pavilion, which runs in the west-east direction, comprises the main entry, double-height living and formal dining room, all topped by a linear skylight stretched from one end to the other. A bridge with a glass block floor links the smaller, opposite-side pavilions on the upper level. The side-pavilion at the front houses a two-car garage, a foyer on the ground floor, and a master bedroom over it. The side-pavilion in the back contains a kitchen below and a guest bedroom above with a large terrace overseeing the central garden. Just as the name implies, the house is predominantly made of glass inserted into steel frames. There are clear glass panels, frosted glass blocks, and a full-height section at the entry hall with a screen of steel grating. Bright and scarce artworks and furniture pieces are strategically placed, each bringing just the right ambiance to the space around it. A solid, brown-brick wall the height of a person provides privacy at the front of the house, while a similar wall along the alley on the opposite side masks the back of the house and a small rear garden. The house won a National AIA Honor Award in 1986.

Photo: Timothy Hursley

Courtesy of Krueck Sexton Partners

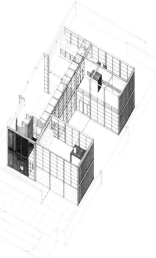

Photo: Phillip Turner

Orchard East
1875 North Orchard Street
*Wheeler Kearns Architects
(Chicago), McKay Landscape
Architects (Chicago)*
2007

058 B

Photo: Vladimir Belogolovsky

🚊🚊 To Armitage
🚌 73 to Armitage & Orchard; 9, 72 to
North Ave & Orchard

Orchard East is a private residence in the central part of Lincoln Park, one of Chicago's most affluent neighborhoods. It is situated in the middle of one of the most exclusive urban blocks on the east side of North Orchard Street. This unequivocally modern dwelling contrasts sharply with the predominantly oversized McMansions dressed up in all kinds of historical suits— neoclassical, French chateau, Italian palazzo, and other pseudo-palatial types. Most houses on the block could easily be the center of attention elsewhere, but they feel somewhat uncomfortable here. They appear quite tense in their self-conscious competition with one another to feel noticeably expensive. Orchard East is different. Casually occupying five typical 25-by-125-foot (7.6-by-38-meter) lots, it is one of the biggest houses on the block to be sure—about 9,000 square feet (836 square meters)—but its size is not the priority here. The house takes over slightly more than a third of its site. It disengages from the street as much as possible through generous setbacks and by allowing the landscape to come close, deep inside, and on top. There are three levels. Besides the ground floor that opens itself almost entirely to the surrounding garden through glass walls and sliding panels, there is one floor below ground and one seemingly floating above with cantilevers up to 40 feet (12 meters). The landscape comes down into the sunken outdoor areas, glazed interior courts, and extends vertically throughout, blurring the boundaries between inside and outside to celebrate the rain, snow, and changes of seasons. The structure is built of reinforced concrete and finishes range from stone, wood, and pigmented cement stucco to floor-to-ceiling glass and bronze cladding and detailing. Nearly all the

Courtesy of Wheeler Kearns Architects

building's roof surfaces are covered with plants. // The house is owned by Penny Pritzker, a billionaire businesswoman, member of the influential Pritzker family, former US Secretary of Commerce under President Obama, and one of the world's 100 Most Powerful Women according to *Forbes* magazine in 2005. It was designed by local Chicago firm Wheeler Kearns Architects, who are known for their exclusive, intricately detailed houses for the wealthy. This guide includes their Lake Shore Drive mansion [063], just north of Lincoln Park, which is much more accessible to passers-by. McKay Landscape Architects designed the garden. Its 'wildness' is achieved through the usage of thousands of perennials, ornamental grasses, vines, and bulbs that create an urban oasis for butterflies, bees, and other wildlife. The site also incorporates an extensive garage along the back alley, a vegetable garden, an outdoor dining area, a basketball court, a roof deck, reflecting pools, and a large collection of modern sculptures. One element of this complex that can be examined in every detail is a bronze louvered fence. It artfully controls views from the sidewalk, allowing glimpses into the garden but concealing the main house. It is worth the trip for this long fence alone—it is a genuine work of art.

Education Pavilion and Nature Boardwalk at Lincoln Park Zoo 059 B

Lincoln Park Zoo South Pond,
Lincoln Park
Studio Gang (Chicago)
2010

🚌 151, 156 to Stockton & Armitage

The Education Pavilion designed by Jeanne Gang of Studio Gang is near the edge of the South Pond in Lincoln Park. It is the centerpiece of a much larger project called Nature Boardwalk. Designed by Gang and Chicago-based landscape architect WRD Environmental, the boardwalk is a half-mile path that meanders around and over a man-made pond that was originally built in 1908 and fed by stormwater. The architects removed the pond's concrete edge, increased its depth, cultivated the land around it, and paved the boardwalk with recycled plastic waste. As a result, the 14-acre site was transformed into a lush, prairie-style garden filled with native trees and plants and brimming with birds, frogs, fish, turtles, and insects. Lincoln Park Zoo manages this new ecosystem. The Pavilion serves as a shelter for open-air exercise classes and other formal and informal events. Measuring 46-by-33-feet (14-by-10 meters) and reaching a height of 16.5 feet (5 meters), the honeycomb-like,

Photo: Tom Harris

12-bay pavilion is inspired by a tortoise shell and bolted together as an assembly of prefabricated glulam wood ribs and pod-like translucent fiberglass domes. Each element was designed to be light enough to be handled and installed by hand. The whole structure touches the ground lightly, as it sits on pin-connections, allowing all the necessary movement to transfer shear forces. The Pavilion's arching form frames Chicago's skyline due south and serves as a perfect photo opportunity. At night, the lattice piece itself attracts all the attention, as it is dramatically lit from below to render a field of petal-like openings formed by gently curved wood ribs that bend in three directions, bringing the pavilion delightfully to life.

Photo: Tom Harris

Photo: Kendall McCaugherty, Hall+Merrick Photographers

2400 North Cannon Drive,
Lincoln Park
Ross Barney Architects (Chicago)
2018

060 B

🚌 151, 156 to Stockton & Webster

The Searle Visitors Center serves as a dynamic east-gate pavilion to the Lincoln Park Zoo. It comprises two buildings: a small stone-clad box housing public bathrooms to the south and a larger C-shaped, glass-clad welcoming structure arrayed around a courtyard to the north. They are tied together by a single L-shaped canopy that connects the two structures and the two ends of the main building. It is this fractured canopy that makes the center particularly interesting and remarkably dynamic. The canopy is an assemblage of seven identical, overlapping aluminum planes that support and hang from one another. Each of these elements features a pattern of layered branches that filter light as if composed of tree branches. They cast densely interwoven shadows onto the permeable pavement and are reflected in the glass façades below. // The larger building contains visitors' information, administrative offices, a members' lounge, guest services, and a lost and found office. This compact, campus-like project was designed by Carol Ross Barney of local firm Ross Barney Architects, a leading voice in support of the regeneration of the Chicago River and the firm behind the Chicago Riverwalk [008]. While the zoo is open 365 days a year and free for visitors, purchasing a membership is encouraged, and it includes free parking at the Lincoln Park Zoo parking lot. A monumental gate with a layered branch pattern, similar to the one that distinguishes the canopy, rolls across the entry to lock the space between the two buildings. The gate's pattern was designed to discourage climbing.

Photo: Kendall McCaugherty, Hall+Merrick Photographers

Peggy Notebaert Nature Museum

2430 North Cannon Drive, Lincoln Park
Perkins&Will (Chicago)
1999

061 B

🚌 76 to Cannon & Nature Museum/Fullerton; 22, 36 to Clark & Fullerton; 134, 143, 151, 156 to Stockton & Arlington

Opened in 1999, the Peggy Notebaert Nature Museum looks like an abstract suprematist painting from above. Named after the wife of one of its sponsors, it is composed of several rectangles, triangles, trapezoids, and even an 'X' that serves as a pier extending into the North Pond in Lincoln Park near the acute corner defined by N Cannon and W Fullerton. The museum's fractured forms, built in concrete and glass, are expressed in angular masses that collide into one another and integrate dramatically into the surrounding landscape. Some are topped by green roofs. The low-rise building, largely hidden by overgrown shrubs and much taller trees, is entered through an incision in the landscape. As you approach the pond, the incision turns into a miniature ravine, emphasizing the building's integral and organic relationship with the site. Bridges and elevated walkways enable visitors to interact both with the building and the surrounding landscape. // The museum grew out of the Chicago Academy of Sciences. Founded in 1857, it possessed one of the finest collections of natural history specimens in America. It was originally located in the Loop, but the Great Chicago Fire of 1871 destroyed both the academy's building and its holdings. In 1893, the creation of the Field Museum at the Museum Campus south of Grant Park, with one of the largest natural history collections in the world, challenged the academy's status. It occupied the Matthew Laflin Memorial Building across from the Lincoln Park Zoo from 1894. It flourished there as a research institute, but struggled as a museum. The outdated Laflin Building was absorbed by the zoo in the mid-1980s and transformed into its administration office, while the city offered the academy its current location alongside the North Pond. // The once-again reimagined and rebuilt Peggy Notebaert Nature Museum is best known for its premier exhibit: the Butterfly Haven. Inside this 2,700-square-foot (250-square-meter) greenhouse there are over 1,000 free-flying butterflies of 40 exotic species and several bird species from the southern hemisphere. There are also serene pools of water, a lush garden with tropical trees, flowers, and a 14-foot (4.3-meter) waterfall. The building was designed by Ralph Johnson of Perkins&Will. Since the museum's completion, Johnson has worked on a number of projects that engage with the landscape and explore natural history in America and other parts of the world, most notably, a much larger Shanghai Natural History Museum that opened in 2015.

061 B

View over Peggy Notebaert Nature Museum and
North Pond Natural Area in Lincoln Park from the southeast

Wrightwood 659

659 West Wrightwood Avenue,
Lincoln Park
Tadao Ando (Osaka, Japan)
2018

062 B

🚇🚇🚇 To Diversey or Fullerton
🚌 22, 36 to Clark & Deming; 8 to Halsted & Wrightwood

Since 2018, Chicago's affluent Lincoln Park residential neighborhood has been home to Wrightwood 659, a private gallery for exhibitions on architecture and socially-engaging art. The gallery is named after its street address. Designed by Pritzker Prize-winning Japanese architect Tadao Ando, the new structure is hidden within the shell of what was a 1930 four-story, 38-unit apartment building. It was entirely gutted and only its neo-American federal-style front façade and perimeter walls were preserved. // The gallery, run as a Kunsthalle by the Chicago-based grant-making Alphawood Foundation, was commissioned by its owner: entrepreneur and philanthropist Fred Eychaner. He lives next door at 665 West Wrightwood Avenue in a 1997 Ando-designed house that was the first freestanding structure by Ando in the United States. The two buildings could not be more different. Rather than merely reflecting one architect's signature style, they are tributes to the times in which they were created. The house was built during a decade that obsessively celebrated the unique identities of leading international architects. It turns its public face—a blank concrete front that could be mistaken for the loading dock

of a suburban warehouse—away from the lovely historicist townhouses and apartment buildings all around to focus on a self-referential inner world of the architect's oeuvre. // In striking contrast to that, the new Wrightwood 659 is almost entirely hidden behind the existing historical façade. What awaits one behind it is the kind of architecture that is no longer pure; it is multi-referential, which is a clear nod towards increasing respect for context and infatuation with preserving not just ruins but anything that is old. From the outside, Ando's intervention reveals itself only at the very top where the architect added a minimalist, see-through penthouse structure. The building's main façade acts as a mask, which is freed from all floors and clad without marking former floor divisions in so-called Chicago 'common brick' with its characteristic beautiful amber color on the interior side. The new 'building within a building' of Ando's trademark exposed concrete is pushed back to form a soaring three-story atrium where the gorgeous brick wall is celebrated as the key dramatic feature. This atrium space, the absolute gem of the new gallery, is reminiscent of Ando's 2009 restoration of Punta della Dogana art museum in Venice. But in Venice, the architect kept the original seventeenth century red bricks in place. In Chicago, the bricks were carefully removed, not only from various parts of the building, but even from other structures demolished in the area, and then reassembled into an abstracted, beautifully textured plane to commemorate the original structure by celebrating its material. The bricks, with deeply recessed mortar-joints and lit indirectly, add a sense of solidity and depth. // The new interior is built as a composite of steel frame reinforced with both structural and non-bearing architectural concrete. The space comprises a non-public partial basement with administrative offices on the ground floor. The second and third floors have white-walled galleries connected by a concrete feature stair cantilevered from a freestanding fin wall. Finally, the top fourth floor, which is reached through the back stair, offers an enclosed gallery, flexible event space, outdoor terrace, and long narrow gallery along a glazed western wall. This latter space offers expansive views over the surrounding low-rise neighborhood and a bird's-eye view of Ando's house next door, which is wrapped around an organically shaped reflecting pool. The admirable quality of its concrete was achieved through multiple mock-ups for every critical component personally reviewed and approved by Ando. As a result, many independent experts agree that the building has the highest quality concrete ever achieved in America and is comparable to the finest examples built in Japan, where building industry craftsmanship, particularly when it comes to producing this material, has reached a cult-like status.

5

062 **B**

Wrightwood 659: an object-like exposed concrete stair within a soaring three-story atrium clad in recycled amber-colored brick behind the original façade of a former apartment building

Lake Shore Drive
3000 North Lake Shore Drive,
Lake View East
*Wheeler Kearns Architects
(Chicago)*
2011

063 B

🚇🚌 To Wellington
🚌 77 to Lake Shore Drive & Wellington

Although it has a North Lake Shore address, this single-family residence is the last building on West Wellington Avenue, which allows its east end to look directly onto Lincoln Park toward Lake Michigan. The three-story, 5,000-square-foot (465-square-meter) home sits comfortably on its 1.6-acre (0.65-hectare) corner site with no neighbors to the north. It puts itself almost entirely on display from just about every side, and the house is ready for that, as everything appears classy and thoughtfully designed. What immediately stands out is the building's sculptural form, which is meant to be appreciated from different sides as it rises at a gentle angle, growing towards the east, bringing two mostly solid upper stories forward and over a predominantly glazed first floor. The house sits on a plinth that grows into a single-story garage towards the back. Both are clad in split-faced limestone and interlock with the rest of the house, which is faced in smooth limestone. The roof over the projecting garage forms an L-shaped second-floor terrace. The house's asymmetrical volume is further abstracted by a variety of large and

small openings oriented both vertically and horizontally, with a pair of uneven double-height corner apertures with inset windows on the eastern face. On the opposite side, the property is separated from the neighboring apartment building to the west by a backyard and driveway. // The residence was designed by Wheeler Kearns Architects, with the interiors designed by KADLEC Architecture + Design. Inside, the split-level plan and a freestanding snug stair create inviting spaces of various scales. The interiors, although decisively modern, are warm and cozy thanks to the use of wooden floors and window frames, as well as bespoke built-in wood benches, cabinetry, and movable privacy screens. The home shows a preference for natural light, earthy-colored materials and furnishings, and last but not least, the dominating presence of grown trees that surround the house on all sides.

House Etch ↗
4156 North Paulina Avenue,
Lake View
Studio Dwell Architects (Chicago)
2017

064 B

🚇 To Irving Park or Montrose
🚌 780 to Irving Park & Hermitage; 78 to Montrose & Paulina

House Etch in Lakewood is an appealing assemblage of orthogonal volumes and planes of board-formed concrete, stained cedar, and clear glass. Furthermore, solid walls are crisscrossed by ribbon windows

5

to bring additional natural light, while also assuring privacy. The corner house stretches for half a block, from the mid-block service alley to its formal entry on North Paulina, without breaking for a typical backyard in the middle. There is a generous front garden, while the interior courtyard is tacked behind the house on the south side towards the eastern end of the property. The ground floor—a double-car garage, mudroom, study space, family room, kitchen, and double-height great room—bluntly reveals itself through extensive glazing right next to an active sidewalk along West Berteau. There are additional common spaces and a guest bedroom in the basement, and the top floor, accessed by an open-riser steel-and-glass stair, houses the master bedroom and kids' bedrooms. The master bedroom cantilevers over the outdoor deck below and its large west-side window looks over the back garden. Concrete walls and full-height glazing on the ground floor mark public areas, while cedar-clad surfaces upstairs shield the

private quarters. // The house was designed by Studio Dwell Architects, a practice that focuses on designing private dwellings in Chicago. Here, the architects responded to the client's request to rely on the mid-twentieth century modern aesthetics of Latin American architecture with an emphasis on expressing natural materials. The house's name is reflected in the fact that two of its key materials are interrelated—concrete poured against rough boards has become etched with wood textures that mimic the natural exposed cedar. There is an abundance of natural light throughout the house thanks to a variety of windows that allow open and controlled views of the tree-lined streets. Inside, white-painted drywall is mixed with accents of board-formed concrete, such as a cantilevered fireplace in the great room and partial walls elsewhere. Expressive furniture, light fixtures, and artworks add dynamic ambiance throughout the house. At night, the dwelling turns into an abstract form sculpted by warm light.

Claremont House

065 B

3909 North Claremont Street,
North Center
Brininstool + Lynch
2007

To Irving Park
80 to Irving Park & Oakley; 49 to
Western & Grace

Claremont House occupies a narrow lot that runs from its front on North Claremont to a service alley in the back. Its west-facing façade is bookended by traditionally-looking single-family houses and modestly scaled brick-clad apartment buildings on a typical residential block in the St. Ben's neighborhood on the city's North Side. At first glance, it does not strike one as an oddity. Its single-lot bulk, setback, and plantings match most other buildings here and the red brick of its façade is almost identical to some other neighboring houses. Yet there are enough anomalies to make this house quite special, even unique. What appears to be a single-story home is, in fact, three stories—the main floor with the entry, living room, and kitchen is elevated a few feet above the ground. It is the middle level of the house with one floor below that contains a guest bedroom, office or family room, and a patio locked between the house and a two-car garage in the back, and one floor above that contains a master bedroom and two smaller bedrooms. All three floors are linked by a straight-up open riser stair that runs along the south wall from the basement all the way to the second floor in the direction toward the street. The stair's intermediate landing serves as the side entry into the house. This point of entry is the dwelling's main entrance.

Once inside, you either go up a few steps to the main level or directly to the lower floor. There is no familiar front porch with outdoor steps at the front, which is entirely glazed and the landscaping in front butts up against it. The lower part of this window—from the main floor down to the ground—is the clerestory for the floor below. Above that is an oversized picture window that runs from wall to wall and from floor to ceiling. The main mullion-free picture window is as wide as the living room and kitchen behind it and measures 10 by 15 feet (3 by 4.6 meters). The window at the front is reflected in the exact same window on the other side, overlooking the patio below. And there is another matching window directly below, between the lower floor and the patio. The second floor above the front window is entirely clad in brick, as all bedrooms on this level get their natural light from windows lined up along the north wall. // The house's most unusual features include a three-story millwork assembly between the stair and all the other rooms, a sleek stainless-steel kitchen island, a cozy patio, plenty of natural light, and a high level of precision and craftsmanship. And while the house relies on the use of traditional materials such as brick, limestone, and zinc, it is quite radical

in its disciplined geometry, and interior circulation. Its overall minimalist aesthetics such as an open plan, unforgiving transparency, alignments throughout, and the insistence on using the exact same wood color hue for all the cabinetry are also unique. It should come as no surprise that this architectural laboratory of sorts was designed by an architect for his own family. Curiously, Brad Lynch, the founding co-principle of Chicago-based Brininstool + Lynch, put the house up for sale just a couple of years after it was completed. It was eventually sold in 2015, with the new owners putting it on the market again in 2018.

Photo: Pygmalion Karatzas Photography

WMS Boathouse at Clark Park `066` B
3400 North Rockwell Street,
Roscoe Village
Studio Gang (Chicago)
2013

🚌 94 to Rockwell & Devry Parking Lot;
a small parking lot is accessible to the
public

The WMS Boathouse at Clark Park is one
of four boathouses proposed by Chicago
Mayor Rahm Emanuel (2011–2019) as a
cornerstone of his plan to revitalize the
long-polluted banks of the Chicago River.
Studio Gang was commissioned to realize
two of these projects: WMS Boathouse at
Clark Park on the western edge of Roscoe
Village on the North Side and Eleanor
Boathouse at Park 571 in Bridgeport on the
South Side. These facilities have the exact
same program and similar designs, so either one could be visited. The one at Clark

Park was chosen for this guide because
it was built first. Home to the Chicago
Rowing Foundation (CRF) and in partnership with the Chicago Park District,
the WMS Boathouse offers learn-to-row
sessions both in tanks and on the river,
youth and masters team rowing, ergometer training, and rowing-inspired yoga
classes. Due to its unique program, setting, and toy-like scale, this facility presents a fantastic opportunity for an architect to explore ideas that may be imagined
while at school but rarely come about in
real practice. 'The architecture is meant
to visually capture the poetic rhythm and
motion of rowing,' said Jeanne Gang of
Studio Gang, describing her design intentions here. // The key feature of Gang's design is expressed in the boathouse's two
distinctive sawtooth façades—western
overlooking the river and eastern facing
North Rockwell Street. Studio Gang architects translated the time-lapse motion of

Photo: Steve Hall, Hedrich Blessing

Photo: Steve Hall, Hedrich Blessing

rowing into a unique roof system of trusses. They make up a succession of two alternating cross-section profiles—an 'M' and inverted 'V', forming a rhythmic modulation of clerestory windows. Two buildings and a floating launch dock comprise WMS Boathouse. On the south end, there is a two-story training center with a rowing tank, ergometer machines, communal space, mechanical rooms, offices for the Chicago Park District, and a second-floor spacious deck overlooking the river. To the north, there is a single-story indoor and outdoor storage facility for boats, canoes, and kayaks. The two structures are aligned along the river and are separated by a narrow courtyard that cuts across the site towards the launch dock. The façades and roofs are clad in zinc panels and Heathermoor slate. Interiors feature custom millwork and dramatically sloping ceilings that are finished in beautifully stained Douglas fir plywood. The

WMS Boathouse sits within Clark Park and is accessible to the public. The architects worked on site improvements, including the addition of porous concrete and asphalt pathways, native plantings and trees, gravel beds, and gardens. // The Eleanor Boathouse at Park 571 is located at 2828 South Eleanor near the Ashland stop on the Orange Line. The boathouse faces the south branch of the Chicago River at the junction point where it joins Bubbly Creek. This sister of the WMS Boathouse was built three years after its northern prototype on a similar scale and following a similar model in terms of its planning, program, roof design of alternating trusses, site improvements, and even the cladding materials inside and out. The Eleanor Boathouse is home to several rowing teams, clubs, and organizations that brave the Chicago River nearly year-round to train for competitions. A small parking lot there is accessible to the public.

Photo: Steve Hall, Hedrich Blessing

6

067   Chinatown Branch, Chicago Public Library
068   Rodney D. Joslin Campus – Perspectives Charter Schools
069   Williams Park Fieldhouse
070   IIT Innovation Center, The Ed Kaplan Family Institute
071   IIT McCormick Tribune Campus Center
072   IIT State Street Village
073   Morgan Live + Work

Public Library
2100 South Wentworth Avenue,
Chinatown
SOM (Chicago)
2015

 067 C

🚇 To Cermak-Chinatown
🚌 24, 62 to Wentworth & Archer; 21 to
Cermak & Archer

The Chinatown Branch of the Chicago Public Library is located at the crossing of South Archer and South Wentworth Avenues. It directly faces the Cermak-Chinatown stop on the CTA's elevated Red Line. Occupying its own triangular block, this compact freestanding building serves Chicago's Chinatown neighborhood. The two-story structure takes the shape of a triangle with rounded corners, suggesting an abstracted heart in plan—an unequivocal reference of the design's intention to be this community's social hub or literally its heart. Generous setbacks all around the structure allow for abundant landscaping and seating. The building is also topped by a green roof visible from CTA trains. The all-around façade is made up of an ultra-transparent curtain wall. An array of widely-spaced, bronze-aluminum vertical shading fins surround the second floor and jut out, bypassing the roofline to form a ring of spikes against the sky. The library's fully glazed envelope functions as a glowing lantern at night. // The building's entrance is situated on the south side. Once inside, all attention is focused on the central circulation hall—a fluid double-height atrium modeled on a traditional Chinese courtyard plan. A grand curving stair right in the middle of the space is a fantastic alternative to the use of utilitarian elevators. Ascending it under an oculus rewards visitors with a theatrical experience of both floors' full transparency with an emphasis on expansive northern views towards the impressive skyline of downtown. The ground level features an exhibition space and children's zone, while the central community meeting area serves as a flexible, multipurpose room that is also used for special events. Upstairs there is the adult reading zone and the teen area behind a brightly colored acoustic curtain. All spaces are unpartitioned and connect to the central atrium. A combination of waist-height and below eye-level bookshelves creates a sense of openness throughout. There are plenty of informal collaborative areas and intimate reading spots. Opposite the downtown view, the second level displays a mixed-media mural by Chicago artist CJ Hungerman titled *Universal Transverse Immigration Proclamation*. The overhead artwork is eight feet high and measures 60 feet in length (2.4 meters by 18.2 meters). The artist engaged the community in workshops to understand the area's history and gather generations of personal experiences before distilling them into an expression of Chinatown's past, present, and future through paint and markers.

Photo: James Steinkamp

Rodney D. Joslin Campus –
Perspectives Charter Schools ↑
1930 South Archer Avenue, Near
South Side next to Chinatown
Perkins&Will (Chicago)
2004

068 C

🚇 To Cermak-Chinatown
🚇 To Cermak-McCormick Place
🚌 62 to Archer & Dearborn

Appearing quite unexpectedly—more like a fast-moving vessel than a building—the Rodney D. Joslin Campus is a four-story triangular structure in a residential part of the South Loop within the acute angle formed by South Archer and West 19th and bordered on the west side by South Dearborn. Joslin's most noteworthy feature is its eastward pointing corner—a compelling assembly of angled steel trellises and grille panels supporting a deeply projecting canopy that extends at the roofline and hangs precariously in mid-air, ending in a sharp point. The building's three façades are clad in steel siding and dynamically punctured by ribbon windows randomly placed, it would seem. It is the South Archer Avenue side that presents itself most effectively as it is here that the building's low brick base gets separated from the rest of the steel façade by a ribbon window that stretches continuously along this entire façade. This does the trick of making the building appear to float or 'swim' above ground or, in this case, above a strip of grass and trees on the two longer sides. The short, west-facing back side abuts a parking lot. // Joslin is one of five open-enrolment, tuition-free public schools managed by Perspectives, one of the first charter schools in Illinois. It was designed by Perkins&Will with a focus on interaction and socialisation among students and staff. Small-group spaces allow for a variety of uses and encourage chance encounters outside the classrooms. The Cornerstone Community Church, which is a part of the school, stands at the southwest open corner under an extensive metal canopy that floats across, turns all the way up the height of the building, and comes down diagonally along the western façade to become a fully integrated part of the building. The school was designed as a system of interconnected volumes and planes; nothing is an add-on or afterthought—a quality that is more common to machines and vehicles than buildings.

WILLIAMS PA

Williams Park Fieldhouse ↓   069 D
2850 South State Street,
Dearborn Homes
STLarchitects (Chicago)
2016–2019

🚆 To 35th-Bronzeville-IIT
🚌 29 to State & 28th Street; 1, 4 to
Michigan & 28th Street

Coincidentally, a short walk due north from the IIT Innovation Center [070] is another project clad in a unique material. In fact, it is the first building in Chicago to be fully clad in vibrant, iridescent, stainless-steel shingle tiles that follow a dragon scale pattern, giving the building a constantly changing, chameleon-like appearance. Located in Bronzeville, the Williams Park Fieldhouse acts as a community anchor strategically placed in the park at the heart of Dearborn Homes, a public housing complex that is a part of the Chicago Housing Authority. The single-story rectangular building is situated on a north-south axis parallel and just off S State. It is locked between a small rectangle of greenfield to the east and a football/soccer field to the west. The new facility can be entered from either its main entrance along the west side or from the east side. A single, slanted roof defines the fieldhouse. It rises towards its south end to capture as much sun as possible. Its south and north end-walls are slanted as well and form right angles with the roof. The walk-through entry lobby slices the building in two unequal parts: reception, a basketball court with spectator seating, offices, storage, mechanical rooms, and restrooms to the south, and two multipurpose community/club rooms, a pantry, and storage rooms to the north. // The building's exterior takes multiple chromatic and reflective expressions—each shingle responds to different light conditions, appearing to change hues when viewed from different angles. This play of colors fluctuates profusely throughout the day and with the changing seasons. In contrast, its interior is restrained. The main attraction inside is its slanted ceiling with exposed long-span glulam beams. // The building's architects, José Luis de la Fuente and Luis Collado, have run STLarchitects since 1996. They came from Spain where they studied at the ETSAM, the Higher Technical School of Architecture of the Technical University of Madrid. Both architects worked at SOM in Chicago. The partners also designed the Spray Pool on the east side of the building.

6

Photo: Ignacio Espigares

IIT Innovation Center, The Ed
Kaplan Family Institute
3300 South Federal Street,
Bronzeville
John Ronan Architects (Chicago)
2015–18

070 D

🚆 To Sox-35th
🚆 To 35th-Bronzeville-IIT
🚌 29, 31 to State & 33rd Street

Named after the Chicago-based bar code technology entrepreneur, the Ed Kaplan Family Institute for Innovation and Tech Entrepreneurship—commonly referred to as the IIT Innovation Center—is a new ground-up building added to the north end of the Mies van der Rohe-designed IIT campus in 2018 near West 31st between S Federal and S State. The first new academic facility built on the IIT campus in nearly 50 years, the center is devoted to fostering collaboration, innovation, and entrepreneurship between students, faculty, alumni, and partners. The building was designed by Chicago-based architect John Ronan (b. 1963), an IIT professor and the architect behind several projects in this guide, most notably the Poetry Foundation [030]. The freestanding, two-story rectangular volume with proportions of two to one (or two squares in plan) fits perfectly into the original 24-square-foot (7.3-square-meter) campus grid that also governs the structural module within the building. Two open-air courtyards—the building's 'eyes' and

'lungs'—serve as entry points and bring in natural light and ventilation. // The building's most striking feature, however, is the milky-white skin of its upper level, cantilevered over the glazed ground floor. This distinctive façade is wrapped in three horizontally stacked segmented bands of pillow-like cushions made of a polymer called ethylene tetrafluoroethylene, commonly abbreviated as ETFE. Its puffy, supple appearance contrasts greatly with the sharpness and precision for which the IIT campus is known. The ETFE envelopes are not entirely novel: they were used in much earlier structures such as the Water Cube of the 2008 Beijing Olympics (PTW Architects) and the Eden Project in Cornwall in England (Grimshaw Architects), which opened in 2001. Still, its application remains rare and this is the very first example in Chicago. The panels consist of several layers separated by air chambers, which are inflated and deflated automatically to alter the amount of sunlight coming inside and reduce glare and energy usage depending on the weather. Blair Kamin, an architectural critic at the *Chicago Tribune*, wrote that the Innovation Center 'exemplifies an emerging trend in architecture—a "dynamic façade" that can tune a building to its climate'. Still, the intrigue is: how does it feel to be inside a cloud-like space with such limited visibility? // The building is accessed through either one of two neatly planted courtyards that direct visitors to an open lobby space. There are

exterior stairs that lead straight to the second floor, acting as direct emergency exits. Instead of being compartmentalized, the lobby unfolds rather like a casual flow of open spaces. Eyes are immediately drawn to a wide bleacher-style stair that faces the larger south-end courtyard and is peppered with colorful foam pads. The space acts as a large auditorium and is open and connects the two floors. Circulation seems to be entirely casual and spontaneous. The interior concrete flooring and exposed steel columns and ceilings all contribute to an overall industrial and informal atmosphere. There is a coffee shop near the entry and a loop of open-plan studios, media labs, workshops, collaborative hubs, and lounges. Some of these spaces are more open than others. Many can be subdivided by curtains or movable partitions. // The second floor hosts the Institute of Design, a graduate design school founded in 1937 as the New Bauhaus, with László Moholy-Nagy (1895–1946) as its first director. The façades upstairs allow you to see ghost-like outlines of adjacent trees, but you will always come across exterior views while walking around and looking down and through the interior courtyards, which are glazed from floor to ceiling. There is a sense of suspense here nevertheless—spaces are very sleek, very futuristic, and predominantly white all around with brightly-colored chair upholstery, movable privacy partitions, and dry erase boards. // During the center's walkthrough with John Ronan, the architect said: 'I wanted the building to float. I wanted it to look like a cloud as if it would float away if it weren't held down. I wanted to make Crown Hall look heavy in comparison. I wanted to propose a building that would feel ultralight.' He succeeded. Visually, the space is very stimulating and seems fitting for a collaborative environment. Some complain about the ETFE's sound performance. It is not like glass and occasional traffic noise is noticeable. Yet there is a very acute sense of being almost outdoors, which can be refreshing. The building is intended to be open 24/7, so the ETFE façade is designed to glow like a lantern all night. This is achieved by running a continuous LED strip light along the perimeter; it is also a part of the emergency lighting system. This effectively turns the entire Innovation Center into a building-size light fixture, animated by moving shadows within, attracting students from all over the university campus while also making it feel safer.

6

Photo: Philippe Ruault

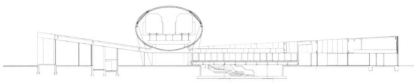

3201 South State Street,
Bronzeville
Rem Koolhaas of OMA (Rotterdam),
Jeanne Gang of Studio Gang (Chicago)
1997–2003

071 **D**

 To Sox-35th
 To 35th-Bronzeville-IIT
 29, 31 to State & 33rd Street

The McCormick Tribune Campus Center, a 2003 addition to the famed Mies van der Rohe-designed campus of the Illinois Institute of Technology (IIT) in Bronzeville on the South Side, was Pritzker Prize-winning Dutch architect Rem Koolhaas's (b. 1944) first completed building in the United States and is so far the only one in Chicago. Koolhaas, the founder of OMA, is a cult-like figure in the profession and a trendsetter. His buildings often become game changers and case studies for both architects and students all over the world. Keen on critical site observations, these projects disrupt common practice by exploring untested programmatic and formal possibilities. The center, which was a collaboration between Koolhaas and Jeanne Gang (she previously worked at his headquarters in Rotterdam) in partnership with Holabird & Root and ARUP, is a case in point: it was conceived as a strikingly vibrant contrast to IIT's orderly lines, squares, boxy minimalist buildings, and their calibrated alignments master-planned by Mies, the school's director from 1938 to 1958. // The Campus Center's design is defined by its unlikely location—underneath and on either side of the CTA's elevated Green line, which Koolhaas and Gang wrapped with an oval tube of concrete and clad in corrugated stainless steel. This 530-foot (160-meter) tunnel, which is meant to muffle the noise from the passing trains, is held precariously in place by seven reinforced concrete V-shaped prongs—five thrust upward from within the building, punching through its roof, and two others placed immediately outside, one at each end. The structurally independent, sleeve-like tunnel is the most striking element of the new building. It appears to crash through the center's roof right in the middle, seemingly causing its V-shaped appearance. The irregularly-shaped, single-story space under its inverted, pitched roof provides a focal point for social life on campus. The late *New York Times* architecture critic Herbert Muschamp described the dynamic space as 'a bazaar of a building, a souk of sensations that stands in vibrant contrast to the immaculately modern desert around it'. The building's cross-axial composition is based on a diagram that the architects drew as they connected the most well-attended buildings and areas on campus, all around the building's central location, effectively turning the new structure into an urban intersection. It is a network of interior streets and plazas

that convey the feeling of an around-the-clock neighborhood—a microcosm of commercial, entertainment, academic, and recreation activities. Inside, the dynamic collision of multiple ramps and levels running into and around a sunken courtyard-like cafeteria offer seemingly borderless zones. Apart from a cafeteria, they are intended for programs such as a coffee shop, mini-market, auditorium, computer center, bookstore, game areas, and a variety of informal spaces for meeting, socializing, and studying. It also embraces the adjacent Commons Hall, originally designed by Mies in 1953 and now repurposed as a food court. // Situated directly across East 33rd from Helmut Jahn's State Street Village [072], which was also completed in 2003, the student welcome center's design was selected in the 1997 international competition. Some 56 invited architects participated, including masters such as Norman Foster,

Fumihiko Maki, Toyo Ito, and Daniel Libeskind. Alongside Koolhaas, the other finalists were Peter Eisenman, Helmut Jahn with Werner Sobek, Zaha Hadid, and SANAA. Once completed, the building became the first new structure on IIT's campus since 1971. Apart from programmatic intensity, the architects introduced a rich material palette, particularly with the emphasis on industrial materials and bold colors. There are rough materials, unfinished surfaces, and exposed joints that unequivocally transmit the idea that education is a process—open-ended, unruly, undefined, overlapping, and with multiple meanings. The hybrid building is a playful response to the dogmatic 'less is more' aesthetic of Mies, whose full-height Op Art portrait on glass at the west entry is used as a provocative sign of both reverence and irony. The building is a seemingly impromptu assembly of referential elements—from painted black 'I-beam' columns to unplastered Sheetrock ceilings. What could be more satisfying for Koolhaas than to insert the most Post-Modernist gesture of his career right across the street from one of the most treasured temples of mid-twentieth century modernism—S. R. Crown Hall (1956), home of the IIT's School of Architecture and the finest work by Mies in Chicago? The pair constitute the most striking juxtaposition of neighboring buildings anywhere.

6

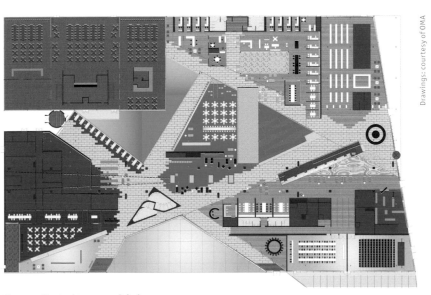

Campus Center's cross-axial plan

IIT State Street Village
3303/3333/3353 South State
Street, Bronzeville
*Murphy/Jahn (since 2012, JAHN,
Chicago)*
2001–2003

 072 D

🚇 To 35th-Bronzeville-IIT
🚇 To Sox-35th
🚌 29, 31 to State & 33rd Street

What appears to be a single 550-foot (168-meter) low-slung building, tightly tacked in between South State and the CTA's Green Line elevated train, is actually an alignment of three interconnected U-shaped structures in a row, each accessed through its own central entry court. These three five-story buildings are joined by two semi-covered walk-through courtyards and are referred to as the 'north', 'middle', and 'south' sections. They make up a 367-bed residence hall and are shaped by two distinctive full-length façades—the front on the west side and the back on the east. The former addresses tree-lined South State and is defined by a single extruded curve that transitions into the building's roof, which is an appealing assembly of profiled and perforated stainless-steel panels. The latter is a straight-up plane of

specially engineered glass that blocks the noise of the trains that zip by literally just a few arm's lengths away. Apart from its primary function, the building serves both as a space-defining visual wall and sound barrier for the college's grassy Main Quadrangle directly across the street, which is due north of S. R. Crown Hall, the iconic 1956 centerpiece of the IIT campus. Without any pretense, it is safe to say that the dormitory building designed by Helmut Jahn, himself a former IIT student, withstands the test that comes of facing one of the most refined structures of mid-twentieth century modernist architecture. // To the north across East 33rd, the building faces the Rem Koolhaas- and Jeanne Gang-designed IIT McCormick Tribune Campus Center [071], which is a competition-winning structure for which Jahn was also a finalist. Both buildings were completed in 2003 and were the first additions to the IIT campus in more than 30 years. If the Koolhaas building is defined by its striking and ironic contrasts to the IIT's campus architecture, the building by Jahn is an attempt to refine and even enrich it by example. In fact, situated right between the Crown Hall and the 'L' train, it is hard to imagine a more fitting solution. The high-tech

6

Photo: Pygmalion Karatzas Photography

Photo: Pygmalion Karatzas Photography

structure is a poured-in-place concrete frame with expressive steel-and-glass façades masterfully integrated with nature that is imaginatively pulled into the building's 'pockets'. The west façade is particularly ingenious. It is animated by alternating solids and voids, a succession of see-through steel panels, courtyards, and terrace openings that from a distance resemble streamlined stainless-steel train cars. Up close, the façade's components directly and indirectly produce a delightful interplay with birch trees, plants, grass, leaves, and ivy, forming unusually sleek juxtapositions. // Courtyards are fenceless and entirely see-through. The trees are beautifully enclosed by and reflected in the glass all around them, while each space is centered on a panoramic elevator and partially covered by curved perforated canopies, entirely and effectively fusing the boundaries between architecture and nature. Dorms occupy the first four floors, while common areas, student lounges, and open terraces are lined up along the top, ship-like deck embraced by tree crowns. The interiors feature unfinished concrete with stainless-steel furniture designed by Jahn. Among the most remarkable design features here are the far-reaching steel-and-glass extended planes that turn this building's south and north ends into appealing abstractions that effectively help to block the noise coming from passing trains.

Photo: Matthew Messner

Morgan Live + Work

3209 South Morgan Street,
Bridgeport
UrbanLab (Chicago)
2011

To Ashland
31 to 31St Street & Morgan

The Morgan Live + Work project transmits its meaning quite literally: it is a home and office on Morgan Street in Bridgeport, a working-class residential neighborhood on the South Side. It was designed and is owned by husband-and-wife team Martin Felsen and Sarah Dunn, who run the architecture and urban design firm UrbanLab, which was founded in 2000. They had to demolish a run-down grocery store before it was possible to build this three-part structure, which is made up of two rectangular volumes and a self-erected hill. They used the debris to form the mound at the back of the site. The store was replaced with a new single-story, box-like office space at the front. Another rectangular box—an apartment unit—spans the space between the prairie-grass-planted mound and the office. One end of the apartment opens on a green roof over the office below; the other offers direct access to the mound and surrounding landscape below, although it is quite steep. On the Morgan Street side, the office is skinned with perforated Corten steel panels to withstand the wear and tear of street life. Raw aluminum panels wrap all the other façades. The upper unit is a prefabricated structure. It has extensive glazing on the south side overlooking the backyard. Through this large opening, a chaotic pattern of steel supports is visible directly behind the glass. These thin columns help stiffen the box and make the interior look like a bridge truss. The eastern end of the apartment opens entirely with a garage-style door. // Both architects teach at local schools: Felsen at the Illinois Institute of Technology and Dunn at the University of Illinois at Chicago. Before opening UrbanLab to focus on projects ranging in scale from houses to cities, Felsen worked at Peter Eisenman's office in New York, while Dunn worked at Rem Koolhaas's OMA in Rotterdam. This explains their house's original concept-driven design and sentiment for inventing memorable buildings in the most surprising ways. The architects' position is quite ambitious: 'Our primary interest is in forward-looking projects that speculate on a more resilient and resourceful tomorrow.'

Hyde Park, Woodlawn, and Grand Crossing

7

074 Joe & Rika Mansueto Library
075 Max Palevsky Residence Commons
076 University of Chicago Booth School of Business, Charles M. Harper Center
077 Gordon Parks Arts Hall
078 Reva and David Logan Center for the Arts
079 David Rubenstein Forum
080 The Keller Center – Harris School of Public Policy
081 South Campus Boiler Plant
082 The Barack Obama Presidential Center
083 City Hyde Park
084 Hyde Park Art Center
085 Gary Comer College Preparatory School and Gary Comer Youth Center

Joe & Rika Mansueto Library   074 E
1100 East 57th Street, University
of Chicago: Hyde Park
*Murphy/Jahn (since 2012, JAHN,
Chicago)*
2011

To Cottage Grove then Bus 4 to Cottage
Grove & 57th Street
171, 172 to Ellis & 57th Street

Located on a compact corner site at the
intersection of South Ellis and East 57th
in the heart of the University of Chicago
campus, the Joe & Rika Mansueto Library
appears to be buried deep in the ground
with just the upper part of the egg-
shaped glass roof visible. The futuristic-
looking structure is surrounded by an eclectic collection of buildings to which it
is attached surreptitiously by an angled
glass walkway. Yet the unusual building is a logical solution to an improba-
ble brief: to find a space large enough to
store up to 3.5 million books with precise environmental control, as well as
a reading room and preservation facilities—all on a tight, 160-by-360-foot site
(49-by-110 meters). To make the reading
room and the preservation department

as pleasant as possible, the architect opted to conceive the building as two parts, one on top of the other. Books went below grade—55 feet (17 meters) below to be precise—where their environment could be better controlled to achieve the desired constant temperature and humidity at a lower cost. All public spaces are located at ground level inside a minimal elliptical glass dome that rises to a height of 35 feet (10.7 meters) at its center. This space is divided into the grand reading room on one side and labs for preservation, conservation, and digitization on the other.

The column-free space under the dome is achieved through the use of steel crisscrossed curved beams that carry glass panels—see-through at eye level with added ceramic frits to block out UV rays and solar heat overhead. // The library is the third building on campus designed by Helmut Jahn. The other two are utility plants and are examples of high-tech architecture: the West Campus Chiller Plant, barely one block away from the library at the corner of East 56th and South Maryland, and the South Campus Boiler Plant, south of Midway Plaisance Park [081].

7

Courtesy of JAHN

Photo: Lourdes Legorreta

Max Palevsky Residential Commons

075 E

1101 East 56th Street, University of Chicago: Hyde Park
LEGORRETA + LEGORRETA (now LEGORRETA)
2001

🚇 To Cottage Grove then Bus 4 to Cottage Grove & 56th Street
🚌 171, 172 to Ellis & 57th Street; 55 to 55th Street & Ellis

Located on the University of Chicago's campus, which is home to many distinctive buildings featured in this guide, the Max Palevsky Residential Commons, often abbreviated to 'Max P' or just 'Max', is an extensive low-rise, three-building dormitory complex. It sits next to the university's main library and the Joe & Rika Mansueto Library [074] on a double block directly north of the main campus quad, which is defined by late nineteenth-century Collegiate Gothic residential halls. The three buildings are clad in orange brick and topped by bright slanted blue roofs. These understated building blocks are distinguished by ordered rows of square, recessed windows of various sizes and are particularly notable for spacious entry atriums, each celebrated in its own color—purple, yellow, and pink. The complex is further broken down into walkways, grass beds, and articulated corners with a series of setbacks, open spaces, and patios. // The building's bright colors, expressed in window mullions, is a giveaway of its famed designer, Mexican architect Ricardo Legorreta (1931–2011). The prolific architect and recipient of the 2000 American Institute of Architects Gold Medal was a disciple of Luis Barragán, who was particularly well known for his use of bold, primary geometric forms painted in striking colors, similar to the three colors used here. The architect's large international practice, now called LEGORRETA, is headed by his son Victor Legorreta, who joined his father's firm in 1989 and became his partner and managing design director in 2001—the year this project was completed. His sister Lourdes Legorreta, an architectural photographer, provided her photo of Legorreta's only built work in Chicago for this guide.

University of Chicago Booth School of Business, Charles M. Harper Center

076 E

5807 South Woodlawn Avenue,
University of Chicago: Hyde Park
Rafael Viñoly Architects (New York)
2004

🚇 To Cottage Grove then Bus 4 to Cottage Grove & 58th Street
🚌 1/2 to Woodlawn & 58th Street; 171, 192 to 59th Street & Kimbark

Chicago Booth, or simply Booth, was founded in 1898 and is the second-oldest business school in the US. *The Economist* ranked the school number one globally in 2019. It is associated with nine Nobel laureates—more than any other business school in the world. Its Hyde Park campus at the University of Chicago on the South Side occupies a large part of the northern portion of its block, which is just above Midway Plaisance Park. The building's composition is centered on the University of Chicago's Career Advancement office at Ida Noyes Hall, situated immediately to the south. More importantly, the building sits between two historically and architecturally significant landmarks: the university's Gothic-style 1928 Rockefeller Memorial Chapel to the west across South Woodlawn Avenue and Frank Lloyd Wright's 1910 Robie House, which is an example of his Prairie style and a UNESCO World Heritage Site directly across East 58th to the north. // The business school was designed by New York architect Rafael Viñoly, who won the commission in an international competition. His NEMA Chicago [040] is the tallest tower in the South Loop and his Center for Care and Discovery, a 10-story hospital with a heliport on its roof (not included in this guide), is just a few blocks away from Booth at the crossing of South Maryland and East 57th. Booth constitutes a well-balanced and sensitive composition of terraces, setbacks, and deep cantilevers that effectively break down its bulk, evoking a sense of the horizontality and lightness of Wright's Robie House. The building's lower floors are clad in horizontal panels of Indiana limestone, a material widely used on this campus, and topped by glazed volumes. Yet it is the building's

7

interior space that deserves your close attention. // The school is planned around the natural light-flooded Winter Garden, a six-story glass atrium and the building's central place of circulation. Its airy interior is ringed by student services, lounges, study areas, meeting rooms, classrooms, and lecture halls, all connected by open stairs on the lower floors and below-grade levels. Teaching facilities, and administrative and faculty offices are upstairs. The central square below is big enough to be used as a ceremonial quad where fairs and exhibitions can take place. The Winter Garden's glass roof is gracefully held by four main structural columns that simultaneously resemble the tree branches in a garden and Gothic vaults—a direct reference of the nearby Rockefeller Chapel and other structures designed in the Collegiate Gothic style throughout the university campus.

These massive yet elegant structures are built of tubular steel and utilized to channel rainwater into a special reservoir. // The new building provides an attractively landscaped streetscape, especially along South Woodlawn Street. The Winter Garden's glass cube with steel Gothic arches, clearly a Post-Modernist gesture, is visible from the outside and serves as a unique symbol of the school—a see-through cathedral of knowledge. Its design also evokes Viñoly's celebrated Tokyo Forum (1997), an eye-shaped glass atrium where two columns carry a gigantic truss from which two curved glass curtain wall façades are draped down. Booth's ambitious program enabled the architect to develop a generous scheme that turned a mere pragmatic project into an exemplary civic space. One of the most compelling buildings of the architect's oeuvre, this enthralling space is open to the public.

Photo: Barbara Karant

Gordon Parks Arts Hall 077 E

5815 South Kimbark Avenue,
University of Chicago: Hyde Park
*Valerio Dewalt Train Associates
(Chicago) and FGM Architects (Chicago)*
2015

To Cottage Grove then Bus 4 to Cottage Grove & 58th Street
172 to Woodlawn & 58th Street; 171, 192 to 59th Street & Kimbark

Gordon Parks Arts Hall, the most recent addition to the north end of the University of Chicago Laboratory School's main campus, is situated across South Kimbark from Rafael Viñoly's Chicago Booth [076]. It was built in place of the demolished Belfield Hall, which was a single-story workshop. Like Booth, the building's design is inspired by Collegiate Gothic architecture, which is common across the campus. Here though, the inspiration is formally much more direct, although it is made interpretative through extensive use of glass and the geometry of sweeping angles. The three-story hall comprises the middle school and high school arts programs with spaces for music and performing arts education. Facilities include a two-story 750-seat in-the-round theater, a 250-seat black box theater, and an art gallery. The new building maintains a connection to the existing East and West Belfield Halls through glass-enclosed corridors. The Arts Hall faces Scammons Garden to the north and the Lab Schools' central courtyard to the south, both of which are used for outdoor play and teaching. The building's north façade is the most rewarding in terms of its unusual design: folded glass curtain wall and ribbed metal panels assembled into the dramatic construct of an angular gabled roof interrupted by four 'solar chimneys'. Solid areas of the exterior are clad in Indiana limestone to complement the surrounding buildings. Impressive double-height interiors are formally much more abstract and expressed in a stern palette of limestone, metal panels, and unpainted concrete, including oversized round columns. Large expanses of the building's flat roofs are planted.

Photo: Steve Hall, Hedrich Blessing Photographers

Photo: Steve Hall, Hedrich Blessing Photographers

Reva and David Logan Center for the Arts

078 E

915 East 60th Street, University of Chicago: Woodlawn
Tod Williams Billie Tsien Architects (New York)
2007–2012

🚇 To Cottage Grove
🚌 2 to 915 E. 60th Street; 4 Cottage Grove & 60th Street; 61st Street & Ingleside

The Reva and David Logan Center for the Arts is prominently located on the northern edge of the Woodlawn neighborhood on the campus of the University of Chicago right in front of the Midway Plaisance, a one-mile-long public park designed by Frederick Law Olmsted and Calvert Vaux for the 1893 World's Columbian Exposition. The center houses departments of visual arts, film, music, and theater programs that were previously scattered throughout the campus. The new complex comprises three interconnected buildings grouped around a public plaza: a two-story horizontal structure with the artist studios topped by a field of north-facing skylights, a partially sunken formal proscenium theater, and a 10-story tower. The tower evokes an abstract painting and from different vantage points, it may appear as if parts of it are missing, which is achieved through the use of large expanses of reflective glass. This building consists of a café that spills outdoors, an auditorium, black-box spaces, film production and dance studios, galleries, offices, music practice rooms, and classrooms. The top floor is reserved for performances, lectures, and parties and offers expansive views of Lake Michigan and downtown Chicago. // From the outset, the university intended to build the Logan Center as a very special signature piece. Its design was selected in an international competition that initially invited more than 60 accomplished architects. The winning project was designed by the New York husband-and-wife team of Tod Williams and Billie Tsien. Other finalists included Hans Hollein (Austria), Thom Mayne (Los Angeles), Fumihiko Maki (Japan), and Daniel Libeskind (New York). Logan is the architects' first built work in Chicago, as would have been the case if any of the other finalists had succeeded. Curiously, the building is just a stone's throw from the site of the architects' other important Chicago project: the future Obama Presidential Center [082], which was also won in a prestigious international competition. // The architects' solution for the Logan Center is both a vigorous contextual response to its location—physical and cultural—and the development of their personally-driven sculptural oeuvre with its masterful use of stone, concrete, wood, tiles, and fabrics. While the low buildings convey the sense of horizontality of Frank Lloyd Wright's Prairie School, the tower is a nod to Chicago's tradition of building tall. The building's façades are entirely clad in warm, multi-hued Missouri limestone. These panels are cut into four-foot-long bars and laid out as 'Roman' bricks (longer and flatter than typical modern bricks) in another nod to Wright and the Prairie School. The tower's design seems to refrain from any repetition, both inside and outside, in the architects' desire to create a unique place where different art disciplines overlap. Inside there are puzzle-like spatial surprises of rooms, and every side and corner are treated with a personal touch to play subtly with what is expected. Different floors are connected with generous elevators, dramatic stairways with custom-made tiles and felt paneled walls, and an emphasis on treating the building like a vertical street—a spatial adventure full of surprises and chance encounters. There are various communal places and secret pockets just right for spending some time alone.

David Rubenstein Forum 079 E
1201 East 60th Street, University
of Chicago: Woodlawn
Diller Scofidio + Renfro (New York)
with Brininstool + Lynch (Chicago)
2015–2020

Metra To Univ. of Chicago/59th St.
🚇 To Cottage Grove
🚌 2, 171, 172 to 60th Street & Woodlawn;
59 to 61st Street & Woodlawn

Barely three short blocks to the east of
Tod Williams Billie Tsien Architects' Logan
Center [078] along East 60th on the south
side of the Midway Plaisance that sepa-
rates the Hyde Park neighborhood to the
north from Woodlawn to the south, we
find the next landmark building in our
Chicago 100 guide: the David Rubenstein
Forum. Unlike the original north side of
the Chicago University campus, which
was designed predominantly in a mixture
of the Victorian Gothic and Collegiate
Gothic styles patterned on the colleges of
the University of Oxford in England, here
on the south side, architecture is much
less rooted in historical context. On our
short walk from Logan, we pass the Crown
Family School of Social Work, Policy, and
Practice by Mies van der Rohe (1965) and
the University of Chicago's Law School
by Eero Saarinen (1959). The other side
of the new Rubenstein Forum is home
to the Keller Center – Harris School of
Public Policy (1963), which was originally designed by Edward Durell Stone and

recently transformed and reviewed in this
guide [080]. // The forum is the first building in Chicago by renowned New York firm
Diller Scofidio + Renfro. It is composed
of two parts: a two-story, low podium-
like building and a 10-story tower. It comprises a dining room for conference at-
tendees and an elevated wine bar and café on the ground floor. A keynote event
space is located in the University Room
upstairs—the largest room in the facility
that can seat more than 600 guests. The
tower at the corner of East 60th Street and
South Woodlawn is a 166-foot (51-meter)
boldly organized stack of meeting spaces that the architects call 'neighborhoods'. It salutes the university's
prime symbol: the 217-foot (66-meter)
Rockefeller Chapel slightly diagonally
across the Midway. The forum is a kind of
inside-out building that communicates
what's happening in its 'belly'. Wrapped
in glass and silvery, shiny zinc, it is conceived not as a singular icon, but as an assemblage of parts that resembles a column of haphazardly piled books—single
and double-height multi-purpose meeting spaces intended for workshops, sym-
posia, and lectures that can accommodate from 25 people to auditoriums that
seat 185 and 285 people. It culminates in
the 10th-floor meeting room with impressive downtown views. Instead of putting
all the meeting rooms on one side and all
the pre-function rooms on the other, the
architects rotated some of the floors 180
degrees, giving the building its dynamic

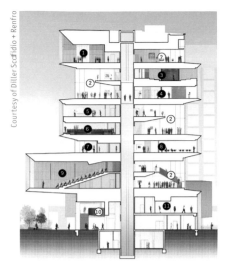

profile with various levels poking in and out and framing views toward the north and south. Along 60th Street the terrazzo paving extends from the sidewalk into the fully glazed double-height lobby, blurring the boundary between inside and outside. Directly above it on the third and fourth floor, Friedman Hall steps forward and forms a 40-foot (12-meter) cantilever that acts as a welcoming canopy. // The forum's interiors are distinguished by their full-width two-story picture windows and blackened steel staircases that the architects loved to bend and twist and extensive wood finishes, all highlighted using important artworks and historical documents selected from Rubenstein's personal collections. The forum's stacked design resembles another building the architects completed in New York in 2016: the Vagelos Education Center for Columbia University Medical Center. However, the Chicago version is more tightly organized. A handsome bosque of 20 maple trees on the building's south side connects to the university's Campus South Walk. Green roofs such as the one above the podium and a Japanese garden above Friedman Hall provide unique elevated views over downtown Chicago.

The Keller Center – Harris School of Public Policy

080 E

1307 East 60th Street, University of Chicago: Woodlawn
Woodhouse Tinucci Architects (Chicago) & Farr Associates (Chicago)
2019

Metra To Univ. of Chicago/59th St.
To Cottage Grove then bus 63 to 63rd Street & Kenwood
2, 171, 172 to 60th Street & Kenwood

The Keller Center, the vibrant new headquarters of the Harris School of Public Policy, is just a short block east of the David Rubenstein Forum [079] on East 60th Street and facing the Midway Plaisance on the University of Chicago's South Campus. An adaptive reuse project, the Keller Center is technically an interior design project, which this guide does not cover. Yet the resulting transformation is so complex and so outstanding that it would be an oversight not to include it here. The original three-story building was designed by Edward Durell Stone (1902 1978). The 1962 building initially served as the Kellogg Center for Continuing Education, a conference center, and hotel for visiting scholars. It later became a dorm for graduate students. The temple-like, imposing structure sits atop a five-foot (1.5-meter) plinth and is distinguished by slender, full-height concrete pillars encircling a limestone façade. They provide support for the deeply-cantilevered roof—a flat concrete slab with long air slots all around the perimeter's edges. The building recalls renowned works by the architect such as the US Embassy in New Delhi, India (1959) and the John F. Kennedy Center for the Performing Arts (1971; preliminary designs date to 1959). Projecting a highly institutional, even imperial character, the structure was never loved by students who called it 'the least lovable ugly building on campus'. // The architects transformed this monumental building in the most radical way by opening its core and inserting a four-level atrium called the Harris Forum—three floors above the plinth and one within it. This new central collaboration space was then topped by extensive new skylights. An additional fourth floor with glass exterior walls was built over the original roof. It sits around the skylights and is set back from the building's front just enough to be visible

from the street and give this hefty edifice a lighter appearance. This symmetrical top-floor addition comprises the Executive Education Suite that supports specialized training for alumni and executive-level professionals. The building's platform has been made less intimidating with the help of a wheelchair-accessible ramp and a flight of stairs that has been cut into the northwest corner. // The new atrium is an airy, sun-streaked, welcoming space extensively clad in wood and glass. The wood interiors are made from ash trees that Chicago officials cut down in public parks during the emerald-ash-borer beetle infestation that originally struck the city in 2006 and keeps recurring. Theaster Gates, a local artist, oversaw the process of cutting trees into lumber and finished panels at a mill that was set up just south of the project site, where he provided job training to people from Chicago's South Side. The sunken and plinth-level floors comprise open-terraced areas designed to encourage collaboration and informal learning, while the second and third floors contain classrooms, team rooms, quiet zones, and faculty offices. // Another interior highlight is a handsomely-detailed set of multi-story

switchback stairs wrapped in a frame of blackened steel just off the atrium. There are traces of the building's transformation throughout this highly-dynamic space. Visitors will encounter unfinished cuts in the concrete floor slabs, exposed steel inserts, remnants of old rebars, and open columns and beams with rough concrete surfaces that contrast greatly with the new glass walls, plaster, and refined wood finishes. These collisions of old and new, and an abundance of glass that allows visibility of material layers and various activities inside classrooms, emphasize the process of transformation and the fact that collaboration and engagement are important aspects of education itself.

South Campus Boiler Plant 081 E

6053 South Woodlawn Avenue,
University of Chicago: Woodlawn
Murphy/Jahn (since 2012, JAHN,
Chicago)
2010

Metra To Univ. of Chicago/59th St.
To Cottage Grove then Bus 63 to 63rd
Street & Dorchester
2 to 60th Street & Blackstone; 59 to
Dorchester & 61st Street

The University of Chicago's South Campus Boiler Plant was conceived as a rudimentary container to house machines, not people. Yet it is designed as an elegant display case, a Center Pompidou in miniature to showcase machines converting electricity and natural gas into chilled water and steam for distribution across campus to heat and cool the university and hospital buildings. The stainless steel-and-glass container displays everything inside and puts on view how it is assembled—concrete walls, steel structure, zigzagging stairs, columns, girders, beams, floor decks, light fixtures, and particularly the multi-colored machinery (ducts, pipes, and control valves), all clearly visible from the street in the most proud and even voyeuristic fashion. The architect

Helmut Jahn designed dozens of buildings in Chicago, eight of which are covered in this guide. He tried to remove the subjective aspects of design and aesthetics by replacing them with a rational approach based purely on function and performance. Yet the result is quite celebratory—a beautiful object masterfully wrapped in a floor-to-ceiling ultra-clear glass curtain wall supported on steel bar mullions and metal screens and perforated in places where the building needs to 'breathe'. The piece is rounded along the top edges to improve its proportions, give it a finishing touch, and to make a point that this is not an abstract modernist box but a building with distinctive aesthetics and a clear intention to turn a mere utilitarian facility into a shimmering, silvery object that the university would cherish like a treasure.// The building continues the relatively recent tradition of treating utility plants ceremoniously, particularly on American university campuses. Boston-based Leers Weinzapfel Associates set this trend in 2000 with their University of Pennsylvania Gateway Complex in Philadelphia. The South Campus Boiler Plant here is coupled with another Jahn-designed facility—the West Campus Chiller Plant at 5801 South Maryland Avenue, near his Joe and Rika Mansueto Library [074].

Rendering: Tod Williams Billie Tsien Architects

The Barack Obama Presidential Center
082 E

South Stony Island Avenue and
East 60th Street, Jackson Park
*Tod Williams Billie Tsien Architects
(New York)*
Under construction after 2021
groundbreaking

Metra To Univ. of Chicago/59th St.
To Cottage Grove then Bus 63 to Stony
Island & 64th Street
6, 15, 28 to Stony Island & 60th
Street; 59 to 60th Street & Stony Island

The Barack Obama Presidential Center is being constructed in Jackson Park on the South Side of Chicago, close to where former First Lady Michelle Obama was born and raised and where her husband was first elected to public office. The new complex, devoted to the 44th President of the United States, will include a library with Obama's presidential archives and a museum dedicated to his presidency (2009–2017). Chicago was chosen as the center's host city, beating bids from Honolulu, the President's city of birth, and New York, where he was a student at Columbia University. The project was developed in partnership with the nearby University of Chicago.

The original vision was for the center to seamlessly integrate into the park and the community and include diverse public spaces such as new gardens, an enlarged playground, and scenic paths for jogging and biking. The Great Lawn, with its gentle slope, will offer opportunities for activities all year round, including sledding in the winter and picnics and movies in the summer. Jackson Park, a 500-acre (202-hectare) park, is located in Woodlawn, a low-income, predominantly African-American community bordering Lake Michigan. Named after the seventh president, Andrew Jackson, the park was first developed as the host site of the 1893 Chicago World's Fair to celebrate the 400th anniversary of Christopher Columbus' arrival in the New World. The fair, colloquially known as 'The White City', was designed as a prototype for what its planners and architects John Wellborn Root and Daniel Burnham saw as a model for an ideal city that would follow Beaux Arts principles of design. The landscape, with its intricately shaped lagoon, was designed by Frederick Law Olmsted, the famous designer of New York's Central Park. // The Obama Center will be located southwest from the Museum of Science and Industry, which resides in the only

7

remaining structure from the fair, the old Palace of Fine Arts. The new complex is being designed by New York architects and husband-and-wife duo Tod Williams and Billie Tsien, who are best known for notable works such as the American Folk Art Museum in New York (demolished in 2014 to accommodate the 2019 MoMA expansion by Diller Scofidio + Refro), the Barnes Foundation in Philadelphia, Asia Society in Hong Kong, and the Logan Center for the Arts [078] just a few blocks to the west of here at the University of Chicago's south campus. The architects were chosen over the other six finalists in a 2016 international competition with an initial list of 140 applicants. The other finalists were David Adjaye, Diller Scofidio + Renfro, Renzo Piano, SHoP, Snøhetta, and John Ronan, the only Chicago-based architect. It was the first international design competition to select an architect for a presidential library. // Ralph Appelbaum Associates, headquartered in New York, was chosen as the exhibition designer. The Obama Center is designed as a campus framed by Sunny Stony Island Avenue to the west, a promenade in front of the Lagoon to the east, Midway Plaisance to the north, and an existing track and field to the south. The three main structures—the Museum Building, Forum Building, and Chicago Public Library—are planned around a small rectangular plaza facing the avenue near 60th Street. There will also be a new low-rise Program, Athletic, and Activity Center in the southern part of the site. The landscape architecture that wraps around the buildings and continues over the planted roofs of the forum and library buildings has been designed by New York landscape architect Michael Van Valkenburgh. // Building America's presidential libraries is a modern tradition that started in 1939 when Franklin Roosevelt donated his personal and presidential papers to the federal government. The presidential library system is currently composed of 13 completed libraries, starting with the Herbert Hoover Presidential Library and Museum. They are administered by the Office of Presidential Libraries, which is part of the National Archives and Records Administration (NARA). These archives and museums house documents and artifacts of US Presidents and their administrations. Each library provides a complete record of a presidential era. It was the 1955 Presidential Libraries Act that established a system of privately erected and federally maintained libraries. The act encourages presidents to donate their historical materials to the government and ensures their preservation and availability to the American people. // According to the design, the Museum Building, anchoring the northern end of the plaza, is the center's most prominent feature, reaching a height of 180 feet (55 meters), while all the other buildings are single-story structures integrated organically into the surrounding landscape. It will house educational and meeting spaces, including a ground-level restaurant that opens seamlessly onto the adjacent public garden. The building's tough-looking, monolithic, and somewhat grounded form is distinguished by faceted sides and cutaway corners. It evokes four hands coming together, reflecting the architects' initial idea that it takes many hands to shape a place and community. All three buildings around the plaza are clad in light-colored textured stone. The Forum Building's roof garden escapes architecture's rigid orthogonal geometry, spilling organically right over the surrounding terrain. This design echoes many architects' current fascination with integrating nature into buildings. As a result, there is no longer a clear distinction between where the architecture stops and the landscape begins. The Obama Presidential Center was originally planned to open in 2021 at a cost exceeding $500 million. Delays were caused by the federal review process, the National Environmental Policy Act, the National Historic Preservation Act (due to Jackson Park's historic designation), and approval needed from the Federal-Aid Highway Act for road improvement work. All the permits were finally obtained in late 2020 and construction started in mid-2021. It is expected to open by 2025.

City Hyde Park
5105 South Harper Avenue,
Hyde Park
Studio Gang (Chicago)
2016

083 E

Metra To 51st/53rd St. (Hyde Park)
🚆 To 51st then Bus 15 to E Hyde Park &
Lake Park
🚌 172 to E Hyde Park & Lake Park; 2, 6,
28 to Lake Park & E. Hyde Park Blvd; 28 to
Lake Park & 52nd Street

Completed in 2016, City Hyde Park was built in place of a suburban-style strip mall and surface parking with the intention of creating an urban, active-living complex. The project is situated in the northeast corner of Hyde Park at a busy intersection of East Hyde Park Boulevard and South Lake Park Avenue, conveniently adjacent to a Metra train stop near Harold Washington Park on Lake Michigan. Occupying its own block, the structure comprises a 14-story slab of rental apartments along East Hyde Park Boulevard and a two-story commercial plinth with a large grocery store, fitness center, co-working space, small retail, cafes, and amenities for residents. There are also two underground floors of parking. The project follows pretty much the same typology as Perkins&Will's Skybridge [050] on the Near West Side, which also consists of a tower over a podium with a parking garage and a large grocery store. The residential tower here is placed perpendicularly to the lake, which enables all the units

to view it from their windows. The apartments are accessed from central double-loaded corridors—half of them face north with distant downtown views, while the rest are oriented to the south. All the units on this side have balconies overlooking the supermarket's green roof. // It should be apparent that the project, designed by Jeanne Gang of Studio Gang, is included in this guide due to its zigzagging façades, particularly its diamond-shaped balconies on the south side. This façade is made up of a playful array of stacked concrete panels that form so-called 'stems'—tree-like assemblies of columns, bays, sunshades, and balconies. Together these elements bring vertical loads all the way to the ground, which allows an effective thermal separation between the balconies and the apartment interiors, which in turn reduces energy consumption. The building's various balcony conditions offer residents oblique views from one another and different levels of privacy and sun exposure. Their intricate arrangements continue the architect's preoccupation with animating residential façades by playing with what she refers to as 'residents' chance encounters' and, more broadly, the idea of cultivating a sense of community within large residential complexes. This fascination has led to the creation of many original residential buildings distinguished for their dynamic façades, both in Chicago and around the world. The most emblematic example in this guide is the Aqua Tower on the New Eastside [011].

7

Hyde Park Art Center
5020 South Cornell Avenue,
East Hyde Park
Doug Garofalo (Chicago)
2006

084 E

Metra To 51st/53rd St. (Hyde Park)
To 51st then Bus 15 to E Hyde Park &
Lake Park
6, 28, 172 to E Hyde Park & East End

The Hyde Park Art Center (HPAC) is a non-profit visual arts organization and the oldest alternative exhibition space in Chicago. Before moving to its current building just north of Hyde Park Boulevard near Harold Washington Park on Lake Michigan in 2006, HPAC had occupied about a dozen spaces since it was founded in 1939. The center is a hub for contemporary arts. It serves as a gathering and production space for artists and the broader community beyond the city through diverse educational programs offered by Oakman Clinton School, exhibitions that take place in six flexible galleries, residencies for local and international artists, and free public events. The new building was converted from an old army warehouse leased indefinitely to HPAC by the University of Chicago for $1 a year. The two-story building's design deals with the idea of softening the institutionalized boundaries between an arts organization and the public by highlighting ideas such as transparency of the art-making process and experimenting with technology and concepts. The building's most notable feature is a section of its façade along South Cornell Avenue where it is centered on East 50th Street overlooking the lake and framed by several residential towers. The ground floor here is assembled out of five metal garage-style doors that open up to the main double-height gallery behind and spill out onto the street. These graffiti-painted doors support the second-floor projection screen, which measures 10-by-80 feet (3-by-24 meters). // The new center is a rare building by the Chicago-based, internationally-recognized architect and educator Doug Garofalo (1958–2011) of Garofalo Architects. Garofalo was a respected professor at the University of Illinois at Chicago, serving as its acting director from 2001 to 2003. He helped to initiate ARCHEWORKS, an alternative design school focused on social causes. The architect was one of the early pioneers of parametric design. Together with Greg Lynn of FORM in Los Angeles (then based in Hoboken, New Jersey) and Michael McInturf Architects in Cincinnati, Garofalo was one of the co-designers of the Korean Presbyterian Church (New York; 1999), the first building fully conceived and executed with the use of advanced computer-aided design and fabrication technology.

Kelly Kaczynski, *Olympus Manger* installation, 2008

Photo: Tom Van Eynde; Courtesy of Hyde Park Art Center

Gary Comer College Preparatory School and Gary Comer Youth Center

085 E

7131 S South Chicago Avenue and 7200 South Ingleside Avenue, Grand Crossing
John Ronan Architects (Chicago)
2006 and 2010

🚌 30 to South Chicago & Ingleside or South Chicago & 71st Street/Cottage; 71 to 71st Street & Cottage Grove/S. Chicago

The Gary Comer College Preparatory School and the Gary Comer Youth Center, both designed by John Ronan, the founder of John Ronan Architects, are part of a school campus on a long rectangular site stretched along S South Chicago Avenue in the Grand Crossing neighborhood on Chicago's South Side. The two rectangular buildings are pulled apart by a large parking lot that doubles as a practice parade ground. The two-story charter high school at the southwest end of the campus comprises a large, glazed lobby space, lecture room, classrooms, and administrative offices. This building's envelope is an appealing assembly of bright yellow and green aluminum-composite panels fronted with corrugated stainless-steel siding and perforated metal screening on the outboard side of the windows along both long façades. The school's perimeter is topped by an extensive green roof, and two continuous rows of skylights in the center run the building's length over the interior hallways on both levels. They also bring natural light to classrooms through glass walls along the hallways. // The school is designed to be used in conjunction with the adjacent Gary Comer Youth Center at the southeast end of the site. The three-story building houses a large gymnasium that can be converted into a 600-seat performing arts theater, a cafeteria, music and dance rooms, a recording studio, costume design shop, art rooms, exhibition space, and computer lab space. The building is marked by an 80-foot-tall tower surmounted by an LED sign that announces programs and events. // The youth center facilities are shared with the school. Similar to the school building, the center features extensive glazing to allow visual access between the different programs. Exhibition spaces and other program facilities located around the perimeter on the third floor overlook a planted roof garden in the middle that serves as an outdoor horticultural classroom. Skylights that dot this landscape bring natural daylight into the gym and cafeteria below. The youth center provides space for various youth educational and recreational programs and supports the South Shore Drill Team and Performing Arts Ensemble, a 300-member dance performance group for children aged eight to 18. The group regularly performs in parades and on stage. The building's exterior is clad in cement board panels that are arranged in a random pattern of various shades of red and blue, as well as black, white, and glass—all the same size—to allow for their replacement over time in response to damage or vandalism. In a sobering reminder of the realities of this tough neighborhood, bullet-proof glazing is used on both buildings' perimeters—an attempt by the architect to create an inviting but secure environment.

8

086   **Eight-Unit Condominium Building**
087   **Pfanner House**
088   **Brick Weave House**

Eight-Unit Condominium Building

086 C

2016 West Rice Street,
Ukrainian Village
Vladimir Radutny Architects (Chicago)
2019

To Chicago and then bus 66 to Chicago & Damen

50 to Damen & Iowa

Located in the heart of the Ukrainian Village neighborhood in West Town, the 2016 West Rice residences comprise a puzzle-like block of eight condominium units—four uniquely configured duplexes and four single-story apartments stacked above them in a design that responded to the client's request to maximize the site's buildable area. Organized as a small community of individual dwellings, the building is wrapped in one continuous corrugated metal skin with some of the public area windows behind it. This technique gives the complex a decisively sleek and fresh appearance, highlighting atmospheric changes brought forth throughout the day and indeed by the seasons. Unlike apartments in typical high-rises, each of the residences here is designed to face more than two directions and includes plenty of outdoor space, which maximizes daylight as well as cross breezes. // Ukrainian-born architect Vladimir Radutny has been living in Chicago since he was 11 and studied architecture at the University of Illinois at Urbana Champaign. He opened his local practice in 2008 and combines it with teaching at the Illinois Institute of Technology. His small studio has become well known in Chicago, winning numerous local and national awards for exquisitely built neo-modern interiors, many of which are executed at Chicago's most prominent landmarks, including Lake Shore Drive towers by Mies van der Rohe and the SOM-designed John Hancock Center.

Pfanner House

1737 West Ohio Street,
West Town
Zoka Zola Architecture (Chicago)
2000–2002

087 C

To Chicago and then bus 66 to Chicago & Wood

65 to Grand & Wood

Sitting at the northern end of its block and stretched in an east-west direction, Pfanner House is both contextual and entirely unique. The brick-clad timber-framed house occupies a compact corner lot in a residential part of West Town just south of the East Village and Ukrainian Village neighborhoods. Despite its appropriate scale, restrained form, and agreeable materiality—its entire surface is finished in the same orange brick with matching mortar as most other buildings around it—there is something quirky about this house. First, it

is reversed—while other neighboring structures, predominantly single-family houses, face North Hartland Court with their formal entries and front yards, Pfanner House shows its back here, namely a garage door. The dwelling is entered from the opposite end of the lot, where other houses have their garages lined up along the service alley in the back. While the house is built right against the sidewalk on its northern edge, its garage-side on the west is set back a few feet to allow for an extra-wide sidewalk. Despite this generous move, since there is no front yard, the house is closer to the street than all the other houses, and all its floors are aligned. This straight-up elevation is largely solid except for a large opening in the middle. It turns around the building's northwest corner with a deep terrace behind it. The opposite side has an open garden; there is a door there, but the main entrance is on the long side, from West Ohio Street. // The house is a

8

Photo: Doug Fogelson

sturdy orthogonal block characterized by subtle shifts and recesses in the brick skin, punched by a few apertures and openings that seem to have been placed randomly—some very large, others more moderately sized. The overall composition is somewhat reminiscent of the 1930 Villa Müller by Adolf Loos in Prague—nothing seems to be out of the ordinary, but the result is quite special—abstracted and strangely familiar at the same time. While the most intriguing element from the outside is the missing corner above the garage, the most striking part of the interior is a double-height space that reveals itself right from the sidewalk on West Ohio Street through a very large window with a low sill. It measures 14 by 9.5 feet (4.3 by 2.7 meters) and is aligned with one of the two large sidewalk trees, which provides privacy from passing cars. // Zoka Zola is both the home's architect and owner. Born in Croatia and educated in Zagreb and London, she started her practice in London and came to Chicago with her family in 1997, following her husband Peter Pfanner, an industrial designer who the house is named after. It is the architect's first building in Chicago. The space behind the big window and solid, main entry door next to it is the architect's studio. It occupies a double-height space that is split between two levels—a narrow strip at the level of the sidewalk

along the front and the rest is recessed 4.5 feet (1.4 meters) into the ground. The space is dramatized by an open stair. This striking sculptural element shifts and changes direction as it rises from the pit to the entry, then to the low-ceilinged mezzanine-level library with a reading niche. It then rises again to another intermediate landing overlooking the studio, and finally shoots straight up to the third floor, which is split into the living room and kitchen, each at its own slightly different level. The large west-end opening over the garage houses a terrace with a wooden floor and an outdoor fireplace accessed from the living room, while the kitchen on the opposite end leads to a smaller setback terrace overlooking the garden below. The kitchen is a handsome room with a window wrapping around the southeast corner directly above the stainless-steel L-shaped countertop sitting over white oak cabinets. The sleeping quarters on the top fourth floor comprise a master bedroom with its own bathroom, with two other bedrooms sharing the second bathroom. This private level has the advantage of being a full floor above all neighboring houses to the south. This fact is celebrated by large panoramic windows on the southern wall, both in the master bedroom and its bathroom where the top of the bathtub is aligned with the window's sill. //

Photo: Roland Halbe

The house is a continuous loop of circulation and masterful spatial fluidity, all achieved by relying strictly on orthogonal geometry. Openness is the key spatial principle here. It is all composed of white walls, white oak floors and built-in cabinetry and stairs, spare and clean-lined classic furniture, a striking lack of ornamentation, and the conspicuous absence of clutter. The architect questioned the very fundamental character of a house in her home manifesto: 'Why do we so easily create prisons for ourselves? Is it because a balance between security and freedom is hard to maintain? How can our houses not trap us in? As an architect of my own house, how is it possible not to be housed inside my own limits?' The house is reportedly often complimented by passersby who may say: 'This is the best house in Chicago!' The architect has said that complete strangers roll down their car windows to tell her how much they love the house. Critics love it, too. It received *Architecture* magazine's Home of the Year award in North America in 2003 and architectural historian Kenneth Frampton included it in his 2008 revised edition of *American Masterworks: Houses of the 20th and 21st Century*.

8

Photo: Doug Fogelson

Brick Weave House
1922 West Race Avenue,
West Town
Studio Gang (Chicago)
2009

088 C

🚇 🚇 To Ashland
🚌 65 to Grand & Wolcott; 50 to Damen &
Grand

Brick Weave House sits in the middle of an eclectic residential block in the lower part of West Town, just south of East Village and Ukrainian Village. Visiting this tiny project is highly encouraged since it will allow the reader to get a feel for its surroundings and experience the exceptionally rich variety of residential types so characteristic of Chicago. The city is extremely tolerant of the fact that any model is possible, whether historicist, modern, Post-Modern, or uncompromisingly futurist. This view, for example, is entirely absent in conservative New York. In fact, when it comes to the scale of single-family houses, this particular block on West Race Avenue holds more diversity than all of New York's boroughs put together thanks to their stubborn insistence on endlessly repeating just a few types of colonial houses. This is why 12 of the 100 buildings featured in this guide are houses, and many more could easily have been included. // Designed by Jeanne Gang of Studio Gang, Brick Weave House is of particular interest not merely because it is the artistic vision of a famous architect, but it is also a thoughtful renovation entirely rooted in the history and circumstance of its predecessor. The new building occupies the footprint of a century-old stable. It was completed on a modest budget and responded to the client's desire to salvage as much as possible of the older structure. The design strategy was also driven by the fact that the historical building had sustained heavy fire damage. It was this fact that led to the decision to cut away the damaged parts and weave about a third of the remaining original structure into the new construction. The front walls and roof were removed, creating a garden surrounded by a two-story porous 'brick weave' screen. The brick screen is what makes the house truly unique. It animates the garden and interior with appealing filtered sunlight. Rectangular voids in the screen throw hexagonal patterns of light onto interior surfaces. At night, the house glows like an abstract lantern, giving its entire block a characteristic

Photo: Steve Hall, Hedrich Blessing

8

reference point. // Variations in ceiling heights and floor levels connect the two-story part of the house at the front with the double-height living room volume in the back through a cascading section. The original structure's lot size is about a third wider than is typical. Two-thirds are occupied by the house—from end to end. The other third to the east is reserved for the garage, set back and accessed from the front, as well as the back garden directly behind the garage. The garden runs parallel to the living room. The main entry door is inconspicuous, on the east side and in the corner, right in front of the garage.

9

089   Independence Library and Apartments
090   Northtown Library and Apartments
091   Ardmore House

Independence Library and Apartments

4024–4024 North Elston Avenue, Irving Park

John Ronan Architects (Chicago)
2019

To Irving Park then take bus 80 to Irving Park & Elston/Monticello

In 2016, when Chicago was undergoing a revitalization of its existing libraries and looking for opportunities to build new ones, a remarkable solution was found: it was dubbed co-location. The idea was to combine two different building types—a community library on the street level and a housing block for seniors on top. The benefit of such unusual mixing of programs is two-fold. First of all, this strategy is more affordable and efficient. Two different agencies, in this case the Chicago Housing Authority and Chicago Public Library, can use the same lot where otherwise two lots would need to be purchased separately. Secondly, shared community spaces can be made much larger and therefore more attractive to the local community. By 2019, Chicago had opened three so-called co-located projects across the city. Two of these hybrid buildings are included in this guide. The third, the Roosevelt Square Library and Apartments on the city's Near West Side, was designed by SOM. The two reviewed here are in nearby neighborhoods on Chicago's North Side: the Northtown Library and Apartments in West Ridge [090] and this one, the Independence Library and Apartments complex in Irving Park. // The library-cum-public housing complex in Irving Park is a four-story affordable housing block and two-story community library. It stretches along North Elston Avenue near the intersection with West Irving Park Road, three short blocks to the east of small Independence Park. This festive, uncompromisingly modern building is a refreshing addition to its largely monotonous suburban surrounding—red and yellow brick and stone houses, bungalows, and commercial storefronts that are mostly one to two floors and nothing higher than a few four-story prosaic apartment blocks. The building's lower part, a local branch library, is built in line with its neighboring buildings of similar height on both ends. Its minimalist flat façade is sliced into two horizontal bands of similar width—the top is clad in large dark stone panels, while the bottom is continuously glazed in tinted, mullionless, and highly reflective glass. The interior is a singular double-height space with cushion-covered bleacher-style seating leading to a mezzanine level with direct access to an elevated park with grass and trees planted over the ground floor parking garage, which is entered from the back street. // The remainder of the library's interior is lined with uninterrupted ribbons of glass on both long sides. White surfaces dominate here—walls, ceiling panels, parapets outlining the mezzanine, bookshelves, furniture, and even light fixtures. The space is also peppered with bright colors—carpeted zones, chairs, cushions, and of course, the books' jackets. A grid of unpainted concrete columns that hold the residences above organizes the space. There is a large community multi-purpose room that supports public lectures, gatherings, and events. // Apart from the previously mentioned setback on the garage side, the four-story 44-unit affordable apartment block steps back from North Elston Avenue, leaving space for a narrow strip of grass on the library's roof at the front. The building's apartments are arranged on both sides of the double-loaded central corridors. All the units feature brightly-colored recessed balconies arranged in a checkerboard pattern. This playful design not only makes the building appealing aesthetically, but also lets residents identify their apartments from the street. The same colors are applied to the respective apartments' entry doors, door frames, and floor areas in front of them. The building's façades demonstrate masterful use of imaginative combinations of solid and perforated metal panels that make the building's surfaces quite sensual. The Independence Library and Apartments were designed by Chicago architect John Ronan. His IIT Innovation Center [070] on the IIT campus on the South Side has some parallels with this library's interior, particularly its airy openness, use of vibrant colors over white backgrounds, and palpable materials and finishes.

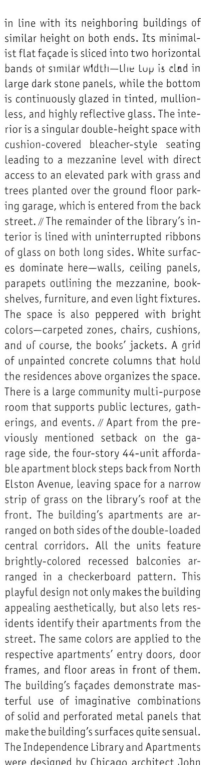

9

The Independence Library and Apartments complex is made up of a four-story 44-unit affordable housing block with brightly-colored recessed balconies arranged in a checkerboard pattern over a two-story community library.

9

Northtown Library and Apartments

6800 North Western Avenue,
West Ridge
Perkins&Will (Chicago)
2019

090 **A**

Metra To Union Pacific/North Line to Rogers Park

49B to Western & Pratt

The Northtown Library and Apartments, located diagonally across from the northwest corner of Warren (Laurence) Park in West Ridge on Chicago's North Side, is another take on co-location—a new type of mixed-use building program explained in the previous entry for Independence Library and Apartments [089] in nearby Irving Park. The Northtown library-cum-public housing complex has the exact same program—an affordable housing block with 44 apartments for seniors on top of a community library. The building takes over its own block. The ground floor is fully transparent and features generous setbacks utilized for planted areas and pockets of public spaces. The library is anchored at both ends—a large double-height lobby and community room on the south side, while the north side houses the YouMedia learning lab. The lobby supports community performances and includes a space for an artist-in-residence. Here, all attention is focused on *Eclectic Current*, a full-height, colorful mixed-media mural by neighborhood artist Chris Silva, who created it with input from local residents. These public areas are accessible after regular library hours. A much smaller second floor includes offices, community meeting spaces, a fitness

center, laundry room, and the library's green roof with pathways and benches. One particularly interesting feature inside the library is an open-roof internal reading garden. Triangular in plan, this appealing courtyard is glazed all around and, in addition to providing secure outdoor space, it floods the interior with daylight and visually brings in landscaping, even if only glimpsed between the bookshelves. This east-side space should be visited in the first half of the day before the sun goes west. // The apartments are stacked on the third and fourth floors within a serpentine structure that incorporates central double-loaded corridors. These floors are precariously cantilevered at both ends. The curved geometry helps to fit in more units, while the resulting setbacks allow for deeper and more useful green-roof areas on both sides. These two top floors incorporate glazed community spaces distinguished by bright yellow that perhaps symbolizes the inhabitants' golden years. These areas, as well as all the apartments here, grant expansive views over the immediate low-rise neighborhood. The building's structure is particularly playful on the south end where it is supported by muscular V-shaped round columns that, together with the building's snake-like body and color, contribute to the perception of this whole structure as a giant caterpillar. Each apartment has one designated parking spot on the ground level to the west of the building. Northtown was designed by Ralph Johnson of Perkins&Will, the architect of several other projects in this guide, including his iconic butterfly-shaped Rush University Campus Transformation Project [051] on the Near West Side.

9

Ardmore House

1326 West Ardmore Avenue,
Edgewater
*Kwong Von Glinow Design Office
(Chicago)*
2020

🚇 To Bryn M
🚌 36 to Broadway & Ardmore; 84 to
Ridge & Glenwood

Ardmore House is named after the avenue it sits on in the central part of the
Edgewater neighborhood on Chicago's
North Side. It owes a lot of the quality of
its appearance to the L-shaped service alley that hugs it along two of its edges—
short on the northern end and long on the
western side. It is this gap to the west of
the site, which resulted in a 50-foot space
between it and any other building along
the alley, that attracted the husband-
and-wife architectural duo of Lap Chi
Kwong and Alison Von Glinow (he is originally from Hong Kong and she grew up
in the northern suburb of Lake Forest) to
the teardown that once occupied the site.
Where others saw mainly disadvantages,
namely the lack of privacy and additional noise from passing cars, the Harvard-
trained and former Herzog & de Meuron
apprentices saw a unique challenge. To
realize the project, they acted not only as designers but also as their own contractors and homeowners. Moreover, they
moved their practice here—Kwong Von
Glinow Design Office, which they founded in 2017. // The house, which may appear
ordinary at first glance, is in fact full of
surprises and inventions. Its simplified,
largely traditional bulk, clad in a dark
color palette of finishes, sits on a rectangular footprint under a standard pitched
roof. The off-the-street entry door is accessed by a narrow, single flight of open
stairs. Ribbons of windows wrap around
the second floor. What is very unusual
here is how the house is organized within. There is a twist, or two twists to be precise. First, the entire interior is rotated 90
degrees. Instead of a typical succession of
rooms, visitors enter into a double-height
curved atrium (the curve is a segment of
an imaginary circle) that runs lengthwise
from the front door to the back door. The
architects call this sliced space an interior
courtyard. It is an informal multi-purpose
relax-play area with reading nooks and
bookshelves. Immediately upon enter-
ing, you notice that the house is reorient-
ed in an east-west direction, with the line
of symmetry falling right in the center of
its long west wall where there is a 7-by-
10-foot (2-by-3-meter) mullion-free,

clear glass picture window. What seems to be the sidewall from the outside, suddenly turns into the front façade from within, with the central window acting as a visual entry. Interestingly, at 56 feet (17 meters) this façade is among the widest single-family front elevations in Chicago. // The second twist is a sectional flip of the two main floors. There are three bedrooms with two in-between bathrooms on the first floor, right off the atrium. The family living space is on the second floor, accessed by a semi-enclosed stair. The upstairs is a succession of unpartitioned spaces—a living room, dining room, kitchen, kitchen island, and the only enclosure, a small island powder room. These zones are demarcated by the unevenly spaced solid triangles of the structural trusses above. These divisions in the cathedral ceiling allow for slightly different atmospheres and lighting qualities within each zone. Here, in a beautiful light-filled room, you are surrounded by wide panoramic windows on all four sides. Especially noteworthy is a long 'smile' of picket railing and two ribbon windows. One runs the full length of the alley façade and opens on the informal backyards of the neighboring houses—balconies, fire escapes, streetlamps, and meandering cabling. The street-wall window, also from side to side, frames century-old tree crowns. // The two above-mentioned floors sit on top of a partially sunken basement, which is the couple's workspace. Plenty of daylight enters through several medium-sized square windows along the avenue side and the alley 'front'. There is a restrained palette of colors and materials throughout the house—white walls and white oak wood floors, built-in cabinetry, window frames, shelving, and furniture. The basement is built of poured-in-place concrete, while the rest is a wood-frame construction. Externally, the cladding reflects the making of the house. The unfinished concrete base is followed by a treated-wood exterior façade system. The bottom half of the first floor is clad in gray wood, while black wood lines the rest, including two identical canopies at both ends. // The house is the architects' manifesto of sorts. It is an exemplary case study that poses some of the most fundamental questions about its relationship to the surrounding context and the internal family space structure. Curiously, the project has an intriguing resemblance to Robert Venturi's famed 1964 Vanna Venturi House in Philadelphia, particularly in its wide axis primary orientation, play with symmetry, as well as reliance on employing curves, niches, and irony, of course.

9

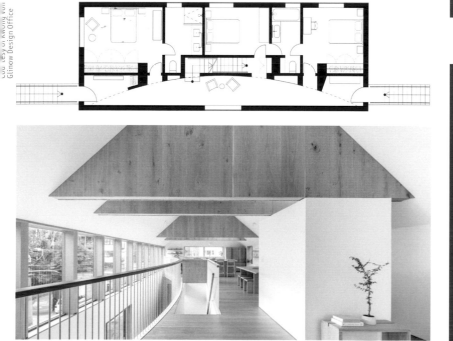

10

092   **Northeastern Illinois University, El Centro Campus**
093   **United Airlines Terminal & O'Hare CTA Station, O'Hare International Airport**

Northeastern Illinois University, El Centro Campus

3355 North Drake Avenue, Avondale
JGMA (Chicago)
2015

To Belmont
82 to Kimball & Avondale/Henderson

Vibrantly colored and intriguingly twisted and truncated, the boomerang-shaped object that landed in 2015 just off the eastern edge of the Kennedy Expressway in northwest Chicago's Avondale neighborhood is called El Centro. Motorists see this dynamic structure as a rhythmic array of dark blue vertically-angled painted fins on their way to O'Hare International Airport. Heading back towards downtown, they see the opposite sides of the fins, which are painted a golden yellow. The chameleon is the first component in a satellite campus for Northeastern Illinois University (NEIU). Its main campus lies less than three miles due north from here. Programs housed in El Centro provide educational, career, and cultural opportunities primarily, though not exclusively, to the local Latino community. The sculptural form responds to both its location and NEIU's desire to advertise its programs within as a kind of three-dimensional billboard. The attention-grabbing structure uses its fins to succeed both visually and acoustically. The structure celebrates the university's colors, helps divert direct noise from the expressway's roaring traffic, and effectively diffuses the intensity of the setting western sun. According to students, the building's interiors are surprisingly quiet. The colors stand out strongly in Chicago's predominantly monochromatic urban fabric and are associated well with the local Latino community. // The building's designer, Juan Gabriel Moreno, the founder of JGMA, is well known for his bold forms and colors, as exemplified by two of his other buildings in this guide: Daley College Manufacturing, Technology & Engineering Center [099] and SOS Children's Villages Illinois [053], both in the southwest of the city. // Inside, the building demonstrates a similarly robust and fluid geometry in the double-height multi-purpose lobby, glazed hallways, object-like stairs, informal seating areas, and entry-level security desk, which are all sculpted as fully integrated elements of the overall energy flow. There is a two-level library and resource center, a reading room with city views, a Latino community center, a student lounge, and a lush green outdoor terrace. Fully-glazed, single-loaded corridors on the highway side act as a sound barrier in front of the classrooms stacked on the second and third floors. A linear gallery within the solid portion at the building's base houses the university's art collection. // This review could end here, but a noteworthy controversy lurks over this all-in-all good building. After it earned an award from the Chicago chapter of the American Institute of Architects, it was revealed that the architect's submission package included photos that were digitally edited. Bulky air-cooling equipment haphazardly stacked on the sleek building's roof was removed from the photos commissioned by the architect. Would the jury uphold their decision had they known about this? In any case, Moreno admitted that these units were far larger than he anticipated and that options for screening them 'had proved prohibitively expensive', as he put it. In other words, the unsightly part of the building remains unfinished, at least for now.

Photos: Tom Rossiter

United Airlines Terminal & O'Hare CTA Station, O'Hare International Airport

093 A

10000 W O'Hare Avenue, O'Hare
International Airport
Murphy/Jahn (since 2012, JAHN, Chicago)
1986, 1984

🚇 To O'Hare
Shuttle buses to O'Hare from Downtown
and Metra Station

Unlike most older airports, whose designs were based on railroad and bus stations with high-ceilinged ticketing areas and modestly-scaled gates, the United Airlines Terminal was the first to reverse this hierarchy in its admirable attempt to celebrate the immediate arrival and departure experience. The most successful of these later terminals is arguably the Richard Rogers-designed Barajas Airport (2006) in Madrid, Spain, with its straightforward linear diagram and a clear progression of spaces for departing and arriving passengers. Here at the United Terminal, these grand processional spaces are memorable for their unique triumphal steel frame and glass arcades leading to and from the gates. Over the years, the asymmetrical arches adorned by perforated, white-painted, straight and curved steel beams have become iconic. This elaborate high-tech look that contributes so much to the airport's overall futuristic atmosphere symbolizes the experience of arriving in Chicago. There is something powerful, even celebratory about this design that evokes the grand European railroad stations, which were in fact the main inspiration for the terminal's architect Helmut Jahn, who grew up in Germany, but whose acclaimed professional career kicked off in Chicago. Throughout the concourse, 50-foot-high (15-meter-high) skylights and vaulted corridors provide plenty of daylight. They stir up the romance of travel.//In our interview, the late architect said he designed the profile of the iconic 'broken' arch intuitively and surely would have done it differently if he had more experience. He said: 'Now I think that that roof with an arch and a straight kink is something like high-tech baroque. Architecture is about space and light, but I prefer when form follows force rather than function.' Nevertheless, O'Hare is a powerful design statement. Its visual symbolism is as exhilarating as spaces inside Jahn's Thompson Center [001] in the Loop, which was designed around the same time. To

get the full Jahn experience at O'Hare, visit his CTA Blue Line station that terminates at the airport and the underground tunnel between the B (landside terminal) and C (satellite terminal) concourses, which features a dazzling display of color, sound, and light that transcends the typical tunnel experience. // The Chicago Transit Authority's O'Hare station on the Blue Line is Chicago's westernmost station and terminus. Constructed beneath the existing airport parking structure, the station is attached directly to a pedestrian concourse that links it to the airport hotel and Terminals 1, 2, and 3. The long station measures 600 feet (183 meters) in length, 70 feet (20 meters) in width, and 30 feet (9 meters) in height. It contains three tracks and two island passenger platforms. Large post-tensioned concrete girders bridge this broad space overhead in their gutsy effort to transfer the load of the parking structure across the station's entire width, enabling the platforms to be entirely free of columns. There is a strong sense of horizontal movement conveyed by side waves— full-height glass block walls on both sides. This dynamic notion is heightened by the changing transparency of the glass and the use of soft colored light behind

it. The lights are white, while the color comes through from brightly illuminated painted pipes, ducts, and concrete walls on the other side of the glass. // The tunnel mentioned earlier is often described as the most memorable experience at O'Hare. Four moving walkways grouped in the center take passengers through the 744-foot-long (227-meter-long) light sculpture entitled *Sky's the Limit* designed by California artist Michael Hayden. This computer-operated, zealously theatrical installation erupts with continuously changing rainbow neon color lights abundantly covering wavy sidewalls and canopies and phosphorescent glass tubes floating overhead and reflected in the mirrored ceiling. This parade of visual whimsy is synchronized with music. Jahn's intention here was, of course, to cheer up arriving and departing visitors who otherwise would have to drag themselves through a windowless corridor for at least two minutes. Responses are mixed. While many accept the discotheque-like experience as an upbeat distraction, others have grown tired of it over the years and now go as far as avoiding it altogether by switching to a different airline when they can. Either way, to see it you will need a ticket on a United Airlines flight!

10

A dazzling display of color, sound, and light, the 744-foot-long (227-meter-long) light sculpture entitled *Sky's the Limit* at the tunnel between the United Airlines Terminal B (landside terminal) and C (satellite terminal) concourses

Photo: Rainer Viertlböck

10

093 A

Northern Suburbs: Evanston, Wilmette, Glencoe, and Skokie

Northern Suburbs

11

094   Lipton Thayer Brick House
095   Gillson Park Beach House
096   Writers Theatre
097   Holocaust Memorial Foundation of Illinois

Photo: Marty Peters

Lipton Thayer Brick House

094 A

2600 Thayer Street, Evanston
Brooks + Scarpa (Los Angeles)
2018

Metra To Central Street then CTA Buses: 201, 206 to Central Street & McDaniel

When people pass this unusual mid-block house on the south side of Thayer Street in northern Evanston, it is not quite clear what exactly draws their attention so intently. Are they intrigued by its façade's dynamically assembled brickwork? Or the spaces that are unexpectedly revealed through it? What is visible from the street is merely a sand-colored box—an open-top rectangular container with brick cladding on all sides. There is an L-shaped two-story glass house inside with a spacious courtyard in the northeast corner. It is the front wall that gets all the attention. Try to move one way or another and the entire surface will start dissolving by opening and closing with vertical strips of spaces behind it. The moiré-like pattern is not repetitive, so there is a lot of dynamism here. What visitors are looking at is an array of twisted columns of bricks threaded onto hidden steel rebar like kebabs on skewers. These full-height, slender columns are braced horizontally every couple of feet from the courtyard side. The steel frame is only visible when viewed straight ahead, but disappears entirely from most angles, adding a sense of mystery and even thrill at the thought of how the whole thing can possibly support itself. // The house was designed by Lawrence Scarpa and Angela Brooks, a husband-and-wife team of architects from Los Angeles-based Brooks+ Scarpa. Their work is known for experimenting with sleek volumes and surfaces that often fracture, break apart, disintegrate, engage with the program, the sun, and explore how to bring a sense of movement into architecture. Brick is their fascination here. They particularly liked the so-called Chicago 'common brick', known for its color irregularities and imperfections. Ironically, these are qualities that long made it unpopular with homeowners. The architects saw it as their challenge to use a prosaic building material to achieve something special and beautiful. It worked twofold. The multi-angled brickwork absorbs light beautifully. This hand-sculpted, almost baroque foil turns the house into a delightful interplay of continuously shifting geometric patterns of light and shadows. // The garden in front plays along quite fittingly with a full-width field of wheat spikelets cut by a diagonal shortcut entry passage that disappears from the frontal view. Together they work quite well. There is something rough, candid, and earthy about this juxtaposition with a profound sense of domesticity, which somehow turns into something quite urban, polished, and refined once you pass the façade and get in front of the see-through house. At night, the dwelling transforms quite beautifully, creating an appealing glow from within.

Gillson Park Beach House
101 Lake Avenue, Wilmette
*Woodhouse Tinucci Architects
(Chicago)*
2019

095 **A**

🚇 To Linden

The strikingly graceful, serpent-like Gillson Beach House is just a few blocks north of Linden, the final stop on the CTA's Purple Line, immediately above Chicago's northern suburb of Evanston and barely 100 feet (30 meters) from the shoreline of Lake Michigan near Wilmette Harbor. Stretched in a relaxed wavy posture on the edge between Gillson Park and a white sandy beach, this public facility comprises restrooms, concessions, and a lifeguard station. The designers are Chicago-based Woodhouse Tinucci Architects, the same firm that modernized the University of Chicago's Keller Center [080]. They used sand dunes and a classic dune fence as an obvious but effective design inspiration. The ingenuity of this project is in its elemental composition and attractive materials. The architects placed park and beach amenities inside simplified volumes made of durable in-situ light-colored concrete patterned with vertical wood board strips. These 'rooms' are pulled apart to leave plenty of space for in-between walkways and seating and are linked by a continuous curvilinear roof and back wall on the park side. Both roof and wall are assembled from widely-spaced weathered larch, supported by a non-intrusive light steel frame that makes the wood trellis look like it is hovering without any visible support. The effect is amplified as one moves along and around this highly dynamic structure, which constantly surprises with its ever-changing play of shadow patterns. There is a large parking lot right in front of it, also designed by Woodhouse Tinucci. The see-through beach house allows an uninterrupted visual connection between the beach, parking, and park. A short walk from here, and visible right from the beach, is the Bahá'í House of Worship. Completed in 1953, it is one of only seven Bahá'í temples in the world.

Serpent-like Gillson Park Beach House stretches in a relaxed wavy posture on the edge between Gillson Park and a white sandy beach on Lake Michigan. View from the north.

11

Writers Theatre
325 Tudor Court, Glencoe
Gang Studio (Chicago)
2016

096 **A**

Metra Union Pacific/North Line to Glencoe

🚌 213 to Green Bay Rd & Park Ave

Situated in the heart of Glencoe, a northern suburb of Chicago, the Writers Theatre is designed like a compact village—a cluster of interconnected buildings. The award-winning professional theater troupe was founded in 1992 and dubbed 'America's finest regional theater company' by the *Wall Street Journal*. The theater's new home was designed by Jeanne Gang of Studio Gang and sits directly across the street from the Metra station, which is a 40-minute train ride from the Ogilvie Transportation Center [044] in the West Loop Gate. Situated in a park zone and surrounded by single-family houses, the building is entered from Tudor Court. It faces a commercial block with small restaurants, art galleries, banks, stationery stores, and beauty salons. The two-story structure with the top floor projected out and wrapped in thin crisscrossed wood members, which evoke shoelaces or more aptly, vintage typewriter typebars or strikers, marks the theater's lobby. It is surely the most appealing and intriguing part of the complex, at least architecturally, both on the outside and within. The double-height, glazed space contains informal stair-stepped seating areas (one of them doubles as a concessions area in the back) and is designed to accommodate multiple uses, including informal performances, talks, and community events for up to 350 guests. Sliding glass doors dissolve the east side and seamlessly connect the lobby with the adjacent park. // The second-floor space with the aforementioned striker-like members is the luminous outdoor Grand Gallery Walk, which is suspended around and over the atrium. It is nicknamed the 'canopy walk', hovering as it does above the sidewalk at the same height as the tree crowns. Theatergoers are welcome to stroll here before and after performances. In addition to interesting views both

Photos: Steve Hall, Hedrich Blessing Photographers

inside and out, the structure itself is of interest. This gallery is structured by great timber trusses with an elegant assembly—a delicate lattice of cedarwood battens supporting the lower beams by using flared wedge fastener connections dubbed 'cat's paws'. These peculiar details were developed by Studio Gang in collaboration with craftsmen and timber specialists. The lobby's main design concept was to expose the theater's connection to the life of the local community. This connection is celebrated through the transparency and flexibility of the gathering spaces and their availability for the community. The complex comprises a 255-seat three-quarter thrust stage theater, a 99- to 200-seat traditional black box space with innovative staging and seating configurations, rehearsal spaces, a lounge, a rooftop terrace, and offices. At night, when the building is lit from within, it glows like a lantern.

11

Holocaust Memorial Foundation of Illinois

9603 Woods Drive, Skokie
Stanley Tigerman McCurry Architects (Chicago)
2009

097 A

To Dempster-Skokie then CTA Buses: 54A, 97

The Illinois Holocaust Museum & Education Center is situated in sub-urban Skokie on the edge of northern Chicago. Surrounded by single-family houses, a high-rise condominium complex, and parkland, the building's main façades face the I-94 highway that zips by just about 30 feet (9 meters) to the east. The museum was founded in 1981 in response to a neo-Nazi group's 1977 attempt to march through Skokie, where many Holocaust survivors had settled—reportedly 7,000 at the time, the largest per-capita concentration outside Israel. More than half of Skokie's population is Jewish. After battling this provocation in the courts, which involved the US Supreme Court, a rally ultimately took place the following year at Federal Plaza in downtown Chicago in the name of the observance of the First Amendment in America. // The museum originally occupied a small storefront on Main Street. Its mission statement, to 'remember the past and transform the future, and

to preserve the legacy of the Holocaust by honoring the memories of those who were lost, and by teaching universal lessons that combat hatred, prejudice, and indifference', was the starting point for the new building's architect, Stanley Tigerman, who was born in Chicago to a Jewish family originally from Hungary. He chose storytelling, a Post-Modernist design strategy, as the main representation approach for this emotionally-charged project. // Just like the other Tigerman-designed projects featured in this guide, particularly his Self Park in the Loop [006], the Holocaust Museum is rich in symbolism and specific messages that it intends to send to visitors and passers-by. The museum is split into two similarly-scaled but distinctly designed steel- and aluminum-clad wings—one 'dark' and the other 'light', reflecting on the story of the Holocaust, which is embedded in the building's design. Going through the building is a one-way progression, a linear journey, just like in real life. Visitors enter through the 'dark' angular building where there is no daylight, and move down a gentle slope to learn the dark history of the Holocaust, reaching the 'hinge' between the two wings. It symbolizes the rupture in humanity that occurred. From that point, visitors start their ascent towards daylight. The 'light' wing symbolizes reflection and intolerance toward crimes

against all people. In fact, the museum educates about genocide beyond the Holocaust. The inaccessible in-between space between the two wings houses the centerpiece artifact: a vintage 1934 German railcar—the type used to transport millions of Jews to concentration camps. It was brought here from Germany in one piece and installed before the rest of the building was constructed around it. It is the most powerful moment in the exposition, representing 'ineffability'. Exposed piping, ducts, conduits, and concrete blocks throughout the interiors define permanent exhibition spaces and reflect on German industrialization. // On the building's front, the two wings come together to form the cleave marked by two wireframe torch-like objects. They represent two columns from the First Temple or Solomon's Temple, as described in the Bible—with the exact height, diameter, and space between. They no longer guard anything; they are just outlines or ghosts of the real columns. The two hinged wings have a particular orientation that is not directly related to its immediate site. The 'dark' wing is oriented six degrees towards the West Wall in Jerusalem, while the 'light' wing faces due east in anticipation of a Messianic age. The central cylindrical feature above the roof is crowned by six candle-like objects that symbolize six million murdered Jews. // The museum contains exhibitions, an art gallery, an education center, an auditorium, and a library. The upper level of the building's light side houses reflective spaces, including a memorial, the Book of Remembrance surrounded by soaring walls etched with the names of Holocaust victims, and the Hall of Reflection, with 12 seats representing Israel's tribes. The use of symbolism signifies an act of defiance to those who would contemplate the elimination of any culture and its history. It was the Skokie controversy that ignited a passion for the creation of the US Holocaust Memorial Museum in Washington, D.C. When the museum's new building opened in Skokie in 2009, former President Bill Clinton, who opened the Washington museum in 1993, was the keynote speaker.

11

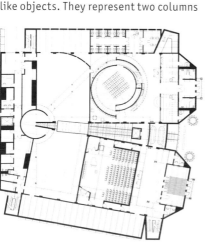

Courtesy of Stanley Tigerman McCurry Architects

The Hall of Reflection with 12 seats representing Israel's tribes at the upper level of the building's 'light' wing

11

12

098   Chicago Park District Headquarters
099   Daley College Manufacturing, Technology & Engineering Center
100   Ford Calumet Environmental Center

Rendering: John Ronan Architects

**Chicago Park District
Headquarters** ↑
4800 South Western Avenue,
Brighton Park
John Ronan Architects (Chicago)
Under construction; occupancy in 2023

098 D

🚇 To Western

🚌 48. 49, 94 to Western Orange Line
Station; 47 to 47th Street & Western
Avenue; 51 to 51st Street & Western
Avenue

After spending two decades in its
Streeterville location, the Chicago Park
District Headquarters will move to a massive new 17-acre (7-hectare) campus now
under construction in the Brighton Park
neighborhood on the Southwest Side.
The headquarters will encompass a two-story, pancake-like building designed
by Chicago architect John Ronan. He located his creation at the eastern end of
the site and extended the park's pathway
right through the building, splitting it into two similarly sized halves. The zigzagging passage forms two central open-air
courtyards, bringing light and air into the
large building's core. The split building
will house the agency's administrative offices and the park's fieldhouse with a slew
of amenities open to the public, including a fitness center and multi-purpose
rooms. There will be numerous outdoor
meeting and recreation spaces for headquarters and fieldhouse staff. While the
split divides the offices and fieldhouse
on the ground floor, the second-floor
headquarters' offices extend over the
fieldhouse and have views into the fitness center below. While the building's
circumference is almost entirely glazed,

and the upper floor is wrapped by a delicate metal shading screen like a frilly
skirt, many of the split's interior walls are
clad in recycled brick that came from demolished buildings in the area. // The rest
of the campus will feature two artificial-turf athletic fields, a grand lawn, a nature
play area, a playground, a spray pool, and
parking for hundreds of cars and bicycles. The new park zone is being built over
the reclaimed industrial property where
the city has already undertaken environmental clean-up work and capped the
area with a layer of clean soil. The Park
District, which is a separate agency from
the City of Chicago, manages more than
600 parks, 27 beaches, 230 fieldhouses,
78 public pools, dozens of sports and recreational facilities, several boat harbors,
two botanical conservatories, a zoo, and
11 museums. The headquarters is expected to be completed by late 2023.

**Daley College Manufacturing,
Technology & Engineering
Center** ↗→
7500 South Pulaski Road,
West Lawn
JGMA (Chicago)
2019

099 A

🚌 67 to 76th Street & Daley College; 390
to Richard J. Daley College

The state-of-the-art Daley College Manufacturing, Technology & Engineering
Center (MTEC) is an unusual-looking addition to the main Daley College building in the West Lawn neighborhood on
the Southwest Side. The new structure
hooks up to the southeast corner of the
conventional older building, and then

Photo: Tom Rossiter, courtesy of JGMA

rises to the second-floor level and turns into a bridge that diagonally crosses over West 76th to position itself casually on a long rectangular site across the street. The new facility houses a high-bay manufacturing space, labs, classrooms, administrative offices, and communal areas for students who are here to obtain the skills and training needed for highly specialized, technology-oriented careers. // The center was designed by Juan Gabriel Moreno, who founded his architectural practice JGMA in Chicago in 2010. Born and raised in Colombia and trained at California State Polytechnic University, Moreno has developed a visually-dynamic language of architecture by utilizing sleek angular geometry and high-tech materials, often expressed in bright colors. These choices are highly appropriate here. The architect was inspired by the students' pursuit of manufacturing careers as a sophisticated and high-tech learning path. The building evokes a conveyer belt that snakes eagerly across and over the site, which was entirely featureless before this new structure. The resulting fluid form can be likened to the non-stop linear flow of the manufacturing process. There is transparency everywhere to showcase machines, equipment, and manufactured products. The manufacturing industry is celebrated with metal panels, exposed steel, glass, and extensive areas of bright yellow, orange, and red. The pedestrian bridge is intentionally oversized to accommodate plenty of informal gathering spaces for students. Architecture is an organic thing here—playful, vivid, and engagingly educational. The exterior is distinguished by sculptural, wavy patterns of gill-like features appearing and disappearing along the sleek metallic façades.

Photo: Tom Rossiter, courtesy of JGMA

12

Ford Calumet Environmental Center
11555 South Stony Island Avenue, South Deering
Valerio Dewalt Train (Chicago)
2021

100 A

Parking is available on site

The industrial-looking design of this small environmental center reflects the history of its site—a former dumping ground for slag from nearby steel mills. The building is the center point of the 280-acre (113-hectare) Big Marsh Park that opened in 2016 on the southeast side of Chicago. It includes a 40-acre (16-hectare) bike park and walking trails. Completed in 2021, the education hub serves as a gateway to eco-recreation opportunities throughout the region. The building is a mass timber structure made up of a single-story rectangular volume entirely clad in a rain screen of Corten steel and topped by a pair of large binocular-like rooftop light monitors lined in exposed nail-laminated timber. These two perching and deeply projected elements embrace the entry below and effectively double the height of the exhibition space within. In addition, this open-plan, daylight-flooded exhibit hall is distinguished by glue-laminated beams and comprises classrooms, offices, restrooms, storage, and a bike repair area. Ten-foot (3-meter) floor-to-ceiling square windows are punched into all four sides of the building. Large hydraulically operated hangar doors made of steel hinge downwards to fit flush with the exterior wall, covering windows to secure the facility when it is closed. The doors' perforated metal screens preserve visibility to the interior. When raised, these door-canopies not only provide shade, but also block reflections from above to ensure that birds do not fly into the glass.

12

Illustrations: Natascha Meuser

Stanley Tigerman:
'I am an American Architect. I am a Hybrid'

Architect's Chicago office
17 April 2012

Stanley Tigerman (1930–2019) was born in Edgewater, a lakefront community area on the North Side of Chicago. His start in architecture was as hurried as it was irrational. He left MIT after just one year, apprenticed with Chicago architect George Fred Keck for one year, and then rushed to open his own practice, which quickly failed. He then spent four years in the US Navy, serving in the Korean War. After returning to Chicago, Tigerman worked for several years at top local offices such as Skidmore, Owings & Merrill and Harry Weese and then was accepted to the Yale School of Architecture graduate program under Paul Rudolph, even though he never earned his bachelor's degree. He established his own practice upon graduating in 1961 and combined that with his position as the American correspondent of *L'architecture d'aujourd'hui*. He then worked for a decade in Bangladesh. Tigerman rose to prominence in the mid-1970s when he boldly undermined the then undisputed authority of mid-twentieth century modernism, particularly modeled on how Mies saw it, which by then had turned into a religion-like dogma with a widespread following. The young architect played a crucial role in forming the first-generation Post-Modernist group of architects in Chicago that went into the history books as the Chicago Seven. From 1986 onwards, the practice he led with his third wife, Margaret McCurry, was called Tigerman McCurry. The architect was a prolific writer and actively involved in teaching. He was director of the University of Illinois Chicago School of Architecture from 1985 until 1993 when he was let go because of his outspokenness. In 1994, Tigerman co-founded ARCHEWORKS with designer Eva Maddox as an independent architecture school with a focus on progressive, socially-oriented design. The architect designed hundreds of memorable projects, over 200 of which were realized. This guide features four: Self Park in the Loop, the Anti-Cruelty Society in River North, the Holocaust Museum in Skokie, and his 1978 Library for the Blind, which opens the Post-Modernist chapter in Chicago's architectural history as the earliest building in this book. Tigerman was one of 20 architects to participate in the 1980 seminal exhibition *La Strada Novissima* at the 1st International Architecture Biennale in Venice. Tigerman's drawing archive was transferred to Yale University's Manuscripts and Archives depository in 2012.

I would like to start with your current exhibition at the Graham Foundation. It marks the 2012 transfer of your drawing archive to Yale University's Manuscripts and Archives depository. Could you talk about this archive and your passion for drawings?
I am an 81-year-old architect and like architects of my generation such as Peter Eisenman, Frank Gehry, John Hejduk, and all my peers, we have to draw. Architecture has to be drawn. I studied at Yale under Paul Rudolph and I had to draw a lot. I was also a painter and studied with Josef Albers, so drawing is my passion. I'm still drawing.

Stanley Tigerman (1930–2019)

Your website says that your office is committed to the creation of a contemporary and authentically American architecture that is characteristic of its own time and place. Could you explain what you mean by authentically American?

America is a hybrid. This is not our home, unless you are a Native American. For example, you are from Ukraine and my grandparents came from Hungary. Nobody is from here. So, you are automatically alienated here. I wrote a book called *The Architecture of Exile* on this subject.

Wouldn't you say there is such a thing as distinctly American architecture that originated here?

There are no American architectural symbols; the technology—yes, of course, that's what Mies understood so well. But for symbolism, we have to look elsewhere. For example, Post-Modernism was an American movement because we are hybrid and Post-Modernism is a hybrid movement. It's not authentic.

At Yale you studied under Paul Rudolph. You said he was a fabulous teacher. What was it that you learned from him the most?

He was very tough. You have no idea ... During the time I studied with him, one student committed suicide and many ended up on psychiatrists' couches. He was brutal, but he was a great teacher and he demanded no more from his students than from himself. Rudolph was a great role model. When he told me to do something,

it was what he did himself. In one week, he demanded sections, perspectives, models in a big scale and a small scale ... I worked for him, often until the early morning, but I saw him in action, and he worked just as hard or harder than any of us.

Architecture is a very difficult pursuit. You have to be strong to get something built. We had a meeting today here and everybody was trying to put obstacles in front of me. Why? Because I'm trying to do something that's never been done before. And there's always resistance to that—inertia. Try building even a little cottage in a virgin forest and the environmentalists will go against you because you're building something that wasn't intended to be there. So making a new building requires great strength, immense will, fortitude, and belief. Architecture is for tough guys. Everything stands in the way—clients, developers, engineers ... John Hejduk said it all: 'The closer the finished building is to the original drawing, the better the building is.' But it's very hard to do that because buildings get attacked and often lose their poetic content.

In your own work, what have you attempted to do that was never done before?

Ironic buildings—buildings with a sense of irony. The retrospective at the Graham Foundation you mentioned was curated by Emmanuel Petit, who organized all the texts, sketches, cartoons, architectural drawings, and models in relation to themes such as Utopia, Allegory, Humor, Death, (Dis)Order, Identity, and Drift.

097 A

A vintage 1934 German railcar, the type used to transport millions of Jews to concentration camps, placed at the inaccessible in-between space between the two wings of the Holocaust Memorial Foundation of Illinois in Skokie

Why do you think it is important for architecture to possess qualities such as humor and irony?
Well, one of the things you try to do as an architect is to bring pleasure to people. Humor is a part of pleasure. And if I've done anything, that is probably what I'll be remembered for.

What is the most successful project that you have done so far that conveys this notion?
The next one.

Still, looking back, could you pick a particular project and tell me what's ironic about it?

Hejduk wrote in my book that in order to be a good architect you have to do at least one building that has an aura. His words, not mine. And he felt that I have done several buildings that have that quality: The Black Barn at Frog Hollow and my own house in Lakeside, Michigan, are two of those buildings. There is a certain quality in my work that John understood.

What were his exact words?
I don't have them memorized ... Here, why don't you read them from my book *The Architecture of Exile*?

'I am drawn to architecture that gives off an aura. An aura is a difficult atmosphere to define, but as rarely as it occurs, we know when we are in the presence of architecture, drawing, or person that gives off a sense ... Stanley Tigerman is an American architect not in exile but very much at home. The Black Barn at Frog Hollow, with its white swans floating upon the murky catfish pond as organ sounds emanate from the barn, emits an aura of antiquity and of a stillness across an American landscape ... To be named an architect at least one of your works must have an aura. Stanley is an architect.' These words are very precious to me.

You said: 'An architect molds his epoch, rather than reflects it.' What did you mean by that?

Mies said: 'Architecture is the will of an epoch translated into space.' On the other hand, an architect often tells the client or society: 'Come this way—I'll show you a better way!' So sometimes architecture mirrors society and sometimes it leads the way. So one is torn between the two all the time.

You were a founding member of the Post-Modernist Chicago Seven group that started in 1976. What were its main intentions and what is the legacy of the group?

You have to imagine that time. Mies died in 1969. The Miesians, his followers, took over Chicago, and most modern buildings were built as Mies would do them—with the expression of the structural grid. There was no room for anything else. There was no room for people like me or anyone who was not a follower of Mies. So, we did a book on Chicago architects and a show, which debuted at Cooper Union thanks to Hejduk. Then it was shown in Chicago. And unlike the New York Five or Grays, we were not cohesive. We were working in all possible directions. We weren't even good friends. But we wanted to open the city up because it wasn't open to us. We wanted to open it to the next generation.

At the 1980 Venice Biennale, you took part in *The Presence of the Past* exhibit curated by Paolo Portoghesi. What was that like?

The disaster. There is an old proverb: He who walks in another's footprints leaves no mark. What happened there was a re-emergence of the past, namely the Classicism. My purpose was to experiment with the hybridization of architecture, which is so fit for America. But movement toward Classicism—that's a disaster because nothing new is created and that's a problem. In my own project, I was theatrical. It was a façade with a drapery behind which was my work—I was working at the American Academy in Rome then. The work was about irony. It was the theater of the absurd.

There was a split within Post-Modernism with one group pursuing a more literal, classical model and the other being more adventurous and inventive. Yet both groups based their work on historical models. Do you still view your work as Post-Modernist today?

I am an American architect. I am a hybrid. And I always saw architecture as hybrid art. I never saw it as either Modernist, Classical, Deconstructivist, or Post-Modernist.

What are you currently working on?

A client of mine gave me a great project. In 1958, shortly before he died, Frank Lloyd Wright designed a cottage measuring 880 square feet in a forest near a lake in Wisconsin for a postal worker. This postal worker committed suicide and didn't leave any heirs. The cottage was built and over the years it fell into disrepair and became a ruin. In the 1990s, a rich woman rowing a boat on the lake saw the cottage. She liked it and decided to buy it and restore it. She then gave it to the National Trust for Historic Preservation. Four weeks ago, a client came to me, told me this story, and said: 'I want you to design an ultimate Stanley Tigerman cottage measuring 880 square feet.' He will find a piece of land, build the cottage, and donate it to the National Trust for Historic Preservation. So, this is my dream project now. At its very center, this cottage will have an inaccessible cloister with glass on all sides. It will be inaccessible even for maintenance—a totally wild part of nature.

Helmut Jahn:
'Architecture is All About Going with Your Gut'

Architect's Chicago office
17 August 2018

Born in a small town called Zirndorf near Nuremberg in Bavaria, Germany, in 1940, Helmut Jahn graduated from the Technical University of Munich in 1966 and immigrated to the United States the following year. He was particularly keen on settling in Chicago, where he believed architectural breakthroughs were still possible. Once in Chicago, he attempted to pursue his graduate studies at the Illinois Institute of Technology (IIT), but the program proved to be too stringent for his temperament. In 1967, he left IIT in protest and joined C. F. Murphy Associates. By 1973, Jahn had assumed the role of the firm's Executive Vice President and Director of Planning and Design. He took control of the company in 1981. By then it had become Murthy/Jahn. It was renamed to simply JAHN in 2012 and operates under that name today. Among 60 architects cumulatively responsible for the 100 projects featured in this guide, Jahn is the most prolific with eight built works. He has succeeded in becoming Chicago's most eminent architect in recent times.

Jahn came to Chicago at a time when Mies's reputation was as solid as his steel buildings, but his universal language and almost cult-like following began attracting questions a few years after his death in 1969. Jahn joined the young rebellious architects of the Chicago Seven in the mid-1970s. His projects stood out for their reflection of technology and history, particularly his Manhattan Art Deco skyscrapers. His 1985 Thompson Center reinvented the government building typology. It became the closest structure to the true high-tech style ever built in America—an ecstatic spectacle of space, transparency, light, and color. His distinctive towers in Chicago, Manhattan, Philadelphia, Las Vegas, Frankfurt, Munich, Bonn, Bremen, Brussels, Warsaw, Riga, Singapore, Tokyo, Guangzhou, and Johannesburg constitute an extraordinary collection of highrises that metamorphosized dramatically from being overly expressive, even flamboyantly jazzy objects in the 1980s to more recent designs that are highly abstracted and finely chiseled buildings.

… There is so much banality that's being built these days …

Wasn't it always the case?
No, not really. Developers who would love to do buildings are no longer around. I used to know developers who loved going to a construction site and putting their boots in the mud. Now it's all about business and they don't even start before calculating the return on their investment. Constructing buildings now is all about profit-making; everything is so calculated. There is no emotion, no imagination, no invention. There are so many simplistic one-liner buildings …

I think there are architects who will always produce good buildings no matter what the circumstances may be. Let's talk about yours. Some critics call you a 'romantic modernist' and refer to your architecture as 'romantic high-tech'. And you said the following: 'We do not construct decoration; we decorate construction.' How would you define the intention of your architecture?

Helmut Jahn (1940–2021)

Well, these ideas go back to the time right after Mies, shortly after I started working at C. F. Murphy Associates, the predecessor of Murphy/Jahn, and designing my first independent buildings from the mid-1970s. Back then everyone was still working within Miesean dogmatic 'less is more' mode. So, when my early buildings started expressing structure and color, they immediately attracted attention. Then in 1980, the Xerox Center here in Chicago—the one that curves around a corner—was built. It became a real breakthrough. That led to a whole series of distinctive buildings, particularly towers in Chicago, New York, Philadelphia, and Singapore, with the 63-story Messeturm in Frankfurt becoming the most iconic. But that was just one period that led to the next one, which started in the mid-1990s.

What caused that shift and how did your work evolve after that?
I met Werner Sobek, a brilliant German architect and structural engineer. After I met him, my buildings became known for what we called Archineering: a collaboration between an architect and engineer at an early stage of design. It wasn't so much about the aesthetics, but rather about performance, how buildings are constructed, and the use of the materials. I met Sobek in 1994. Our first collaboration was on the design of the Bangkok Airport's roof. The SONY Center in Berlin followed. Sobek was the first person to tell me: 'Helmut, you cannot do this.' Now he often tells me: 'You don't need me. You know your structures.' We work very closely, and we exchange our roles all the

time—the architect thinks like a structural engineer and the engineer thinks like an architect. That collaboration produced buildings on a different kind of level. The Post Tower built in Bonn in 2003 was the marker after which the work became more restrained and refined. Architects need to push for innovation, but today it is so much harder to be inventive because there are so many ways of doing things that are already established. And most clients are afraid to run the risk of making a mistake. That's the biggest handicap in terms of making progress.

Back in the mid-1980s, you said: 'Today we don't have any accepted principles. All the rules, all the styles, are either dead or under observation as to whether they'll survive. For me, it's exciting and exhilarating. It's a kind of freedom we have to enjoy.' You don't seem to agree with this statement today. Do you still feel that all styles are dead and that there is freedom for going forward?
Unfortunately, we no longer have this freedom of possibilities, and it is not the right climate to be able to sell this attitude. Today, clients are big corporations, big banks, and big developers. They all want to be safe. They are skeptical about individuals who have an attitude toward architecture. But doing what is easy will never produce architecture that is new and progressive.

Yet there are still a number of quixotic individuals who fight against all odds.
Sure, I'm fighting, and we still get jobs, but it is much more difficult. And I don't

build as much anymore. We now have just a third of architects compared to before.

You said you are fighting for good architecture and you've been a fighter ever since you came to Chicago from Germany back in 1966.
I came to study at the IIT on a Rotary Club scholarship. One of the first assignments was to design a particular courthouse. I refused. I didn't want any constraints. Then for the course in visual training, we were asked to bring black and white paper. I brought one of each color of the rainbow and my professor said: 'This paper is not black and not white. Get the right colors.' And I said: 'I am not getting any more paper! That's not what I came here for.' [Laughs.]

What did you go there for?
I have no idea! I was just one year out of school. I was this rebellious kid. What did I know? And then George Danforth, the director of the School of Architecture at the IIT, suggested to me that I should take a part-time job at an office. That's how I started working with Gene Summers at C. F. Murphy Associates. I remember how carefully I studied drawings for some of the finished buildings at the office. Who does that anymore? Now everyone is just looking at their computer screens. And where are all the older architects with real experience? It seems that most young architects, fresh out of school, are doing all the work. But people have to learn something before they are given real responsibilities. I remember how in one of the design reviews at Yale, I was on a jury with James Stirling and one student who had a very weak project attacked me for one of my buildings. So, Jim said: 'Helmut, let me take this one.' And he tore that guy apart. He said: 'What the hell do you know about design? We know how to design. But you have to learn something.' Well, I was never a good teacher because I am not a good listener. I have no patience. [Laughs.]

Many architects compare their offices to schools. How do you teach your staff here?

I work with people who I think have the talent, so it's worthwhile to work with them. You need many people to design buildings. So, I rely on many people here. I make endless sketches and ask my designers to build numerous models. I like to think that I teach by example.

When you started your career, you were very rebellious of the Miesian approach that you saw as restrictive. Yet over the years, your work became more refined. Would you admit that his work has more relevance to you now?
I don't try to analyze my own work that way. That's for others to decide. I just go forwards. I am now designing a new tower in Berlin, the Europa Center 2, which is going to be almost three times the height of what is currently the tallest building in the city. The building is very simple, but I made dozens and dozens of models to arrive at that form. And I picked up some ideas from my previous projects. Yet you can't just carry ideas from project to project. Every skyline is different. Every project is a response to very specific conditions. Architecture is not just about pure form-giving. For example, the use of new shading systems can now be embedded into glass panels and that brings new possibilities. The process is endless. What is true about Mies is that you can only achieve excellence with less, not with more. I understood it much more when I met Sobek. Ever since we met, I've started to feel like I was going back to school. Before I was accustomed to figuring out things on my own or relying on what my engineers told me, but with him it was different. I don't just learn a solution from him; I learn the reason for the solution. He sits right next to me when we design and when I drew a truss he would say: 'This part does not want to be there.' So, the work became more responsive to structure. Look at the United Airlines Terminal One Complex at O'Hare that I did back in 1986. Sobek would never let me do that. Now I think that that roof with an arch and a straight kink is something like high-tech baroque. Architecture is about space and light, but I prefer when form follows force rather than function.

Could you comment on your Thompson Center? Now that its future is uncertain, how do you see its place in Chicago's history?

The Thompson Center was a government building turned into a public place. When it opened in 1985, it made history because it became a new public place for the city. It was a new way to integrate private space with public space. Of course, it was never a well-managed public place for political reasons. It is not even open on weekends and there are so many restrictions where people can and can't go. Still, in the future, I can imagine it being used by a private company like Google. The original idea was to open the building from every side. I started with a solid block, but I felt that the building must have a public plaza, so one day I cut the corner off on an angle and curved it to represent the traditional dome of government buildings. When we enclosed the atrium, I felt that the building lost something. That's why 15 years later while designing the SONY Center in Berlin, the atrium there became the open courtyard. I remember when the chairman of SONY viewed the model and said: 'Mr. Jahn, where are the doors?' I said: 'There are no doors.' And he said: 'But then everybody can come in.' So, I said: 'You got it!' [Laughs.] That's what we tried to do, and he never said anything else.

So, it was the Thompson Center that pushed the SONY Center?

Absolutely! SONY is the new kind of urban space for a new society and new preferences. But you can also look at history and learn from there as well. Look at the public piazza in Sienna; that's an inspiration for SONY. One project pushes the next. Then we designed a mixed-use complex with a shopping center, hotels, apartments, and entertainment for the central plaza in Dubai in 2008, but the project was stopped by the financial crisis at the time. That project would have taken SONY to a much bigger urban scale. I think the period from 1995 to 2008 was the most interesting period for my architecture. There was a good push from clients to produce exciting projects.

What you are saying is emblematic because this timeframe coincided exactly with the iconic period when clients demanded their architects build very distinctive, signature-style structures.

If you look at corporate architecture, it was always iconic. But over the last decade, clients are no longer interested in that. Look at Google or Facebook. They have suburban campuses and in New York, they occupy existing buildings. They no longer consider architecture an art form. All they want is to have a roof over their heads. And they're no longer concerned with their image. In the past, these people would wear stylish suits and now they run around in t-shirts. So many corporations no longer build new buildings; they just rent generic spaces from developers.

How can architects fight back?

Well, architecture is so difficult. It is easy to talk about it but very hard to do. You know, good architecture is all about going with your gut. You have something on your mind and you just must go ahead and do it. It's important to keep asking these questions—is it the best way of doing something? Is there another way? You can't stop searching for a better solution, just like architects did after Mies. They really thought he had achieved absolute perfection and from then on, we knew how to do architecture once and for all. But we've got to go forward!

You said: 'Transparency is not the same as looking straight through a building: it's not just a physical idea, it's also an intellectual one.' Could you elaborate on that?

Look, there is no building that's transparent. Every building has things in it. For me, transparency was always about the layers you put in. The idea is to read from one layer to the next. I also like the idea of seeing buildings differently from every side.

As you said: 'I strive for an architecture, from which nothing can be taken away.'

Anything you don't need is a benefit. Not only do you have to have fewer things, but with the things you have left, you must do more.

Adrian Smith:
'To Do Something Conventional Would Be a Complete Waste of Our Efforts'

Architect's Chicago office
7 November 2019

Adrian Smith was born in 1944 in Chicago but grew up in Southern California. He attended Texas A&M University, pursuing a Bachelor of Architecture while being involved with the Corps of Cadets. In 1967, he transferred to the University of Illinois at Chicago while apprenticing at the Chicago office of Skidmore, Owings and Merrill (SOM). He also worked at Perkins&Will for a short period. After graduating in 1969, Smith returned to SOM. He was the company's Design Partner from 1980 to 2003 and a Consulting Design Partner from 2003 to 2006. During his time at SOM, he designed many landmark buildings, becoming internationally known as the 'go-to' skyscraper architect. His creations include Burj Khalifa in Dubai, the world's tallest building since 2010, and Jeddah Tower, now under construction in Jeddah, Saudi Arabia and set to exceed the 1,000-meter mark. Other supertalls include the Jin Mao Tower (Shanghai, 1999), the Pearl River Tower (Guangzhou, 2005), and others in Chengdu, Nanjing, and Wuhan. As the architect was approaching SOM's mandatory retirement age of 65, younger partners began to emerge while his role in the company started to diminish. In 2006, Smith decided to start his own practice. He had the advantage of not needing to do it from scratch. Smith left SOM with 10 active projects and about 50 architects, including his long-time colleague Gordon Gill. Together they christened their new firm Adrian Smith + Gordon Gill Architecture. AS+GG is dedicated to the design of high-performance, energy-efficient, and sustainable architecture. At the time of this interview, it employed 70 people. The architects continue working on some of the biggest and tallest projects on the planet. They call their practice a small-large firm. Since its inception, they have completed over 50 buildings and about 20 more are under construction. AS+GG stands out in Chicago primarily as a global firm. Most of their projects are being built outside of the US—many in China, as well as in the United Arab Emirates, Kazakhstan, Canada, Saudi Arabia, and South Korea. In the US, the architects are working in Chicago, Miami, and New York. This guide includes four projects by AS+GG: the Trump Tower in River North, which was designed while the architects were still at SOM; Steppenwolf Theatre in Lincoln Park; Yard Shakespeare Theater at Navy Pier; and Chicago Architecture Center on the New Eastside. The company also designed Clean Technology Tower, a proposal for a high-performance, net-zero-energy mixed-use development designed both for a specific site in Chicago and as a prototype to demonstrate sustainable architecture principles that can be applied around the globe in the architects' efforts to push potential architectural, technological, and engineering breakthroughs.

Do you mind telling me about your responsibilities in the firm?

Adrian Smith (b. 1944)

Gordon [Gill] and I are both design partners and we design most projects jointly, as we have done since working together at SOM. Even when I was experimenting with Samsung Togok Tower in Seoul back in 1994–1995, I was working with Gordon. At that point we were already working on minimizing waste and maximizing efficiency through understanding how to utilize the 111-story height by incorporating wind turbines, photovoltaic panels, double climate-wall exterior skin systems, open-air atria for wind reduction, tapered and soft corners to mitigate vortices, and even stack effect power generation using the exterior wall cavity space as a chase. That project did not move forward, but we learned so much by exploring its potential.

You are referred to as the ultimate skyscraper architect. Is that how you see yourself?
I see myself as an architect and city planner. We see no limits either in scale or complexity. Our expertise is broad, and we believe we can meet most challenges, large or small. Skyscrapers surely define our practice. The development of this building type preoccupies over half of our time. We work hard to challenge the skyscraper typology. We continuously push the performance and functionality limits, as well as possibilities for hybrid programs. We do a lot of self-initiated research. We analyze density, energy efficiency, vertical transportation, livability,

new construction techniques and materials, and so on. We love skyscrapers—supertalls, as we call them—but what interests us most is addressing very complex urban problems. Our expertise is unique—many of our buildings are a minimum of 300 meters tall. Architecture at this height is rare and it is in this space that our practice is different from most other architects. If you look at our portfolio you will see immediately that when it comes to skyscrapers, and the amount of research that we have undertaken to engineer them, there are very few other firms in the world that can compete with us. We understand how to build very tall buildings successfully, which means that our tall buildings are not just beautiful sculptures, they are performance-driven, well-engineered, meticulously planned and programmed, self-sustaining, environmentally intelligent structures.

Is there one of your skyscraper projects that stands out for you as a particular discovery?
Clearly that would have to be Pearl River Tower in Guangzhou, China, which we designed while at Skidmore, Owings & Merrill. It defined the two key directions for us. The first is large, complex, and tall buildings and the second is on how to ensure that these buildings are outstanding performers. Pearl River Tower is a particularly strong case that works toward the zero-carbon model. The building's unique shape was derived from the behavior of

natural elements on the site and was optimized for local solar and wind patterns, harnessing energy with the help of two sets of wind turbines that integrated into two mechanical floors. Our buildings are designed based on their aerodynamic performance. We also discovered that with or without wind turbines, supertall buildings that have voids in their façades save huge amounts of money because they greatly reduce wind forces and therefore save energy to resist them. They also save costs on the materials used. These buildings must be efficient.

We started talking about high-rise construction and immediately you brought the issue of energy efficiency into the conversation. Is this the number one concern today in building high?
It is high on our list of important criteria. Carbon efficiency, the function of the building to suit its intended use, and beauty are all very important to us. We compare our buildings to a human body. The more fit you are, the healthier and more efficient you become. We don't separate aesthetics from efficiency and overall performance. So, we focus on structure, circulation, quality of light, comfort, energy efficiency, environment, and, of course, beauty, which is very important to us. We mix all these ingredients. But for many people, what is hard to understand about our practice is that we don't base our decisions on aesthetics, not primarily. They think we do because they look at our work and they see that it is beautiful. But that beauty comes from the desire to finetune our buildings and optimize performance. What we focus on is putting our buildings in the most beneficial position from a performance standpoint. It is each location that makes each piece beautiful, not the other way around. Nothing is imposed or forced by our willfulness or something that we bring from another location.

You said you are not mere sculptors, but, as soon as I walked into your office, I saw dozens of beautiful models on display—they are clearly your proud trophies. This is not an engineer's office. Anyone can pick up that message right away. All

these buildings are beautifully chiseled and not to recognize their beauty would probably offend you, is that so?
You have discovered some of our perceived contradictions, specifically from those looking at the firm from the outside. However, none of these buildings are purely sculptural. The design is driven by performance parameters. Our projects are driven by context, not just visual site conditions, but zoning envelop requirements, in other words, how much you can build on any given site, and by the environmental context. So, we deal with required setbacks, solar footprints that we can have on the surrounding existing sites and buildings. First we try to maximize our allowable gross floor area, then we try to maximize value. That's what every developer would want to achieve. The balance is the blend of performance and beauty. Zoning requirements and volumetric constraints define our massing design. Then we analyze our forms and refine them, let's say, as a series of definable arcs rather than random splines. We simplify the geometry to make our buildings easier to construct. Sure, we are architects, we work on achieving beautiful forms, but they are not arbitrary by any means. Our buildings are sculpted to meet specific criteria and they are also site-specific. They are shaped through environmental analysis. We do experiment with ideas such as skin design and we often take a particular component designed for one of our buildings and develop it further for another project.

How high can we go now? What are the limits?
Above 600 meters, the design parameters become complex. One begins to ask the question, why do you want to go beyond that height? Even Burj Khalifa's highest occupiable floor is just about 600 meters tall. Above that mark, you need to climatize the space differently and rethink vertical transportation systems. Just constructing such a tall building straight would be quite a challenge. But structurally, we think current technology can build to a mile high. The best contractors in the world think they know how to do it. Still, we are not quite there.

How would you describe what you do? What is your architecture about?

Architecture must function; it must serve people well. It must be durable. It needs to stand the test of time. It needs to be of its time technologically. It must respond and contribute to the environment in which it is placed. Architecture should be a part of the city and a part of the environment. And it must be beautiful. Yet there is always a need for rationality. Again, we are not sculptors, we are architects. Yet we love making beautiful buildings, and often we are brought to projects, especially in China or the Middle East, where clients own very large developments and they want to create a centerpiece—a landmark that gives an identity to their project or the entire city. However, we all have a need to be connected to nature. That's where most people find themselves happy. We all want to smell the sea, stand in the rain, climb the mountains. No matter what building type we work on, this question always gets addressed. The idea is to make buildings unfold, to reveal something new every time. We work directly with the forces of nature. But there are still certain aspects about tall buildings that we are still learning. It is a process. Still, we have covered many more possibilities than anyone else. We often work with different engineers and we learn a lot from them, so we know enough to ask them very specific questions, which is unusual.

You have designed buildings all over the world. How would you distinguish the character of buildings built right here in Chicago? What makes them special?

Chicago is a densely built city. It is hard to add to it on a large scale. Chicago is not New York. It is very efficient, and it is a city that connects those who come from the East to go to the West. It is a beautiful city on the water. Pragmatism and economy drive Chicago's architecture and aesthetics. It is a gridded city. It is very accessible. It is not constrained by territory like Manhattan; the land is much cheaper here. It is built on technology and cost-efficiency. We can't compete with American coastal cities. Chicago is not

as international. Yet it is a vertical city that rises above the midwestern plains so beautifully as it is approached from land, sea, and air!

What about your Trump Tower here? How do you see this building contributing to the city?

I see it as a building that mediates between two important structures: the Wrigley Building, inspired by the White City movement of the 1893 World's Columbian Exhibition, and the IBM Building by Mies, one of his best buildings. I worked with the context—the height and lightness of detail of the Wrigley Building, the rigor and depth of the IBM building exterior wall, and the curves of the nearby Marina Towers. I call this building a 'hinge' because it connects Michigan Avenue to State Street and the Loop. There are many vistas where it terminates views of streets in Chicago's Loop and the Near North Side. It aligns perfectly with North Wabash Avenue. It sits on a turn of the Chicago River, which allows for full-height views from Lake Michigan. The building has an iconic presence in the city due to its siting and its materiality.

You mentioned that you try to challenge the skyscraper typology. What is it that you aim to achieve?

When we start a project, we always ask the same question—how can we make our building special? We often present our clients with a different perspective on how to think about certain projects. We offer our vision. It is not unusual for us to present something totally different from what a client may expect. In any case, we are always pushing for something very special, yet based on deep analysis and economics. Our solutions are very sound. We will tackle anything, and our clients understand all the whys. We have common goals. We are constantly developing new ideas. If we think of an interesting idea, we initiate our own research that results in books and lectures, and when the right client comes along, we may use these ideas in our projects. We love making things. We love solving problems. We believe that to do something conventional would be a complete waste of our efforts.

Ralph Johnson of Perkins&Will: 'Our Architecture is for People'

Phone interview between New York and Chicago
28 April 2020

Ralph Johnson was born in 1948 in Chicago. He studied architecture at the University of Illinois. Ever since his student days there, he was aware of Perkins&Will, one of the biggest American architectural firms, established in his hometown in 1935. Working there was his dream and it was the main reason for him to return to Chicago after his studies. In fact, his thesis project at the University of Illinois was a real project by Perkins&Will that he analyzed and developed: a community college. After receiving his Bachelor of Architecture in 1971, Johnson was already prepared to practice architecture thanks to rigorous technical courses, but he chose to pursue his Master of Architecture at Harvard's GSD. He also worked at the office of Stanley Tigerman (1930–2019) for almost two years before going to GSD. After acquiring his second degree in 1973 at the beginning of the oil crisis, there were not many options to work on major projects. For the next few years, he helped a friend design a new town project in Florida that was never built. As before, his creative energy was focused on doing many national and international competitions that he did on his own. Some of them he won. That experience gave him enough confidence to apply to Perkins&Will as a design architect.
Johnson joined the firm in 1977. He did well over the next few years, and several of his projects were published. In 1984, his Music Center at Pacific Lutheran University in Tacoma, Washington, was on the cover of *Progressive Architecture*

(P/A) magazine. It received the top award out of 934 submissions that year, although the project remained on paper. Johnson became the firm's head designer in 1985 at a time when it had only three offices—in Chicago, New York, and Washington D.C. Over the years, Perkins&Will has grown into a major company with 25 offices, 10 of which are outside the US. Johnson is a global design director. He has designed schools, universities, hospitals, cultural institutions, and office and residential buildings all over the world. Many of his projects are among the most iconic in the firm's history. Quite a few of them are in Chicago, so it is no surprise that this guide includes seven of his buildings. They include Rush University Transformation Project on the Near West Side, Contemporaine in River North, Skybridge in the West Loop, and Northtown Library and Apartments on the Far North Side. The architect's monographs have been published regularly since the mid-1990s under his own name. Johnson has been a visiting critic at the Illinois Institute of Technology and the University of Illinois, his alma mater.

You worked at the office of Stanley Tigerman for a couple of years between your degrees. What did you learn from him?
I came to work specifically on his Instant City project—a building over a freeway. It was fantastic, although it was a theoretical project. Tigerman was one of the most creative and challenging architects to work for in Chicago at the time. Working

Ralph Johnson (b. 1948)

there was particularly exciting because he was literally connected to the whole world. He was teaching at Cooper Union in New York with John Hejduk at the time and was very engaged in discussing students' ideas and projects. Just to be able to talk to him in the office was very special. Also, he was working on the Library for the Blind at the time, which was fascinating because the building was not just based on the architect's imagination but rooted in the special nature of the problem at hand. It was a fantastic project to learn from. It was very tactile; the building itself was a kind of device to provide guidance to blind people with the help of shapes, surfaces, and bright colors.

The Chicago Seven, led by Tigerman, was active at the time. How influenced were you by their ideas and projects?
Interestingly, my father-in-law, James [Jim] Nagle was one of the original Chicago Seven architects. He also worked for Tigerman before opening his own office in the late 1960s with Larry Booth, a fellow architect at Tigerman's office and also one of the Chicago Seven. Well, it was important to start a new conversation then. Jim recalled that in the 1970s, it got to a point when you would get off an airplane, and you didn't know where you were. So, it wasn't Mies that got boring. It was the copiers that got boring. And my work is based on my strong conviction that every building should be a response to a particular condition. Every building requires its own solution. That was my lesson from the Chicago Seven group,

not the specific language that they chose to express their architecture with. The years that I spent at Harvard were dominated by Miesian ideology, so I understand the architects, such as the Chicago Seven, who revolted against it. Perhaps because of that, my position is not to carry a particular style in a body of work. It is rather about an approach—how do you address the specifics of each project and location? In any case, the Chicago Seven was a major disruption, primarily saying that we need to talk about other things, not just Mies. The Post-Modern movement somewhat undermined his importance, but it opened up the profession nevertheless. And it took a while for his reputation to come back.

In one of your interviews you said about your GSD education: 'Through my direct exposure to a number of great architects, I learned that over time you should develop your own personal approach to architecture.' Do you still believe that?
Sure, but it takes time to get to that level. In my case, this was a process of working for a number of people and doing a lot of competitions, which I did from the very beginning on the side. And very successfully. For example, I did the Pahlavi National Library Competition, a one-million-square-foot building in Tehran. I literally did it out of my kitchen. Out of 600 entries, my project was among the 10 finalists. I was competing against great architects such as Alison and Peter Smithson. Then I was invited to Iran for

the awards ceremony. At the time, I was in my late twenties and had done a very extensive presentation. They thought I was probably SOM or someone like that, because of my high-quality presentation. That competition was won by GMP from Germany, but the whole project abruptly ended with the fall of the Shah in 1979. I also took part in the Roosevelt Island competition. I did the Biscayne Housing competition in the Miami area that I won out of more than 100 entries. Many of them were ideas competitions. Still, for me, participating in architectural competitions was the process of evolving as an architect in search of my personal approach, my own path.

You often work by sketching alone—on planes and at hotels. Could you touch on that?
Every one of my projects starts with a sketch that would point to the main idea. I have a hands-on approach and before meeting with the team I have to spend some time alone to figure out a particular direction. I know that some architects would ask their teams to do five schemes and then they start the critique and choose and pick. My approach starts with my sketches; this is how I have always worked. And it could be just one scheme or more, but I am the one who would make that decision.

How would you describe what you do as an architect? What is your architecture about?
It is about making responsible and responsive buildings that reflect social and environmental concerns. The essence for me is to create humanistic environments that shelter, comfort, and perform on many meaningful levels. What is also important to understand is that architecture is always changing, and our knowledge is increasing. We learn from our own buildings from the past or projects by our colleagues, and we adjust. We learn, and that constantly leads us somewhere else. What I like about the kind of work we do here is that our projects are socially driven. Our architecture is for people. That's why our solutions are driven by performance, not forms. We are not trying to

invent a particular form but address the building type and how architecture can benefit the performance. This has been our approach since the very foundation of our firm. Some architects who work for commercial developers can be a lot more form-driven, but we work the other way around. We do work occasionally on office buildings, for example, but most of our work is driven by a particular program.

I came across some books with your name on the cover. Does that mean that your work has a certain autonomy within the firm? Why did you decide to stay working for a global company, as opposed to opening your own practice?
I think I am very fortunate to enjoy my position within a large corporate firm. It is a rare case. Perhaps architects such as Gordon Bunshaft or Walter Netsch, both working as design principals at SOM— one in New York, the other in Chicago— are rare exceptions. They surely serve as models for me. I admire people who open their own firms, who not only design but also make business decisions. But I didn't want that. I want to concentrate on design only. I love the fact that our firm is in Chicago and we were able to realize many diverse projects here. And I also like the fact that we are a global firm. Right now, one of my projects is in China, another one is in Beirut, and I am working on a competition project in Saudi Arabia. And there's another project that's starting construction in Chicago.

What do you enjoy most about working in Chicago?
More than anything, what I enjoy most is being able to watch my buildings going up day by day and having the kind of control over the building process that you can't have remotely. And being a native, lifetime Chicagoan, it is very satisfying to be able to add buildings right next to so many real masterpieces by some of the finest architects in the history of architecture. Chicago is such an architectural city. It is also a kind of city where it is possible to have a meaningful conversation with many colleagues and exchange ideas about our ongoing projects.

View over Rush University Campus Transformation Project looking east. Its striking five-story, four-winged butterfly-like patient-bed tower hovers over a massive glazed podium of seven floors of diagnostic and treatment facilities. It sits immediately to the south of the Dwight D. Eisenhauer Expressway, which directly links Chicago's downtown with its western suburbs.

What do you think about the creative climate in Chicago right now? Architecture in the city has changed quite drastically since you started at Perkins&Will. What do you think about the transitions over the last 40 or so years?

Chicago was always quite important and influential. Just during my time in the profession, I witnessed the Miesian period or so-called Second Chicago School period from the 1960s to mid-1970s, not just Mies but particularly the influence of Mies. Then Post-Modernism dominated from the mid-1970s to the mid-1980s. And that quickly became the only game in town. It was a total rethinking of modernism, and then it faded away, in a way, transitioning into neo-modern sensitivities, enriched by a lot of questioning and multiple references. I am not sure Post-Modernism was a good diversion, but I think we fully recovered from that. The bad part was the aesthetics that came along with it, but the good part was that it diversified architecture and we never went back to what architecture was before. Architecture became much more informed by urban design, relation to the site, context, nature, and so on. My own work was never strictly modernist. It was always full of meanings and references.

Do you think there is any particular quality that characterizes leading Chicago architects such as Stanley Tigerman, Jeanne Gang, Helmut Jahn, Adrian Smith, John Ronan, and yourself?

All of us have been practicing here in recent times, which are much less cohesive than both the Miesian and Post-Modern periods. It is hard to see us as any kind of school. Each of us has done a lot of interesting projects, but I don't think there is an identifiable character in Chicago anymore. It is now quite diverse, which I think is healthy. I don't think there is even an attempt to create a new Chicago school. There are many interesting buildings created by these highly individual architects, but there is no commonality. I don't see any need for it now. There is a global world now, which is probably the only thing that is tying architecture together right now. Even smaller firms are now doing work internationally. And that seems to have a certain clash with any idea of regionalism and common ideas that come from a particular place. It is hard to categorize the kind of architecture we have today, which I see as a good thing.

John Ronan:
'To Be a Good Architect You Have to Be Fearless'

Architect's Chicago studio
6 November 2019

John Ronan was born in 1963 in Grand Rapids, Michigan. He came to Chicago because he felt a kind of connection with the city that he did not associate with either Los Angeles or New York. He liked Chicago's culture and felt that he would fit in here. He told me that he sensed that 'this is the place where I could succeed'. Ronan earned his Bachelor of Science from the University of Michigan in 1985. He then worked for a couple of years at the office of Stanley Tigerman (1930–2019). That was at the time when Post-Modernism took over and if architects in Chicago had a problem with that, they were a tiny minority. Ronan was one of them, so he applied to Harvard's GSD, which at the time was one of the few lonely fortresses where modernism was still preached under the leadership of the authoritative European architect Rafael Moneo, then chair of the Department of Architecture. Ronan graduated in 1991. Once back in Chicago he worked for Krueck+Sexton Architects (now Krueck Sexton Partners) and Dirk Lohan, the grandson of Mies van der Rohe. And he never parted with academia, having taught design and material culture at IIT since 1992.

Ronan started his own firm, John Ronan Architects, in 1999, the year he won the Townhouse Revisited Competition sponsored by the Graham Foundation. In 2006, the firm was featured in the Architectural League of New York's Emerging Voices and the Young Chicago exhibition at the Art Institute of Chicago. Having built cultural, educational, commercial, and residential projects across the country as well as in Europe and the Caribbean, Ronan's best work is in Chicago. This guide features five of his buildings. The sanctuary-like Poetry Foundation is the architect's strongest and most aspiring project, for which he won an international competition in 2007. Ronan was selected out of a pool of 50 contenders through a lengthy interviewing process. The corner-lot building-and-garden project prominently located in River North was built in 2011. In 2016, the firm was named one of seven international finalists for the Obama Presidential Library, the commission that ultimately went to New York firm Tod Williams Billie Tsien Architects. Ronan's other key project here is the Ed Kaplan Family Institute for Innovation and Tech Entrepreneurship at IIT. The architect's work is informed by Chicago's pragmatism, yet it is sensual and poetic. He likens the process of designing buildings to that of writing books—they unfold layer by layer to reveal originally juxtaposed materials and spatial complexity perceived through one's movement.

Your architecture seems to be quite reserved. Would you agree and would you say this reflects who you are as a person?
Yes, I would agree with that to some degree. It comes from the inside, but it is also imposed from the outside. Yes, I am a more introspective, contemplative type, and personally I am shy and that is reflected in my architecture. The imposed outside part is the influence of the place where I practice—in Chicago. Every place has its own DNA. At the root of the Chicago genetic code is a kind of hardcore brutal pragmatism. It is no accident that,

John Ronan (b. 1963)

for example, Mies van der Rohe succeeded in establishing his career here. There was a perfect match in the DNA of the person and that of the place. And if you look at the list of people who succeeded here, they were those who understood this genetic code well, the severity of Chicago's pragmatism, but also those who could transcend it at the same time and turn it into poetry. Again, Mies would be a perfect example of that. His work here seems almost straightforward, yet very essential and very poetic. Back in my school years, my work was more exuberant and form-driven. I sometimes wonder—why? That's because I am influenced by place but also by time. The clients here are very different from, let's say, New York or Los Angeles. Look at the industries based here—insurance and financial services, which are very low risk, very conservative. Design, fashion, and media companies are not based here. This attitude is reflected in our skyline. This place is very pragmatic at its core, and my work is informed by that.

You worked at Stanley Tigerman's office for a couple of years. Did he represent the Chicago DNA that you are talking about?

First, he did not represent anything. There was nothing typical about Stanley. He became known for protesting against Miesian orthodoxy that was dominating the architectural discourse in the mid-1970s by forming the Chicago Seven, a group of first-generation Post-Modern architects here. They offered a critique of what by then has become an unquestioned mode of practicing architecture. I decided

to work for him because he was the most well-known architect in Chicago. I applied to a number of architects and he was the first to respond and hired me on the spot. I was just 21. But after two years of working for Stanley, I knew I didn't want to do Post-Modernism, which was quite prevalent at the time—almost everybody in Chicago was doing Post-Modernism, one way or another. There wasn't really much of a choice then; if you came to Chicago at that point, you would be a part of some strain of Post-Modernism, basically. That was the time when the Chicago Public Library designed by Tom Beeby was being built. I didn't like nostalgia and was drawn to the rational. At the time, Harvard was one of the few schools still focused on modernism, so that's where I went.

What did you learn from Tigerman?

I learned how to be an architect from Stanley because that was my first job. What I learned most from him was that it is the architect's job to make a project. What I mean is that it is your job, as an architect, to see the possibilities that reside in the brief, even if your client initially doesn't. For example, the brief for the Gary Comer Youth Center on Chicago's South Side, a rough neighborhood, was about the most pragmatic training facility. The owner wanted to use brick and the building's users asked for no windows at all because there were too many drive-by shootings in the area. If I merely listened to my client, it would be just another mediocre building. But I proposed one idea, then another idea. I said: 'What if we did this? What if we did that?' And Gary is the kind of person who would listen to you and then say: 'That's great, but what if we do this?' And he would challenge me to do something even more inventive than what I initially proposed. So, the building became something that went completely beyond the initial brief.

I also learned from Stanley how to thrive on conflict. What I mean is that he was fearless. He didn't back down. Perhaps that's the main thing I learned from him—to be a good architect you have to be fearless. You have to be tough and persevere because there are so many things working against you. To achieve a good building, you have to push people to do things that they may not want to do or are not accustomed to doing at the level you demand. To get a good result you have to be tough. It's about forming an argument and standing by your principles. That's a problem with architecture today— there's often no argument and the result is arbitrary, and mostly about willful form making. There are so many stakeholders in even a small building, and the role of the architect is not simply to say 'yes' to everybody. Architecture is about persuasion; as an architect, you have to persuade people and bring them along with you, so they feel invested in the project ideas and feel a sense of ownership.

How would you describe what you do as an architect? What are the main intentions of your architecture?
My architecture is primarily about space and materiality and less about form. I try to create buildings that are formally simple but spatially complex. I'm interested in the experience of a building rather than the image of a building. I feel there is too much architecture now about one heroic image and how it can be propagated in the media to sell something: it's transactional. I see my work as more of a spatial narrative; I like to explore how buildings unfold and how one moves through them. For me, that's what architecture is all about. I'm not denying that there is a formal red line that runs through my work, but I don't have a priori formal agenda I'm trying to fill. I want my buildings to look different, one from the next, rather than developing a signature style.

I also search for authenticity and attempt to make every project site-specific and culture-specific. I feel that so much of contemporary architecture could be picked up and plopped down somewhere else and you would never know the difference. There is too much contemporary architecture that's placeless or arbitrary. I abhor arbitrariness. I'm rational and have to have a reason for why I do things. Conceptually, I'm inspired by literature. I think of every building as a book. I studied English literature in college. That's why every time I start a new building, I think about it as if I were writing a book. Some of the characters might carry over, but the plot is never the same.

You designed your Poetry Foundation as a building that you said 'unfolds like a poem—line by line'. Could you reflect on such spatial unfolding?
That building is composed of layers of different materials—a layer of birch wood wraps the interior and extends from the library on one end to the performance space on the other. Outboard of that, there's a layer of glass that shifts in and out to compress and expand the exterior and interior spaces. The outermost layer of zinc wraps the whole thing and becomes perforated to reveal the garden, which mediates between the street and building interior. The different layers that comprise the building compress and expand, which you feel as you move through the building. It's a manipulation of these layers that creates spatial sequences. That's what I mean by 'spatial narrative'. The idea is that you, as a visitor, can't consume the building in a single glance; you don't comprehend it immediately; you have to experience it to understand it. The second objective is that every time you come back, you see something else— something new—like a good book you go back to over and over again. Again, the kind of architecture I like is one of formal simplicity but spatial complexity, which I think the Poetry Foundation achieves. The buildings I like are the ones where I don't know what's around the corner, where the story is not given away all at once. I tell my clients: 'I aim to design a building not to be noticed, but to be remembered.'

You often work with humble materials to achieve very special quality. Could you talk about that? For example, you said that with the way you use concrete, you aim to achieve the kind of concrete that no one has ever seen before.

What I attempt to do is to make the ordinary perceived as special. We carefully choose the ingredients. We experiment with the way the materials are produced and finished. I would compare what I do to the job of a chef; chefs all use the same ingredients, but the way they're combined and transformed makes all the difference. So, it's about starting with something ordinary to achieve something that's very special. It's about transformation, not about picking expensive ready-mades as if the design is nothing more than a process of selection. I would further compare the process of architectural design to how poets write beautiful poems relying on the most ordinary words. It is how ordinary words are selected and sequenced that makes them memorable and turns the result into poetry. Likewise, there is no poetry when an architect merely selects expensive materials; anyone can do it. There's no transformation there.

What is your new building, the Kaplan Institute on the IIT campus, about?

The Kaplan Institute is an idea incubator. It poses the question: What should university education be like in the future? Universities were once the place where knowledge was transferred, but with the advent of the internet, the university's mission is changing. It must become the place where knowledge is generated. And for students, it's no longer about what you know, it's about what you can do with what you know. Architecturally speaking, the project is unique because it's surrounded by a very particular context and, as an architect, you have an obligation to acknowledge this important history. Along with the University of Virginia by Thomas Jefferson, IIT is probably one of the two most architecturally significant university campuses in America. Mies described his architecture as skin and bones, and to some extent, the Kaplan building is about what a 'skin and bones' architecture could be today. Crown Hall was lightweight in

appearance for its time, but I wanted to make a building that would make Crown Hall look heavy in comparison. I wanted to propose a building that would feel ultra-light. That's why I chose ETFE, a versatile polymer, to give the new building a cloud-like appearance as if it would float away if not tied down to the ground. The building is in dialogue with the context and it looks to the future.

The ground floor is all transparent and the second floor is atmospheric—like being in a cloud. In this project, we adopted some of the Miesian principles that underpin the campus design, such as the 24-by-24-foot (7.3-by-7.3-meter) planning grid that is still valid, while many others we consciously departed from, such as painting structural steel white instead of black. The site strategy was another departure. Having taught on the campus for many years, I realized that the landscape on the campus was conceived as a residual space to circulate through. There was no destination outdoor space on campus; instead, all the landscape was a left-over space between buildings. That's why I focused on the two courtyards that organize the building and support the Kaplan Institute's mission of creating an interdisciplinary meeting space.

Could you elaborate on the importance of materiality for you? Is it materiality that brings subjectivity into your work? That's your contribution, right?

Yes, that's the consistent and recurring theme in my work—to find inventive ways in how materials can be used to engender space. I don't believe architects invent new materials—and I would be suspicious of any architect making this claim—but architects can invent new spatial relationships using materials. Ultimately, it's about space rather than materiality for its own sake. My objective is to build a kind of space that makes people say: 'My God, I have never been in a space like this before.' So, I would say it is a spatial invention that I'm after, rather than a material invention. I feel quite confident in my ability to use materials, but still have some work to do on the spatial aspects. If I can achieve that, then I'll feel like I've done something.

Jeanne Gang:
'Without an Intellectual Construct, Life is Boring'

Outside of The Standard, High Line hotel in New York
13 September 2016

Jeanne Gang was born outside Chicago in Belvidere, Illinois, in 1964. She is recognized as one of the most prominent architects of her generation. Gang discovered architecture while studying engineering at the University of Illinois. When she signed up for design studio class, she found herself 'hooked'. Her study-abroad program in Europe deepened her love for history and culture. Architecture connected her wide variety of interests in making, geometry, materials, cities, nature, and people. After graduating in 1986, Gang studied urbanism as a visiting scholar at the ETH in Zurich.

She attentively followed many projects that were being designed and built in Europe at the time and went to lectures and reviews by top architects such as Zaha Hadid and Rem Koolhaas. As a teaching assistant to a professor at the ETH, Gang gained insight into an approach that starts with the material, along the lines of the Bauhaus. This and later experience teaching at the Illinois Institute of Technology influenced her work. In her practice, she now explores the quality and character of materials, such as the ways in which wood can be bent, how concrete can be fluid, or how steel can be made flexible. Gang later studied at Harvard's GSD, earning her Master of Architecture in 1993.

Before starting her own practice, Gang decided she wanted to work for someone she really respected. Her first choice was to apprentice at OMA in Rotterdam. Her dream came true and she collaborated directly with Koolhaas on projects in France between 1993 and 1995. At the same time, she was beginning to do projects on her own. She then returned home to teach at IIT and gain additional experience at Booth Hansen in Chicago. Once Gang acquired her professional license, she opened her own practice, Studio Gang, in 1997. In addition to Chicago the firm now has offices in New York, San Francisco, and Paris.

The 2011 MacArthur Fellow architect is teaching at Harvard, her alma mater. Gang met her husband, Mark Schendel, at OMA. He is a managing principal and partner at her firm, which employed 100 architects at the time of this interview. The architect's most celebrated buildings are in Chicago. They range from domestically scaled, pavilion-like boathouses to iconic skyscrapers that now tower over downtown. This guide features seven of Gang's buildings, while many new ones are being planned, including her competition-winning O'Hare Global Terminal, which is expected to be completed by 2028.

Were there good opportunities when you started your practice in Chicago?
Yes, and I always wanted to build big buildings, and somehow I had the impression that I could do it there. It was probably naïve.

And then it happened. What were some of the lessons that you learned from your experience working with Rem Koolhaas?
While at OMA, I was the lead designer on Maison Bordeaux (1994–1998), as well as some other projects in France. I was already predisposed to collaboration, but what I took from him was extra openness

Jeanne Gang (b. 1964)

about how to run an architectural practice, just like a design studio at school; that you could set it up any way you wanted—not just the traditional way. At my studio now we have a very supportive and collaborative atmosphere. I'm always looking for the best talent and best ideas, but simultaneously, I'm investing in our architects and creating a supportive environment so that they can grow professionally to be the best they can be.

Your work isn't about iconic forms, as was the focus of many architects from the late 1990s until the 2007–2008 global financial crisis. Instead, it's more about problem-solving and addressing social and sustainability issues. Where did this idea of using architecture as a tool for solving problems come to you?

I was always a huge observer of relationships, both between people and between people and their environment. When one is very attentive to nature and ecology, one realizes it's all about relationships, not about examining objects on their own. For me, architecture is about changing the way people are interconnected. That's the most exciting part of architecture. I think of architecture as a system; how you set up various opportunities for people to relate to one another, and to be empowered. What are the opportunities for people to interact? How can buildings spark new relationships? This could be through spaces or materials, both old and new, low or high technologies. I pull from everything to find what works best. There's an art to this approach and to constantly honing and adapting one's methodology.

Your particular solutions come from research and work on projects. But where else do you derive your inspiration from? Are there artists or architects that you follow?

Interesting ... I always go back to the work of the Italian-Brazilian architect Lina Bo Bardi. Specifically, a touchstone project for me and my studio is her SESC Pompéia building in São Paulo [a renovation project completed in stages between 1977–1986]. It's urban, it brings together very different people, and it fantastically reinvents so many public programs within what used to be an industrial factory. This is just one project, and I like many works by Brazilian modernists like Vilanova Artigas and Paulo Mendes da Rocha. And, of course, being from Chicago, I greatly admire Sullivan, Wright, and Mies. Yes, there are many influences. Still, many influences come directly from working on projects and from sources that aren't specifically architectural. If you have a curious mind, anything can potentially inform and affect a project.

Will Alsop told me that the art of architecture is putting everything together in your own way. Are you at all interested in finding your own personal way and do you have an artistic agenda apart from the client's requirements?

My artistic agenda is process-driven, but admittedly, it also has formal invention. I think it comes through, but I always try to hold off my formal impressions for as long as possible. I want to avoid having any random tendencies and intuitions. I do that on purpose so that the projects can continue to develop through a rigorous investigative process. Because my work is really about helping a person, organization, or city move to the next level, I have to be able first to listen to what they are saying.

Does this mean that your expression as an architect is suppressed and comes in as secondary to helping your clients?
I wouldn't say so. What's important to me is to reveal things. If you look at our work, it is always about revealing structure, revealing materials. Showing how things can be light or lighter. I am very interested in space itself, and the relationship between light and shadow. The tactile qualities. All that is very important, but our process is not about making something intuitive and turning it into the 'right' solution. Because I feel that it would take away some important part of the gestation process.

Let's talk about your 82-story residential Aqua Tower in Chicago. Each floor plate has different outlines for balconies. I understand that the shape of each floor was dependent on the impact of the wind, and the building's balconies provoke an unusual social interaction among neighbors. But wouldn't you agree that the initial idea was purely artistic, to achieve a certain image?
No, I wouldn't agree with that. I would say the form is important, but that's not how the idea was hatched. As a precursor, I was interested in how tall buildings could be more social and less isolating, more specific with respect to their context, and less generic. We had a site that was surrounded by very tall buildings on all sides. The initial idea was to create hills and valleys, so to speak, on the façades of the building so the occupants could see more of the views from their apartments.
But then, how do you inhabit that topography? That prompted the idea of slicing the hills into horizontal layers and making those exterior spaces into distinctive balconies—all of them unique, each shaped and determined by the wind's impacts, and creating spaces for better social interaction. So, there were many factors. You could say it was done as a

parametric model, but with a social and environmental purpose rather than iteration for form's sake. There is nothing random about the building's shape. Each slight iteration was done for the benefit of the people who live there.

I'm not questioning any of the design sequence steps and your intentions. I think it is a brilliant design. What I am saying is that the initial idea was, nevertheless, an artistic vision, an intuitive vision, if you will. And I'll tell you why I think so. Now you're designing an even taller building, also in Chicago: the 95-story Vista Tower [now St. Regis Chicago]. It has similar wind conditions, the exact same program, and there are many tall buildings around it. But your solution for that building is completely different. There are no 'hills' and 'valleys'. Why is that?
It's a different building, a different site, and a different program, with different opportunities. It follows a different line of research about tall buildings and public space. Our design was a direct response to the fact that this new tower is located right on the border between a public waterfront park and a dense city. This condition prompted the initial idea: How do we lift the building so that people can connect on the ground level? That's how we achieved the three-stem form. The two outer stems support the center one, so the public can easily access East Wacker Drive and the riverfront on the north side from Lakeshore East Park on the south side right under the building.
So, it was about providing an unusual public space bridging two different sides of the building. And we developed a particular building block, shaped like a truncated pyramid, which we flipped and stacked one on top of another and nested together side by side to introduce more corner apartments and unexpected views. I often start these large projects with smaller parts and then build up the form from there. Aqua does this too if you think about the slab as a building element that stacks up to form a building. I never try to produce an iconic image such as a cartoon of a sail, or a ship that would guide the design for the whole project. No, we don't do that [laughs].

This is all great, but let's say, you were commissioned to do a third very tall tower in Chicago. Wouldn't you agree that most likely you would find a way not to repeat yourself and come up with something completely different?

Being sensitive to the specifics of each project makes architecture interesting, but I see our responses as part of a set of interests. Sure, my interests are wide, but not infinite. We learn our lessons and after a number of projects, certain patterns can be detected. There are different lines of research that run through our work, and some projects are more related than others. Not every project is completely different. For example, we developed a whole type of building that we call 'exo-spatial', where we explore spatial and social interaction possibilities outside of the building's envelope, like with the Aqua Tower. So, there are morphologies of building types that we have developed and drawn from.

There are different types and morphologies, but you would not repeat the same idea twice, right?
Sure, we try to come up with different solutions and forms, but I see the ideas as being free of the forms.

What words would you choose to describe your work?
Let's see: people-centric, ecological, spatial, revealing something unexpected, communicative, thought-provoking, tectonic, and beautiful.

Beauty, at last!
It's a kind of unpretentious beauty, but yes, it is still there [laughs].

You said that you see architecture not as buildings but as links to the ecosystem and to how people live. Could you elaborate on that?
I see buildings as facilitators of relationships. I am also interested in exploring how specific sites and climates can affect design. There are always universal aspects to architecture, but I like teasing out the specifics and the differences. For example, when I was teaching at the IIT, I remember how there were design

Photo: Courtesy of Studio Gang

IIT McCormick Tribune Campus Center: its interior responds playfully to the dogmatic 'less is more' aesthetic of Mies, whose full-height portrait on glass is a provocative sign of both reverence and irony.

071 D

courses that gave a program but no site. There were professors who were asking students to design a project in a vacuum.

You would never do that.
Of course not!

You said that architecture enables us to solve problems in our society. Is that really why you like architecture? What about projects such as churches, museums, libraries, and memorials that may be brilliant irrespective of whether or not they solve problems. They are not solving anything; they simply explore spatial, material, and symbolic possibilities.
I don't think every project is about solving problems—sometimes there really isn't a major problem, it's just somebody who wants a building [laughs]. However, I am interested in certain persistent problems and how architecture can be a medium we can use to speak about broader issues and actually make people think about them differently. Climate change and social connectivity are issues I find interesting and important to us and they happen to be very relevant in today's society. So, our mission is not just to solve problems. But I think it is important to be able to problematize projects, not so that they would be 'solved' but because posing a question makes the design more interesting. It can set apart a certain conflict or an issue and help us think about them. Without an intellectual construct, life is boring and we can't progress. It's important to create tension.

The IIT Student Center's hybrid interior confronts visitors with programmatic intensity, a rich material palette, bold colors, unfinished surfaces, and exposed joints that unequivocally transmit the idea that education is a process—open-ended, unruly, undefined, overlapping, and with multiple meanings.

Maps

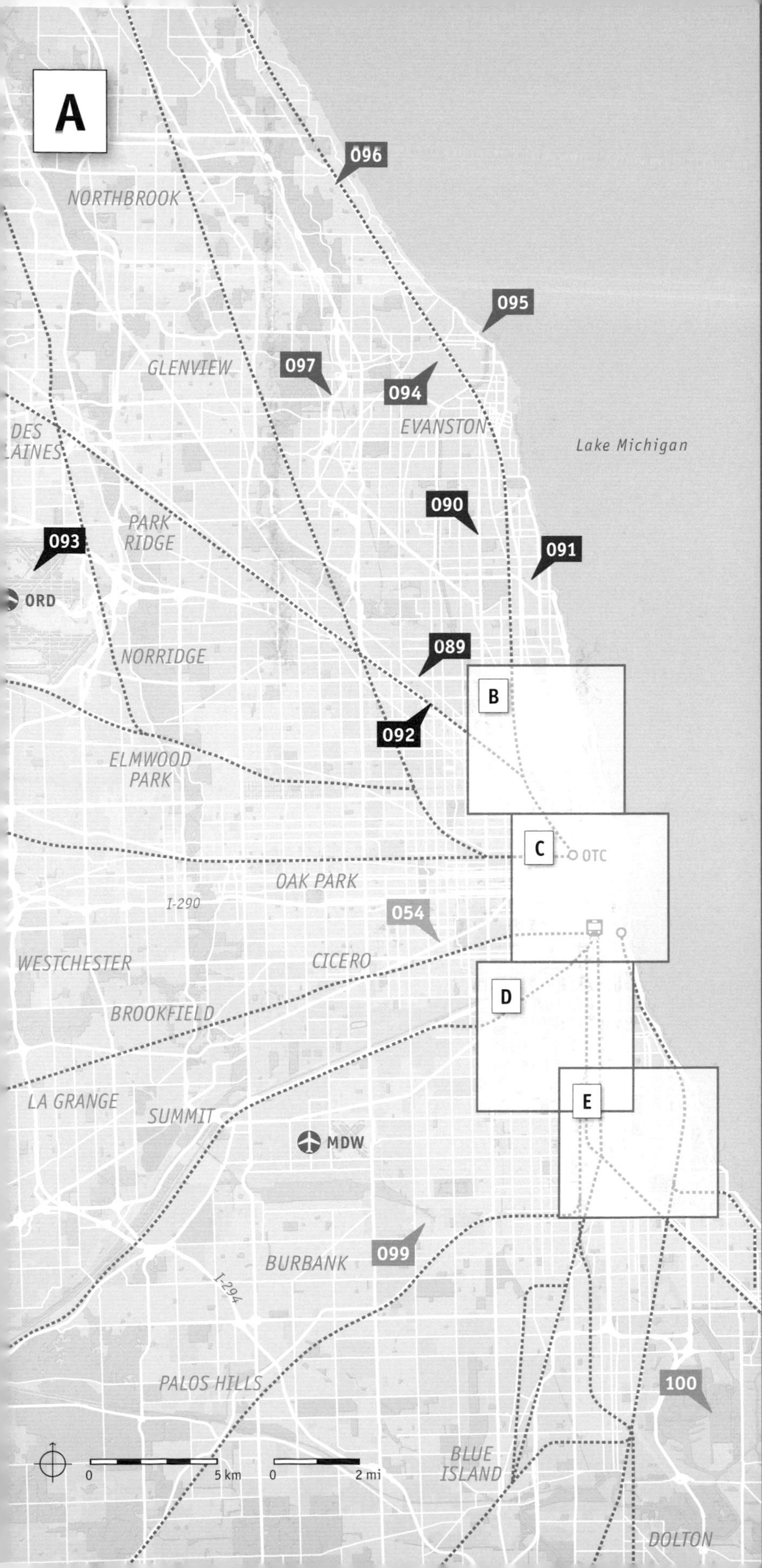

A

096

095

097

094

EVANSTON

090

091

Lake Michigan

093

ORD

089

B

092

C   OTC

054

D

E

MDW

099

100

NORTHBROOK

GLENVIEW

DES PLAINES

PARK RIDGE

NORRIDGE

ELMWOOD PARK

OAK PARK

I-290

WESTCHESTER

CICERO

BROOKFIELD

LA GRANGE

SUMMIT

BURBANK

I-294

PALOS HILLS

BLUE ISLAND

DOLTON

0   5 km   0   2 mi

Sheridan

0   500 m

Lake Michigan

N Clark St

Addison

NORTHALSTED

LAKE
VIEW EAST

Belmont

Wellington

N Clark St

063

S DuSable Lake Shore Drive

Diversey

W Diversey Pkwy

PARK WEST

062

061

Fullerton

LINCOLN PARK

N Clark St

N Racine Ave

N Lincoln Ave

060

059

Armitage

W Armitage Ave

RANCH
TRIANGLE

057

058

Lincoln
Park

056

055

North/Clybourn

OLD TOWN

Sedgwick

N Clybourn Ave

036

C

W Division St — Division
W Division

GOOSE ISLAND

086

W Chicago Ave

N Halsted St

Chicago

W Chicago

031

Ashland Ave

Kennedy Expy

N Ogden Ave

087

I-90

Grand

088

049

WEST LOOP

Ashland

048

Clinton

Union Park

W Randolph St

Ogilvie
Transp.
Cent.

N Ogden Ave

W Madison St

050

04

GREEKTOWN

051

UIC-Halsted

Clint

N Damen Ave

W Ogden Ave

W Harrison St

S Ashland Ave

Polk

Roosevelt Rd

NEAR WEST SIDE

Roosevelt Rd

053

052

Roosevelt Rd

I-90

Addams/ Medill Park

S Blue Island Ave

Dan Ryan Expy

S Damen Ave

Halsted Street

18th

S Ashland Ave

S Blue Island Ave

NEAR
NORTH SIDE

035

N LaSalle Dr

034

033

030

N Lake Shore Dr

N Michigan Ave

W Chicago Ave

032

Chicago

Chicago

STREETERVILLE

RIVERNORTH

029

Grand

028

025

026

008

027

Merchandise
Mart

003

004

007

009

011

012

046

001

005

006

014

NEW EASTSIDE

002

019

015

010

013

045

Washington/
Wells

Clark/Lake

Washington/
Wabash

022

021

020

016

023

017

Millenium

018

Quincy

024

Van Buren St.

037

LaSalle
Street

038

Harrison

043

039

Grant
Park

ago
on
ion

Museum
Campus/
11th St.

042

SOUTH LOOP

040

S Lake Shore Dr

MUSEUM
CAMPUS

041

Northerly
Island Park

18th St.

068

S State St.

067

Not all stations reflected in map.
Please refer to transit map.

0   500 m

S Blue Island Ave

Ashland Ave

S Damen Ave

South Branch Chicago River

■ Ashland

Adlai Stevenson Expressway

South Archer Avenue

MCKINLEY PARK

W 35th St

W 35th St

■ 35th/Archer

Ashland Ave

McKinley Park

W Pershing Rd

W Pershing Rd

S Western Ave

W 43rd St

Ashland Ave

0   500 m

W 47th St

NEW CITY

CHINATOWN

Stevenson Expressway

Halsted

Henry C.
Palmisano
Nature Park

069

ARMOUR
SQUARE

070

W 31st St   W 31st St

BRIDGEPORT   071

073   072

S Halsted St

Dan Ryan Expressway

W 35th St   W 35th St   Sox-35th   35th St.-
Lou Jones

I-90

WENTWORTH
GARDENS

S Halsted St

W Pershing Rd   W Pershing Rd

W Exchange Ave

W 43rd St

S Halsted St   CANARYVILLE

E

47th Ave

FULLER PARK

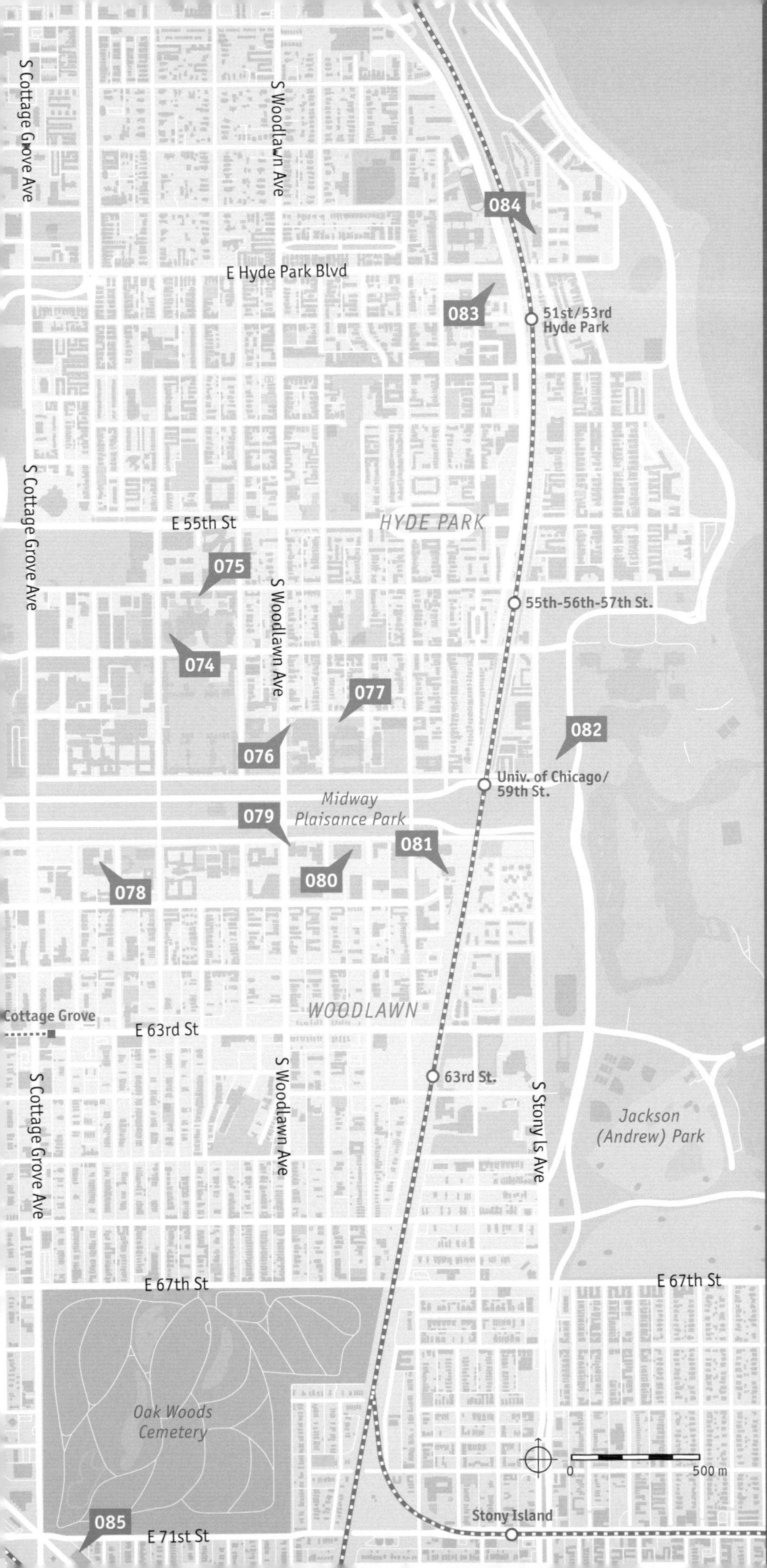

S Cottage Grove Ave

S Woodlawn Ave

084

E Hyde Park Blvd

083

51st/53rd
Hyde Park

S Cottage Grove Ave

E 55th St

HYDE PARK

075

S Woodlawn Ave

55th-56th-57th St.

074

077

082

076

079

Midway
Plaisance Park

Univ. of Chicago/
59th St.

081

078

080

Cottage Grove

WOODLAWN

E 63rd St

S Woodlawn Ave

63rd St.

S Stony Is Ave

Jackson
(Andrew) Park

E 67th St

E 67th St

Oak Woods
Cemetery

0   500 m

085

E 71st St

Stony Island

Index of buildings

Digits indicate project numbers

71 South Wacker
(formerly Hyatt Center) 022
77 West Wacker Drive 004
150 North Riverside 045
333 West Wacker Drive 002
800 Fulton Market 049

A
Accenture Tower
(formerly Citigroup Center) 044
Anti-Cruelty Society 028
Apple Michigan Avenue 026
Aqua Tower 011
Ardmore House 091

B
Blue Cross Blue Shield Tower 013
Brick Weave House 088

C
Chicago Architecture Center 007
Chicago Art Institute,
The Modern Wing 018
Chicago Board of Trade Addition 023
Chicago Horizon Pavilion 042
Chicago Park District Headquarters 098
Chicago Riverwalk 008
Chinatown Branch, Chicago Public
Library 067
City Hyde Park 083
Claremont House 065
Cloud Gate 016
Columbia College Chicago Student
Center 039
Contemporaine 029
Crain Communications Building
(formerly Associates Center) 014
Crown Fountain 017
CTA 'L' Station at State/Lake 005
CTA Morgan Street Station 048

D
Daley College Manufacturing,
Technology & Engineering Center 099
David Rubenstein Forum 079

E
Education Pavilion and Nature
Boardwalk at Lincoln Park Zoo 059
Eight-Unit Condominium Building 086
Erie on the Park 031

F
Ford Calumet Environmental Center ...100
Fourth Presbyterian Church,
Gratz Center 034

G
Gary Comer College Preparatory School
and Gary Comer Youth Center 085
Gillson Park Beach House 095
Glass and Steel House 057
Gordon Parks Arts Hall 077

H
Harold Washington Library 024
Holocaust Memorial Foundation of
Illinois 097
House Etch 064
Hyde Park Art Center 084

I
IIT Innovation Center,
The Ed Kaplan Family Institute 070
IIT McCormick Tribune Campus
Center 071
IIT State Street Village 072
Illinois Center Sporting Club
(now Lakeshore Sport & Fitness
at Illinois Center) 009
Illinois Regional Library for the Blind
and Physically Handicapped
(now Lakeside Bank) 052
Independence Library and
Apartments 089

J
James R. Thompson Center 001
Jay Pritzker Pavilion 015
Joe & Rika Mansueto Library 074

L

Lake Shore Drive 063
Legacy Charter School 054
Lipton Thayer Brick House 094

M

Max Palevsky Residence Commons 075
Mohawk House 056
Morgan Live + Work 073
Museum of Contemporary Art (MCA) ... 032

N

NEMA Chicago 040
Northeastern Illinois University,
    El Centro Campus 092
Northtown Library and Apartments 090

O

OneEleven 003
Orchard East 058

P

Peggy Notebaert Nature Museum 061
Pfanner House 087
Poetry Foundation 030

R

Reva and David Logan Center for
    the Arts 078
River City 043
River Cottages 047
River Point 046
Rodney D. Joslin Campus
    Perspectives Charter Schools 068
Rush University Campus
    Transformation Project 051

S

Searle Visitors Center at Lincoln
    Park Zoo 060
Self Park 006
Skybridge 050
Sofitel Hotel 033
Soldier Field Stadium 041
SOS Children's Villages Illinois 053

South Campus Boiler Plant 081
Spertus Institute 037
Steppenwolf Theatre 055
St. Regis Chicago
    (formerly Wanda Vista Tower) 012

T

The Barack Obama Presidential
    Center 082
The Keller Center –
    Harris School of Public Policy 080
Tower House 036
Trump International
    Hotel & Tower 025
Two Prudential Plaza
    (Pru Two) 010

U

United Airlines Terminal & O'Hare
    CTA Station, O'Hare
    International Airport 093
University of Chicago Booth School of
    Business, Charles M. Harper
    Center 076
U.S. Bank Building (formerly
    190 South LaSalle Street) 021

V

Viceroy Hotel 035

W

Washington-Wabash Station 019
William Jones College
    Preparatory High School 038
Williams Park Fieldhouse 069
WMS Boathouse at Clark Park 066
Wrightwood 659 062
Writers Theatre 096

X

Xerox Center 020

Y

Yard Shakespeare Theater 027

Index of architects

Digits indicate project numbers

A

Adrian Smith + Gordon Gill
Architecture, AS+GG 007, 027, 055
Ando, Tadao 062

B

Bertrand Goldberg Associates 043
bKL Architecture 012
Brininstool + Lynch 065, 079
Brooks + Scarpa 094

C

Charcoalblue 027

D

Diller Scofidio + Renfro 079

E

Epstein & Sons 014
EXP 019

F

Farr Associates 080
FGM Architects 077
Foster + Partners 026
Frederick Phillips & Associates 036
Fujikawa Johnson and Associates 009

G

Garofalo, Doug 084
Gehry, Frank 015
Gensler 034, 039
Goettsch Partners 013, 035, 045

H

Hammond, Beeby & Babka 024
Handel Architects 003
Hoepf, Thomas 019

J

JAHN
001, 020, 023, 044, 072, 074, 081, 093
JGMA 053, 092, 099

J (right column)

John Ronan Architects ....
.... 030, 070, 085, 089, 098
Johnson/Burgee Architects 021

K

Kapoor, Anish 016
Kleihues, Josef Paul 032
Kohn Pedersen Fox Associates, KPF 002
Koolhaas, Rem 071
Krueck Sexton Partners 017, 037, 057
Kurokawa, Kisho 009
Kwong Von Glinow Design Office 091

L

LEGORRETA 075
Loebl Schlossman & Hackl 010
Loewenberg Architects 011
Lohan Caprile Goettsch Architects 041
Lothan Van Hook DeStefano
Architecture, LVDA 054
Lucien Lagrange Studio 031

M

McKay Landscape Architects 058

P

Pei Cobb Freed & Partners 022
Perkins&Will ....
.... 029, 038, 050, 051, 061, 068, 090
Pickard Chilton 046
Plensa, Jaume 017

R

Rafael Viñoly Architects 040, 076
Renzo Piano Building Workshop 018
Ricardo Bofill Taller de
Arquitectura 004
Ross Barney Architects 008, 048, 060

S

Skidmore, Owings & Merrill, SOM ....
.... 005, 025, 049, 067
STLarchitects 069

Studio Dwell Architects 064
Studio Gang ....
     011, 012, 059, 066, 071, 083, 088, 096

T
Tigerman McCurry Architects ....
    .... 006, 028, 052, 097
Tod Williams Billie Tsien Architects ....
    .... 078, 082

U
Ultramoderne 042
UrbanLab 056, 073

V
Valerio Dewalt Train Associates .. 077, 100
Viguier, Jean-Paul 033
Vladimir Radutny Architects 086

W
Weese, Harry 047
Wheeler Kearns Architects 058, 063
Wood + Zapata 041
Woodhouse Tinucci Architects 080, 095

Z
Zoka Zola Architecture 087

Vladimir Belogolovsky (b. 1970, Odesa, Ukraine) is an American curator and critic. He has lived in New York City since 1989. He graduated from The Cooper Union School of Architecture there in 1996. After practicing architecture for 12 years, he founded his New York–based Curatorial Project, a non-profit that focuses on curating and designing architectural exhibitions around the world. Belogolovsky writes for *Arquitectura Viva* (Madrid) and *AZURE* (Toronto) and is a columnist on ArchDaily and STIR. He has interviewed more than 400 leading international architects and has written 15 books, including *China Dialogues* (ORO Editions, 2022), *Imagine Buildings Floating Like Clouds* (IMAGES, 2022), *Architectural Guide New York* (DOM publishers, 2019), *Conversations with Architects* (DOM publishers, 2015), and *Soviet Modernism: 1955–1985* (TATLIN, 2010). Belogolovsky has curated and produced over 50 international exhibitions. Among these are *Architects' Voices Series* (world tour since 2016), world tours on the work of Emilio Ambasz (2017–2018) and Harry Seidler (since 2012, including at IIT's S.R. Crown Hall in 2017), the *Green House* exhibition at the Zodchestvo International Architecture Festival in Moscow (2009), and the *Chess Game* exhibition for the Russian Pavilion at the 11th Venice Architecture Biennale (2008). He has lectured at universities and museums in more than 30 countries. In 2018, Belogolovsky spent the fall semester teaching design studio at Tsinghua University in Beijing as a visiting scholar.

Vladimir Belogolovsky
A selfie at Graceland Cemetery,
Chicago, September 2021

Right: James R. Thompson Center,
plans and interior axonometric views.
Marker drawing by Helmut Jahn

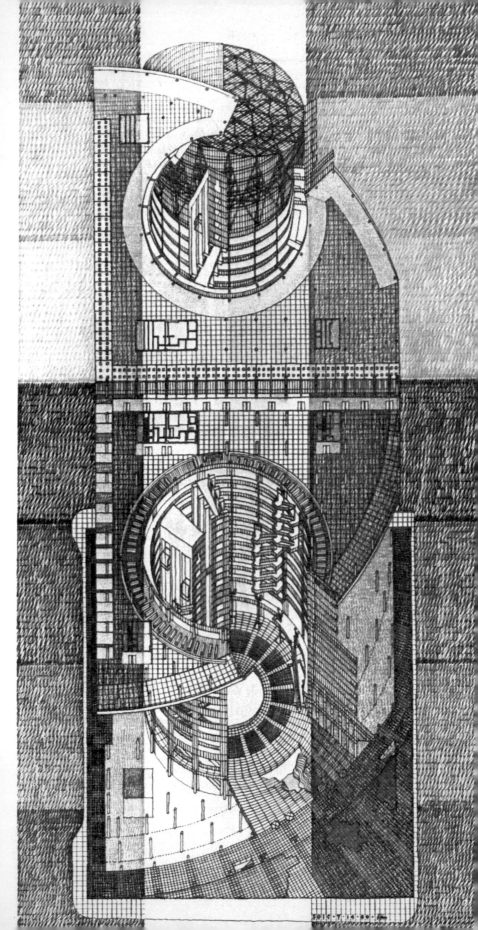

The *Deutsche Nationalbibliothek* lists
this publication in the *Deutsche National-
bibliografie*; detailed bibliographic data
are available at *http://dnb.d-nb.de*

ISBN 978-3-86922-418-3

**DOM
publishers**

© 2022 by DOM publishers, Berlin
www.dom-publishers.com

Editor
Charles Linn

Proofreading
Sandie Kestell

Design
Masako Tomokiyo

Maps
Ee Dong Chen

QR codes
Shaun Thang Yong

Printing
Master Print Super Offset, Bucharest
masterprint.ro

Picture credits:
Unless otherwise indicated, photos,
plans, visualizations, and other graphics
were supplied by the respective architectural practices.